Ruins of Myth Drannor

Prima's Official Strategy Guide

Dan Irish
Daniel Achterman

Prima Games
A Division of Random House, Inc.

3000 Lava Ridge Court, Roseville, CA 95661
(916) 787-7000
www.primagames.com

The Prima Games logo is a registered trademark of Random House, Inc., registered in the United States and other countries. Primagames.com is a registered trademark of Random House, Inc., registered in the United States.

Senior Product Manager: Jennifer Crotteau
Senior Project Editor: Christy L. Curtis
Project Editor: Terri Stewart Bloom

Important:
Prima Games has made every effort to determine that the information contained in this book is accurate. However, the publisher makes no warranty, either expressed or implied, as to the accuracy, effectiveness, or completeness of the material in this book; nor does the publisher assume liability for damages, either incidental or consequential, that may result from using the information in this book. The publisher cannot provide information regarding game play, hints and strategies, or problems with hardware or software. Questions should be directed to the support numbers provided by the game and device manufacturers in their documentation. Some game tricks require precise timing and may require repeated attempts before the desired result is achieved.

ISBN: 0-7615-3018-5
Library of Congress Catalog Card Number: 00-109813
Printed in the United States of America
01 02 03 04 BB 10 9 8 7 6 5 4 3 2 1

Acknowledgements:
First we'd like to acknowledge Dexter Chow for his seemingly eternal endurance and commitment to releasing this game. We're glad you finally made it. To Chuck Yager, thank you for all the prompt responses and for sharing your intimate knowledge of the game with us on so many occasions. Your positive attitude and ability to always see on the bright side made this book come together smoothly. To Bret Berry, thank you for believing in us and allowing us the opportunity to work together on this book, even while working on Myst III: Exile. To Mark, Jack, and the rest of the Stormfront Studios team, thank you for your attention to detail and taking the time to help us get it right.

Of course, our thanks goes out to the editorial staff at Prima: Christy, Jennifer, Terri, and David Knight. We're grateful for your patience and the "elements of style" you brought to this book.

And Dan Irish would like to thank Daniel Achterman for agreeing to work on this project with me, in addition to everything else that we've done. Your passion for the D&D® RPG is stunning, and your knowledge of games unparalleled. It couldn't have been completed without you.

Contents

Contents

PART ONE
The Basics

Introduction

How to Use This Book

Now that you've committed yourself to one of the best adventures Dungeons & Dragons® has to offer, here are a few tips about how to get the most out of this book.

The best way to use this book is to read Chapters 1–4 before playing. These chapters describe the basic strategies for navigating your party through the treacherous waters in Myth Drannor. Chapter 1 describes the changes and improvements the current D&D® Rules contain over the previous ones. Chapter 2 outlines the backstory and describes possible allies and a few of the more common monsters you'll face. Chapter 3 contains some basic guidelines for creating your own unique party with individual strengths and weaknesses, and Chapter 4 highlights some general game mechanics and basic combat strategies.

If you already know how to play and just want to jump to a specific map, each game level is detailed in a different chapter. In each of the walkthrough chapters, the numbers in bold throughout the text match the numbers on the map. Keep in mind that each numbered step gives you only the main action needed to advance in the walkthrough and does not guide you through every possible activity.

Chapter 5 starts the walkthrough section and begins gameplay with an overview of the Stillwater area, the first area of Myth Drannor. This is where your adventure begins. If you are eager to begin, just turn to that chapter and follow along. The way to explore is up to you, and the challenge is yours, but with this book, the roadmap is laid out in front of you.

Good luck!

Chapter One

The New D&D® Games Rules

The new rules for Dungeons & Dragons® have made the game more streamlined and exciting to play. Though many of these changes will be invisible while playing *Pool of Radiance™: Ruins of Myth Drannor* (*Pool of Radiance™: RoMD*), others are very significant, and players who are familiar with the previous rules should be aware of them. Here is an overview of the most significant changes.

Races

The characteristics of the various races have been altered in the latest rules, and a new race has been added: the half-orc. Additionally, there are no longer any racial level or class restrictions. All races can advance to any level in any class. The maximum level in *Pool of Radiance™: RoMD* is 16 in any single class, and the maximum combined level of any multiclass character is 32.

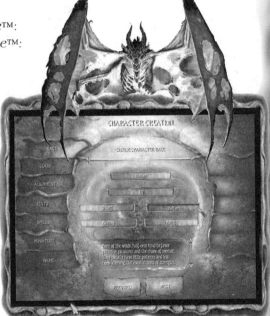

Choose your race at the Character Creation screen.

Classes

Three new classes are available: the barbarian, monk, and sorcerer. In addition, many classes gain special abilities as they advance in levels. For example, at level 2, barbarians learn the Uncanny Dodge ability. These special abilities help differentiate the classes.

The eight available classes in *Pool of Radiance™: RoMD* are: fighter, ranger, barbarian, paladin, monk, rogue, cleric, and sorcerer. See Chapter 3 for detailed descriptions of each of the classes.

Skills

Skills in the new rules replace proficiencies and some class abilities from the previous editions of D&D®. For example, thief abilities such as Remove Traps and Hide in Shadows have been replaced by the rogue skills Disable Device and Hide. When characters advance in level, they are allocated skill points that are divided between their different skills.

Pool of Radiance™: RoMD automatically assigns skill points

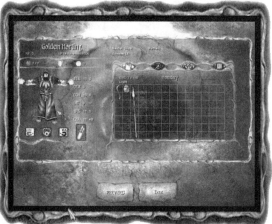

Goldem Horting is a sorcerer with ability scores that favor Intelligence, Wisdom, and Charisma.

when your characters advance in level, depending on their class and Intelligence. See the manual for a detailed description of the available skills in *Pool of Radiance™: RoMD* and how they advance in the game.

Feats

Feats are a new feature in the new D&D® rules. Feats are special abilities that give your characters new talents or improve existing skills and character statistics they already have. For example, Elandor, an elf, has the Improved Initiative feat. This gives her a +4 bonus to her initiative rolls. Unlike a skill, feats have no ranks. A character either has the feat or does not. Characters gain additional feats as they advance in levels.

As with skills, feats are automatically assigned to characters in *Pool of Radiance™: RoMD*, depending on their class. See Chapter 3 for details of which feats each class gains with each level.

Ability Scores

The ability scores used in the new D&D® rules (Strength, Dexterity, Constitution, Intelligence, Wisdom, and Charisma) have not changed from the previous rules, but their bonuses and uses have. In the previous rules, a character had to have a very extreme ability score, such as a 16 or a 5, to get any bonuses or penalties. Now ability scores give bonuses starting at 12 and penalties starting at 9.

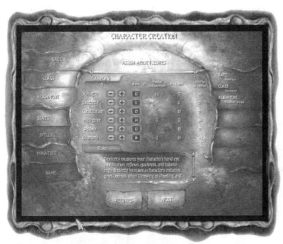

Choose your ability scores wisely. They provide the foundation for your character throughout the game.

Don't place all your ability points in your character's primary statistic to the exclusion of all others. Wisdom helps characters to avoid being surprised, sorcerers need Charisma and Constitution to be most effective, and several rogue skills require a high Intelligence. With the latest rules, a well-rounded character is often best. Usually, a character must enhance three or more ability scores to be as powerful as possible.

Ability scores and their effects are described in greater detail in the game manual. Which ability scores are important to each class is described in Chapter 3 of this guide.

Multiclassing

The multiclassing system in the new D&D® rules is significantly different than in the previous rules. Instead of sharing experience between classes, characters choose what class they want to advance in when they gain a level. This results in lower total class levels than multiclass characters had before, but it's a more flexible system that allows players to carefully control the skills of their characters. Some penalties for multiclassing apply, depending on race and class levels, so make sure you understand the system before building multiclass characters.

See the manual for details of how multiclassing works, and see Chapter 3 of this guide for suggestions about building effective multiclass characters.

Magic

Of the several changes to the spell system, the most significant is the introduction of the sorcerer class. Sorcerers don't need to memorize spells like wizards do. They simply have a set number of spells of each level that they may cast before they must rest, and they may choose what spell to cast at any time, making them very flexible.

Choose your magic!

In *Pool of Radiance™: RoMD*, sorcerers are available, but wizards are not. Additionally, clerics aren't required to pray for spells; they may choose what spells to cast at any time, like a sorcerer. This departure from the new D&D® rules makes your clerics very effective.

6

Chapter Two

Character Guide and Story Setting

The sequel to the original *Pool of Radiance* and Gold Box Games saga introduces you to the Ruins of Myth Drannor. The first computer game to embrace the new Dungeons and Dragons rules, *Pool of Radiance: Ruins of Myth Drannor* is an immersive and challenging role-playing adventure set in a rich, fantastic world.

> *"Already our allies move with purpose through the city—wraith and orog, dragon-kin, and my beloved drow. Here they flock to drink from a Pool of power past all desiring. With the blessing it gives them, they will be our subjects forever, with loyalty to us that endures beyond the grave."*

This chapter describes the legacy of *Pool of Radiance: Ruins of Myth Drannor*. We'll also meet the various characters who can join your trek through the ancient remnants of this Forgotten Realms city, as well as detail the foes you'll undoubtedly encounter.

Introduction

In a time of turmoil, where old leaders and heroes have come and gone, this ruined region is rife with conflict. A new threat to all of the Forgotten Realms comes at its most desperate time. This is where your adventure begins: with a party of brave men and women bound by mutual interests and the desire to restore things to their rightful order.

Backstory

Long ago, a band of fearless adventurers came to the Moonsea area. Stories of opportunity and excitement found in Phlan initially attracted their attention. But, upon reaching the city, they discovered that several run-down portions of the once-proud city were infested with monsters. Their initial motivations of riches and reward forgotten, the adventurers began clearing the city of this dreadful evil. Block by block, they eradicated the threats in areas such as Sokal Keep, Podol Plaza, and Valhingen Graveyard. These exploits earned them a reputation as brave heroes.

In the process, they reaped wondrous treasures, which matched the legends of Phlan. Soon after their exploits, they came upon the larger evil: Tyranthraxus, the Flamed One—an evil dragon that lived beneath the city. He had orchestrated these evils from his hidden den, plaguing the city's inhabitants. Tyranthraxus was using a Pool of Radiance to further his own evil and enhance his power over Phlan. The legendary party faced Tyranthraxus and his minions in an attempt to save all who lived in Phlan. Although it was a difficult and dangerous task, they eventually destroyed the original Pool of Radiance and Tyranthraxus along with it. In doing so, they restored the precious peace to what became known as New Phlan.

New Phlan

But the darkness didn't die with the destruction of the Tyranthraxus. Suddenly, trouble threatens the hard-won peace. The ruined Pool of Radiance awakes with a terrible evil. This evil rapidly spreads outward, tearing through New Phlan, robbing all that it touches of energy and life. Those who can't escape are horrifically transformed into undead. The life force of the entire city would soon be drawn into the Pool.

Elminster, the greatest wizard in all the Realms, hearing of the plight of New Phlan, hurries to the city and begins to investigate. Immediately he suspects that the Pool at Phlan has been awakened and corrupted by the rise of a new Pool of Radiance. This new Pool is spreading evil from Myth Drannor, an ancient elven city that lies in ruins far to the south, across the Moonsea in the Forest of Cormanthyr. Trying to prevent the spread of this terrible evil, Elminster enlists the help of a party of hardened adventurers led by Athan, an experienced warrior. He sends them to Myth Drannor bearing the powerful Gauntlets of Moander. These were used to destroy the first Pool of Radiance.

As New Phlan's best hope, Athan's band of adventurers embarks, dedicated to the destruction of the Pool at Myth Drannor. New Phlan rallies itself to stem the tide of corruption and evil flowing from the Pool.

Heroic Volunteers

As volunteers to help Elminster, Athan, and his band adventurers, you and your companions begin in New Phlan. While on duty, your party spies an unsteady portal opening just in front of them. Hearing weapons clash and glimpsing Athan and the heroes struggling, you suddenly realize that they face a deadly foe. A voice calls through the gate, "You there, in Phlan! By all that is holy, help us!" Without further hesitation, you and your party draw your weapons and jump through the portal.

Arriving on the other side of the portal, you survey the scene. Hours have passed, even though it seemed as if it took only seconds to travel through the portal. The adventurers whose cries for help brought you here are dead. Their lifeless bodies lie at your feet. Some of their attackers have slipped away into the darkness, while a few orcs still loot what is left of their bodies. The responsibility they bore is now your own.

Finding Allies

Suddenly, your party is thrust into the deadly ruins of Myth Drannor, to which not even Athan and his companions proved equal. You have no way home, no promise of reinforcements, and no conceivable hope of victory. Although your party is a carefully prepared group, with each member an expert in his or her field, you're still woefully outmatched. Fortunately, you are not alone in this adventure. You meet many others in Myth Drannor who are sympathetic to your cause and who will join you in your quest. In this section, you'll find details about the characters who can join your party and assist you in the triumph over evil. With this information, you can choose which will best match your party's strengths.

Reading the Stats

Gender: Male or female
Race: A character's race
Class: A character's profession
Level: A character's level when found. This increases as they progress through the game and gain experience.

Caution

This section contains some plot spoilers. If you don't want to learn any story points ahead of time, restrict your reading to the characteristic tables of your potential companions.

Experience: The number of experience points that any ally NPC has when found.

Strength: How strong the character is.

Dexterity: A measure of the character's hand-eye coordination, agility and reflexes, and balance.

Constitution: A measure of the character's health and stamina.

Intelligence: How smart the character is.

Wisdom: How wise the character is.

Charisma: Measures a character's force of personality, persuasiveness, personal magnetism, and ability to lead.

Feats: A list of the feats that a character knows.

Spells: A list of the magic available to a character.

How each character grows and develops beyond the state in which they are found is totally up to you.

> ## Note
>
> The game's manual offers a more complete explanation of the ability scores that affect your characters' quests.

Athan

Summary

This is the heroic leader of the first party Elminster sent on this adventure. He is a disciplined fighter with a soul burning for vengeance.

Your party meets Athan in a secret, underground passageway to Castle Cormanthor detailed in Chapter 21.

Athan's Background

As the leader of the first adventuring band Elminster sent to Myth Drannor, he was entrusted with the valuable Gauntlets of Moander, which were stripped from him by the henchmen of evil.

Once powerful and proud, this warrior's body is now broken. But, a slow fire burns deep within his soul. With a little rest and healing, the vengeance that burns inside of him will blaze brightly once again.

Athan's Characteristics	
Gender:	Male
Race:	Human
Class:	Fighter
Level:	16
Experience:	120,150
Strength:	18
Intelligence:	12
Wisdom:	9
Dexterity:	17
Constitution:	17
Charisma:	11
Feats:	
Point Blank Shot, Precise Shot, Lightning Reflexes, Mobility, Run, Improved Initiative, Combat Reflexes, Great Fortitude, Iron Will, Power Attack, Cleave, Improved Critical, Blind Fighting	
Spells:	None

Bronwyn

Summary

Though she often feels more at home in the woods, this elven ranger's strengths lie in tracking down an enemy. She is a sworn enemy of evil mages and fighters. At one time a secretive and taciturn loner, Bronwyn is now a believer in nature, with little need for the selfishness associated with treasure or the work of hands.

The party meets Bronwyn on the second level of the Second Cellar of the Catacombs. This encounter is detailed in Chapter 17.

Bronwyn's Characteristics

Gender:	Female
Race:	Elf
Class:	Ranger
Level:	12
Experience:	68,900
Strength:	17
Intelligence:	12
Wisdom:	16
Dexterity:	16
Constitution:	15
Charisma:	11

Feats:
Point Blank Shot, Precise Shot, Improved Critical Hit, Great Fortitude, Iron Will
Spells:
Bronwyn has an assortment of 1st, 2nd, and 3rd level ranger spells, plus a number of Orisons.

Bronwyn's Background

As the Sisterhood of Silver Fire assembled a team to investigate the evil of Myth Drannor, Bronwyn emerged as the only one capable enough to guide the team through the dense woods surrounding the embattled city. After successfully guiding them to the outskirts, Bronwyn opted to stay with the team, leaving the comfort and safety of the woods for the dangerous evil lurking within the ruins and dungeons beyond the city walls. Her exceptional tracking abilities, cunning fighting skills, and undaunted scouting techniques prove immensely valuable when seeking the dark, secret evil within Myth Drannor.

Eadred

Summary

An honorable paladin who
has sharpened his skills
with the sword to near
perfection, Eadred is a fair,
muscular, and heroic
young human male.

Your party encounters
Eadred in the Glim
Gardens of House Ammath.
This encounter is detailed in
Chapter 13.

Eadred's Background

In ancient times, a wight of
great strength ruled a
barrow. This evil undead drained the life from
the city. After the city of Myth Drannor grew
above the barrow, one of the city's protector
Knights investigated and found the source of this evil. His role was to destroy it,
and he succeeded, but in doing so he fell under a strong curse. This curse
caused him to fall into a cold, eternal sleep.

As time passed and Myth Drannor came under attack, Eadred entered the
barrow to see if the Knight could be freed. He determined that the curse resided
in the sword stuck into the ground in front of the Knight. Anyone who touched the
sword would take the place of the Knight as the victim of the curse. After setting a
speaking rune as a warning to others about this danger, Eadred touched the
sword. The Knight was suddenly freed and Eadred fell into the endless sleep.

While Eadred slept, Myth Drannor fell. His sacrifice was not enough to
prevent the conquest of evil.

Eadred's Characteristics	
Gender:	Male
Race:	Human
Class:	Paladin
Level:	8
Experience:	29,469
Strength:	15
Intelligence:	9
Wisdom:	18
Dexterity:	15
Constitution:	15
Charisma:	15
Feats:	
Iron Will, Power Attack, Cleave, Improved Critical	
Spells:	
Full complement of paladin spells	

Emmeric

Summary

A humble fighter from New Phlan, Emmeric lacks experience but makes up for it with his abundance of raw courage.

Your party encounters Emmeric in the Halls of Stone, the second level of the Dwarven Dungeons. This encounter is detailed in Chapter 7.

Emmeric's Background

As part of the party assembled by the great Elminster to seek out the mystery of the evil surrounding Myth Drannor, Emmeric had to overcome the belief that he was too young and inexperienced. Using bluster and subterfuge, he managed to join the party just before they teleported to Myth Drannor. He proved himself worthy in the party's efforts to uncover the secret of the new Pool of Radiance under Castle Cormanthor.

When the party was ambushed, he fell victim to a sleep spell and awoke as a prisoner. He searches for any chance to escape, eagerly awaiting your arrival.

Emmeric's Characteristics	
Gender:	Male
Race:	Human
Class:	Fighter
Level:	5
Experience:	13,004
Strength:	16
Intelligence:	16
Wisdom:	9
Dexterity:	13
Constitution:	15
Charisma:	10
Feats:	
Power Attack, Cleave, Improved Critical Hit, Combat Reflexes, Iron Will, Lightning Reflexes	
Spells:	None

Faeril

Summary

Faeril is quick to raise her mace and shield to protect her companions. As a fighter/cleric she is potent in combat, yet able to provide support to her party members through her healing magic.

    Faeril will agree to join your party after you free the Shrine of Mystra. This encounter is detailed in Chapter 11, and Faeril is found in the Stillwater Ruins, described in Chapter 5.

Faeril's Characteristics	
Gender:	Female
Race:	Half-Elf
Class:	
Fighter/Cleric	
Level:	5/9
Experience:	97,801
Strength:	17
Intelligence:	10
Wisdom:	16
Dexterity:	12
Constitution:	16
Charisma:	15
Feats:	
Combat Reflexes, Lightning Reflexes, Mobility, Power Attack, Cleave, Spell Penetration, Combat Casting, Improved Critical	
Spells:	All
Orisons, 1st, 2nd, 3rd, and 4th level cleric spells	

Faeril's Background

Faeril joined the expedition from Elven Court to Myth Drannor knowing that her contribution would prove invaluable. When they were ambushed, Faeril dragged the blind cleric Beriand to safety. She has attended to him faithfully ever since, unselfishly protecting him wit no concern for herself.

    A devout disciple whose faith is without compromise, Faeril belongs to the special sect of Mystra for elven (and half-elven) followers founded by Anorrweyn Evensong.

Jarial

Summary

Jarial's strength lies in the arcane magic that only sorcerers possess. His experience is lacking since he was imprisoned long ago and has been unable to continue his quest to the undercity of Myth Drannor.

Jarial is found encased in stone near Turgild's Square on the 3rd level of the Dwarven Dungeons, The Main Halls. This encounter is detailed in Chapter 6.

Jarial's Characteristics

Gender:	Male
Race:	Human
Class:	Sorcerer
Level:	3
Experience:	3,300
Strength:	11
Intelligence:	12
Wisdom:	8
Dexterity:	16
Constitution:	14
Charisma:	17
Feats:	Spell Penetration, Combat Casting

Spells:
Magic daze (0), detect magic (0), disrupt undead (0), light (0), resistance (0), mage armor (1), magic missile (1), protection from evil (1)

Numbers in parentheses denote spell level.

Jarial's Background

Many years ago, Jarial was a young, intelligent, inexperienced human sorcerer. At the age of 20, he fell in love with an alluring but hot-tempered female sorceress named Ozama. Her passion for acquiring magic led them on a dangerous quest to the undercity of Myth Drannor.

There, in the midst of an argument, Ozama's temper flared. Lashing out, she cast a spell that sealed Jarial in solid rock from the waist down. Even though he pleaded for his release, she coldly refused. She left him there, taunting him with a riddle that she claimed would break the spell. Determined and proud, she stormed off, presumably to finish their quest without him. Throughout the years, Jarial believed that at some point Ozama would return. She never did.

As the years slipped by, he tried every possible solution to the riddle, but to no avail. After yelling his throat hoarse, he finally accepted that he would remain a prisoner of the stone.

Ozama's immobilizing spell has preserved the youth of his body, and his mind has gained patience from the long years of isolation. But his heart still rages with passion for Ozama.

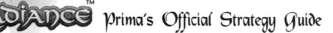

Kellan

Summary

Kellan is a fighter/sorceress, whose combination of magic and strength make her a worthy companion. Her no-nonsense approach makes her a good foot soldier and a valued addition to any party.

The party meets Kellan, along with Bronwyn, on the Second Cellar of the Catacombs. This encounter is detailed in Chapter 17.

Kellan's Background

Kellan is a member of the Sisterhood of the Silver Fire, a secretive organization sent to destroy their arch-nemesis, the Cult of the Dragon. Ordered by the leadership of the Silver Fire to investigate the evil at Myth Drannor, Kellan was perfect for the job. Brave and intelligent, her fighter/sorceress skills are complemented by an excellent sense of strategy and tactics.

Ambushed as they explored Myth Drannor, Kellan and Bronwyn escaped. Together, they evaded the fierce hunt by their evil attackers, only to be trapped in the corrupted city. The two have found a place to hold out, where they can grow in Mystra's faith until rescued.

Kellan's Characteristics

Gender:	Female
Race:	Human
Class:	Fighter/ Sorceress
Level:	7/6
Experience:	85,800
Strength:	17
Intelligence:	11
Wisdom:	9
Dexterity:	17
Constitution:	16
Charisma:	16

Feats:
Combat Reflexes, Combat Casting, Improved Critical, Iron Will, Lightning Reflexes, Run, Spell Penetration, Power Attack, Cleave, Blind Fighting

Spells:
Magic daze (0), detect magic (0), disrupt undead (0), light (0), resistance (0), charm person (1), magic missile (1), invisibility (2), cat's grace (2), fireball (3)

Numbers in parentheses denote spell level.

Tudo

Summary

A dashing young rogue, Tudo ventured into Myth Drannor to pry into its secrets and hopefully uncover much of its lost treasure. In doing so, he meets Nottle, the friendly shopkeeper rogue, who shares his secrets. In collaborating on burgling jobs and the occasional bold heist, they begin to exploit what is left of Myth Drannor for their own causes. However, neither trusts the other an inch. Constant bickering, bragging, and disagreements about the split of the loot cause an uneasy peace between them.

Your party finds Tudo on the Prisons of the Catacombs (the 4th level). This encounter is detailed in Chapter 19.

Tudo's Characteristics	
Gender:	Male
Race:	Human
Class:	Rogue
Level:	12
Experience:	67,801
Strength:	15
Intelligence:	9
Wisdom:	8
Dexterity:	18
Constitution:	14
Charisma:	17
Feats:	
Improved Initiative, Combat Reflexes, Point Blank Shot, Mobility, Run	
Spells:	None

Tudo's Background

A contradiction in terms, Tudo is an honest rogue. With a weakness for stunts, dares, wagers, and quick money, he is easily taken by any opportunity to score at a game of chance. When a rival in Hillsfar bet him a year's earnings that he could not return with a piece of Castle Cormanthor, he eagerly accepted.

When he actually took a piece of the castle, he was detected and imprisoned. Nottle, a friendly villager, scavenger, and shop clerk that your party meets in the Stillwater Ruins, happened to find his cell. He soon learned of Tudo's fondness for wagers and proposed his own.

Monsters

Many creatures in *Pool of Radiance: RoMD* will stand in the way of your party. Some swarm you in groups, some attack silently from the shadows, and some overpower you with magical strength, but all test the limits of your abilities. This section familiarizes you with your adversaries, but it details only a portion of the creatures that you'll face. This bit of knowledge should give you a fighting chance against them.

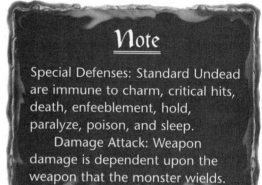
Arraccat

> ## Note
>
> Special Defenses: Standard Undead are immune to charm, critical hits, death, enfeeblement, hold, paralyze, poison, and sleep.
> Damage Attack: Weapon damage is dependent upon the weapon that the monster wields.

	ARRACCAT	BLACK ARRACCAT	GUARD ARRACCAT
ARMOR CLASS:	18	24	20
MOVEMENT:	60	70	60
HIT DICE:	7d10+7	16d10+32	10d10+10
NO. OF ATTACKS:	2	2	2
DAMAGE/ATTACK:	2d4+4/2d6+4	3d10+3/3d12+3	3d4+3/3d6+3
SPECIAL ATTACKS:	None	None	None
SPECIAL DEFENSES:	Immune to paralysis and poison; +5 vs. critical hits	Immune to paralysis and poison; +5 vs. critical hits	Immune to paralysis and poison; +5 vs. critical hits
MAGIC RESISTANCE:	0	10	5
FORTITUDE SAVING THROW:	+4	+6	+4
REFLEX SAVING THROW:	+4	+6	+4
WILL SAVING THROW:	+0	+2	+0
EXP. VALUE:	825	8,400	2,200

Arraccats are aggressive predators, dwelling both above and below ground. These half insect and half feline creatures all have six legs (two are nearly vestigial) and six eyes.

18

Arraccats are aggressive and not very bright, which sometimes leads them to attack creatures larger than themselves. Attack arraccats with ranged weapons and magic before closing to melee range. As a special defense they sport an immunity to poison and paralysis.

Cult Mages and Archmages

	CULT ARCHMAGE	CULT MAGE	CULT OVERSEER
ARMOR CLASS:	12	11	13
MOVEMENT:	60	60	60
HIT DICE:	12d4+24	8d4+8	16d4+32
NO. OF ATTACKS:	2	1	2
DAMAGE/ATTACK:	Weapon	Weapon	Weapon
SPECIAL ATTACKS:	None	None	None
SPECIAL DEFENSES:	None	None	None
MAGIC RESISTANCE:	None	None	None
FORTITUDE SAVING THROW:	+4	+2	+5
REFLEX SAVING THROW:	+4	+2	+5
WILL SAVING THROW:	+8	+6	+10
EXP. VALUE:	3,600	1,500	14,400

These mysterious high-level sorcerers belong to the Cult of the Dragon. They attack your party with powerful magic. Try to kill them before other foes, as their magic can quickly decimate your entire party. They use arcane magic but have few other attacks, and do not last long in melee combat.

Cult Soldiers

	CULT SOLDIER	CULT SOLDIER ELITE	CULT BRIGADIER
ARMOR CLASS:	11	17	12
MOVEMENT:	60	60	60
HIT DICE:	7d10+14	9d10+27	15d10+45
ATTACKS:	Melee +7	Melee +9	Melee +15
NO. OF ATTACKS:	2	2	3
DAMAGE/ATTACK:	Weapon	Weapon	Weapon
SPECIAL ATTACKS:	None	None	None
SPECIAL DEFENSES:	None	None	None
MAGIC RESISTANCE:	None	None	None
FORTITUDE SAVING THROW:	+5	+6	+9
REFLEX SAVING THROW:	+2	+3	+5
WILL SAVING THROW:	+2	+3	+5
EXP. VALUE:	1,000	1,200	18,000

Cult soldiers are human fighters who belong to the Cult of the Dragon. They have the same strengths and weaknesses as any human fighter, and are frequently accompanied by one or more cult mages.

Dark Naga

Armor Class:	14
Movement:	80
Hit Dice:	13d8+26
Attacks:	Melee +7
No. of Attacks:	2
Damage/Attack:	Sting 2d4+2, bite 1d4+1
Special Attacks:	Arcane magic, spit poison
Special Defenses:	Immune to poison, resistant to charm
Magic Resistance:	None
Fortitude Saving Throw:	+5
Reflex Saving Throw:	+7
Will Saving Throw:	+8
Exp. Value:	9,000

Dark naga are fiercely intelligent magical creatures with human faces, leathery purple snake-like bodies, and fanged mouths. In combat, dark naga can spit poison, and any being hit by it must make a Fortitude save (Difficulty Class, DC 23) or take damage. Even worse, dark naga cast spells as 9th level sorcerers, complementing their formidable fighting skills with powerful magic.

When facing dark naga, take them down as quickly as possible with a combination of melee attacks and offensive magic. Keep your clerics out of combat to support your warriors with magic that can neutralize poison and paralysis.

Dracolich

Armor Class:	36
Movement:	80
Hit Dice:	64d12+255
No. of Attacks:	3 (claw, claw, bite)
Damage/Attack:	5d6+17/5d6+17/4d8+8
Special Attacks:	Detect invisible, fear aura, paralyzing gaze, melee chill damage, paralysis, breath weapon
Special Defenses:	Standard undead, plus immunity to cold and fire and +4 vs. magic
Magic Resistance:	35
Fortitude Saving Throw:	+32
Reflex Saving Throw:	+22
Will Saving Throw:	+30
Exp. Value:	75,000

The dracolich Pelendralaar is an undead creature resulting from the unnatural transformation of an evil dragon. Pelendralaar is immensely powerful, combining the power of an ancient red dragon with the unnatural strength of undeath. How such an abomination was created is a mystery.

Pelendralaar retains all the knowledge and abilities of his original form. He can detect invisible objects and creatures, cast spells as a 19th level sorcerer, and cause fear with his mere presence. Furthermore, he can employ the searing heat of his breath weapon once every three combat rounds.

Without a doubt, Pelendralaar is the mightiest foe you will face. For more information on how to defeat a dracolich, reference Chapter 21. We aren't giving away his secrets here.

Pelendralaar

Dragon-Kin

	DRAGON-KIN	DRAGON-KIN CAPTAIN
ARMOR CLASS:	25	28
MOVEMENT:	40	40
HIT DICE:	10d12+7	14d12+9
NO. OF ATTACKS:	2	2
DAMAGE/ATTACK:	1d8+8/1d8+8	1d10+10/1d10+10
SPECIAL ATTACKS:	None	None
SPECIAL DEFENSES:	None	None
MAGIC RESISTANCE:	0	0
FORTITUDE SAVING THROW:	+5	+6
REFLEX SAVING THROW:	+6	+7
WILL SAVING THROW:	+7	+8
EXP. VALUE:	1,800	5,850

Dragon-kin are bipedal humanoids with dragon-like faces, wings, claws, tail, and horns. They are also susceptible to weapons that have bonuses against dragons. They travel and hunt in tribes, and have a weakness for interesting magic items. They are sometimes in league with evil humanoids, who supply them with shiny magical gear in exchange for their service. Dragon-kin have no regard for others, take what they want, and are thoroughly evil.

Dragon-kin prefer to fight in the air, swooping down to rake earthbound opponents with their foreclaws. If forced to bring combat to the ground, dragon-kin move in and use their claws. Face them as you would any other melee opponent.

Freth Drow

Drow Warrior   Drow High Priest   Enthralled Drow

	ENTHRALLED DROW	FRETH DROW ASSASSIN	FRETH DROW COMMANDER	FRETH DROW HIGH PRIEST	FRETH DROW PRIEST	FRETH DROW WARRIOR
ARMOR CLASS:	16	15	13	12	10	13
MOVEMENT:	60	60	60	60	60	60
HIT DICE:	9d12+9	17d6	12d10	16d8	12d8	8d10
NO. OF ATTACKS:	3	3	3	3	2	2
DAMAGE/ATTACK:	Weapon	Weapon	Weapon	Weapon	Weapon	Weapon
SPECIAL ATTACKS:	None	Per rogue	None	Divine Spells	Divine Spells	None
SPECIAL DEFENSES:	Standard undead; +4 vs. turning	None	None	None	None	None
MAGIC RESISTANCE:	17	21	13	19	15	10
FORTITUDE SAVING THROW:	+8	+5	+8	+10	+6	+6
REFLEX SAVING THROW:	+5	+10	+4	+5	+3	+2
WILL SAVING THROW:	+7	+5	+4	+10	+6	+2
EXP. VALUE:	1,200	21,600	3,600	14,400	3,600	1,100

These dreaded creatures were once part of the community of elves that roam the world's forests. Now, these elegant, black-skinned, thoroughly evil elves inhabit black caves and winding tunnels under the earth.

Freth drow are highly trained combatants and attack in patrols with warriors and clerics. They thrive in the darkness, and they like to make quick, surgical strikes at their foes, using long-practiced formations with the warriors. The Freth agreed to help the Cult turn on the Kilsek (another drow clan) and enslave them and take their holdings.

Some Freth drow have trained arraccats. This guard arraccat is a formidable foe. Keep your melee fighters in front and the supporting spell casters in the back. These are frustrating foes and difficult to kill.

However, drow elves are vulnerable to powerful light, which severely impairs their abilities. It is often wise to delay facing them until a way to take advantage of this weakness can be found. They suffer from -1 to attacks in bright light.

Note

Enthralled drow have the same strengths and weaknesses as regular drow, except they have lost all will of their own, have all the regular immunities of undead creatures, and can be turned by clerics.

Gargoyle and Margoyle

	GARGOYLE	MARGOYLE	MARGOYLE QUEEN
ARMOR CLASS:	16	19	20
MOVEMENT:	90	90	90
HIT DICE:	5d10+16	7d10+24	10d10+32
NO. OF ATTACKS:	4	4	4
DAMAGE/ATTACK:	1d4+4/1d4+4/	2d4+4/2d4+4/	2d6+6/2d6+6/
	1d6+6/1d6+6	2d6+6/2d6+6	2d8+8/2d8+8
SPECIAL ATTACKS:	None	None	None
SPECIAL DEFENSES:	+1 to hit	+1 to hit	+2 to hit
MAGIC RESISTANCE:	0	0	0
FORTITUDE SAVING THROW:	+8	+10	+11
REFLEX SAVING THROW:	+6	+7	+8
WILL SAVING THROW:	+1	+2	+3
EXP. VALUE:	1,500	825	1,800

Gargoyle

Hateful and vicious creatures, gargoyles exist only to attack and hurt others. Their race was created when a wizard animated a stone statue. They love nothing more than to lie in wait, then swoop down upon an unsuspecting victim.

In combat, gargoyles favor melee attacks. They are formidable fighters, with four attacks every round! They also frequently attack in groups and attempt to surround the party. Attack with ranged weapons and spells until they close to fighting range, then keep most of your party behind your melee fighters. Characters require a +1 or better weapon to damage gargoyles.

Note

Margoyles are just more horrid forms of gargoyles and are usually the leaders.

Ghast

Armor Class:	16
Movement:	60
Hit Dice:	5d12
No. of Attacks:	3
Damage/Attack:	1d4/1d4/1d8
Special Attacks:	Paralyze
Special Defenses:	Undead, +2 vs. turning
Magic Resistance:	0
Fortitude Saving Throw:	+1
Reflex Saving Throw:	+3
Will Saving Throw:	+6
Exp. Value:	1,200

Ghasts are almost indistinguishable from ghouls, and many a poor adventurer has not noted the difference until it is too late. Ghasts are stronger and tougher than regular ghouls, and they have an even more potent paralyzing touch.

Ghasts often run with packs of ghouls, and they should be fought the same way. Take them out first if possible to negate their carrion stench.

Ghoul

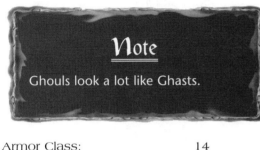

Note

Ghouls look a lot like Ghasts.

Armor Class:	14
Movement:	60
Hit Dice:	3d12
No. of Attacks:	3
Damage/Attack:	1d3/1d3/1d6
Special Attacks:	Paralyze
Special Defenses:	Standard undead, +1 vs. turning
Magic Resistance:	0
Fortitude Saving Throw:	+5
Reflex Saving Throw:	+4
Will Saving Throw:	+3
Exp. Value:	750

Ghouls are disgusting undead creatures that feed on the flesh of corpses. They dwell in dungeons, graveyards, and tombs, where there is plenty of food. Though once humans, orcs, or lizardfolk, they are horribly disfigured, with long, tough tongues, sharp teeth, and claw-like nails.

Ghouls frequently run in packs, and their touch has a chance of paralyzing their opponents instantly. This makes them dangerous foes that should be fought from a distance. Turn them with clerics whenever possible. If you have to fight up close, focus on one ghoul at a time to reduce the number of paralyzing attacks coming your way.

Golem, a Dwarven Statue

Armor Class:	26
Movement:	40
Hit Dice:	14d10
No. of Attacks:	2
Damage/Attack:	2d10+9/2d10+9
Special Attacks:	None
Special Defenses:	Immune to all special attacks and magic, +2 to hit
Magic Resistance:	0
Fortitude Saving Throw:	+4
Reflex Saving Throw:	+3
Will Saving Throw:	+4
Exp. Value:	12,000

These sturdy stone statues will tear your party apart in a hurry if you aren't prepared. Animated by ancient dwarven magic, the dwarven statues have an immense number of hit points, inflict huge amounts of damage with their fists, and are immune to almost all magic.

Make sure your party is at full strength before you face them, and pump your warriors up with spells such as *haste*, *bull's strength* and *prayer*. Have your clerics back them up with healing magic once in combat. Magical gear can help against these stoic guardians, but even with it, these will be tough fights.

Lich

	LICH	ARCHLICH
ARMOR CLASS:	18	23
MOVEMENT:	30	30
HIT DICE:	12th level sorcerer	16th level sorcerer
NO. OF ATTACKS:	2	2
DAMAGE/ATTACK:	Weapon	Weapon
SPECIAL ATTACKS:	Fear aura/paralyze	Fear aura/paralyze
SPECIAL DEFENSES:	Standard undead, +6 vs. turning, +1 to hit	Standard undead, +8 vs. turning, +1 to hit
MAGIC RESISTANCE:	0	0
FORTITUDE SAVING THROW:	+5	+10
REFLEX SAVING THROW:	+10	+15
WILL SAVING THROW:	+15	+20
EXP. VALUE:	12,000	18,000

Liches are undead spell casters, usually wizards or sorcerers but sometimes clerics, who have used their magic to unnaturally extend their lives. Gaunt, skeletal humanoids who hunger for even greater magical powers, they are consumed by a dreadful aura of death and evil.

Be prepared if you face a lich in battle. Have a cleric or other magic user handy with *remove paralysis* and *protection from evil* when encountering them. Like most undead, they are immune to sleep, paralysis, poison, and cold. Turning undead rarely works on them. Use fire magic to wear them down, and try to close to melee with them as soon as possible. Kill them quickly, or their powerful magic will destroy you despite your protections. Keep in mind that your party will not gain any XP until you destroy the Lich's phylactery. Until it is destroyed, the Lich can reappear and haunt your every move.

Lizardfolk

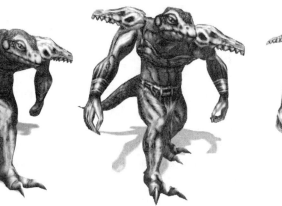

Standard Lizardfolk   Lizardfolk Chief   Stone Lizardfolk

	LIZARDFOLK (ARMED)	LIZARDFOLK TASKMASTER	LIZARDFOLK WARRIOR	LIZARDFOLK FAITH HEALER	STONE LIZARDFOLK
ARMOR CLASS:	15	17	17	15	22
MOVEMENT:	60	60	60	60	40
HIT DICE:	2d8+2	5d8+8	6d8+6	4d8+4	7d8+4
NO. OF ATTACKS:	1	1	2	1	2
DAMAGE/ATTACK:	Weapon	Weapon	1d6+6/ 1d6+6	Weapon	1d8+6/ 1d8+6
SPECIAL ATTACKS:	None	Spells per 4th level sorcerer	None	Spells per 4th level cleric	None
SPECIAL DEFENSES:	None	None	None	None	Immune to all special attacks and magic, +2 to hit
MAGIC RESISTANCE:	0	0	0	0	0
FORTITUDE SAVING THROW:	+1	+2	+5	+3	+3
REFLEX SAVING THROW:	+3	+4	+4	+3	+0
WILL SAVING THROW:	+0	+1	+1	+2	+3
EXP. VALUE:	300	1,200	1,800	900	2,250

Lizardfolk are savage, reptilian creatures that live through scavenging and raiding. Though they generally attack as an unorganized mob, they can be formidable opponents. Lizardfolk faith healers or taskmasters use divine magic against their foes, and a lizardfolk chief presents a tough fight with a massive, powerful enemy.

Because they are unorganized, lizardfolk can generally be picked off one by one by a skilled party. When overrun with rampaging lizardfolk, use area-effect spells to thin their ranks, since individually they have low hit points. Avoid being surrounded, and protect your mages. Stone lizardfolk are susceptible to weapons that are effective against constructs. Constructs are immune to acid, charm, cold, critical hits, death, electricity, enfeeblement, fire, hold, magic, paralyze, poison, and sleep.

Mohrg

Armor Class:	15
Movement:	90
Hit Dice:	14d12
No. of Attacks:	3
Damage/Attack:	1d6+5/1d6+5/1d6+5
Special Attacks:	Paralyze
Special Defenses:	Standard undead; can't be turned
Magic Resistance:	0
Fortitude Saving Throw:	+4
Reflex Saving Throw:	+5
Will Saving Throw:	+9
Exp. Value:	3,600

Mohrgs are the animated corpses of mass murderers or similar villains who die without atoning for their crimes. While they look like zombies or ghouls, they are more dangerous and powerful. They attack with their powerful fists, but melee combat is the best way to face them because of their high hit points. They have relatively low Armor Classes, so warriors can use the Power Attack feat advantageously. Faster than Zombies, they like to move around behind your warriors to attack your magic users.

Orcs

Orc   Orc Chief   Orc Shaman

	ORC	ORC CAPTAIN	ORC SERGEANT	ORC SHAMAN	ORC WARLOCK
ARMOR CLASS:	14	18	17	15	17
MOVEMENT:	60	60	60	60	60
HIT DICE:	1d8	7d10+4	5d10	4d8	6d6+6
NO. OF ATTACKS:	1	2	1	1	1
DAMAGE/ATTACK:	Weapon	Weapon	Weapon	Weapon	Weapon
SPECIAL ATTACKS:	None	None	Spells per 4th level sorcerer	Spells per 4th level cleric	Spells per 6th level sorcerer
SPECIAL DEFENSES:	None	None	None	None	None
MAGIC RESISTANCE:	0	0	0	0	0
FORTITUDE SAVING THROW:	+2	+4	+4	+2	+1
REFLEX SAVING THROW:	+0	+3	+2	+1	+2
WILL SAVING THROW:	-1	+3	+2	+2	+3
EXP. VALUE:	150	4,500	1,200	600	2,250

Orcs are surprisingly aggressive creatures, a warlike humanoid race. They are very strong, but most are poorly trained and only present a challenge to a low-level party.

However, beware of the orc sergeant, orc captain, orc warlock, and orc shaman who are formidable adversaries. Orcs are also trouble when they attack in numbers.

Ormyrr

Armor Class:	18
Movement:	60
Hit Dice:	10d10+10
No. of Attacks:	5
Damage/Attack:	1d6+1/1d6+1/2d6+2/Weapon/Weapon
Special Attacks:	None
Special Defenses:	+4 save vs. poison
Magic Resistance:	0
Fortitude Saving Throw:	+5
Reflex Saving Throw:	+1
Will Saving Throw:	+4
Exp. Value:	4,800

These creatures are seldom seen in Faerûn. It is suspected that they are visitors from another dimension. However, they inflict terrible damage when encountered. They resemble a four-armed, upright worm. They seize weapons and bludgeon their victims with them.

Ormyrr attack with all four arms without penalty, and their immense strength gives them a massive damage bonus. If you get close enough, they'll bite. The best strategy for overcoming an Ormyrr is to gang up on it with melee fighters or use magic spells that work from a distance.

Orog

Orog

The Orog Leader has stats similar to the Orc Captian.

Orog Chieftan

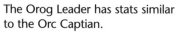

	OROG	OROG CHIEFTAIN	OROG GUARDSMAN	OROG HEALER	OROG HUNTER	OROG MARAUDER BOSS	OROG MARAUDER HOODOO	SOULLESS OROG
ARMOR CLASS:	16	17	18	15	16	19	17	17
MOVEMENT:	60	60	60	60	60	60	60	60
HIT DICE:	3d10+3	10d10+10	5d10+5	4d10+4	5d10+5	9d10+18	12d8+11	7d12+7
NO. OF ATTACKS:	1	1	1	1	1	2	2	2
DAMAGE/ATTACK:	Weapon	Weapon	Weapon	Weapon	Weapon	Weapon	Weapon	1d6+1/ 1d6+1
SPECIAL ATTACKS:	None	None	None	Spells per 4th level cleric	None	None	Spells per 6th level cleric	None
SPECIAL DEFENSES:	None	None	None	None	None	None	Standard undead, +3 vs. turning	None
MAGIC RESISTANCE:	0	0	0	0	0	0	0	0
FORTITUDE SAVING THROW:	+4	+8	+5	+3	+5	+7	+4	+8
REFLEX SAVING THROW:	+1	+8	+2	+4	+4	+4	+4	+0
WILL SAVING THROW:	+1	+8	+1	+5	+1	+4	+8	+6
EXP. VALUE:	500	9,000	1,200	1,000	1,500	3,000	6,000	825

Orogs are a race of great orcs, possibly mixed with ogre blood. They stand taller than regular orcs and are much stronger, but otherwise they share many qualities with their lesser cousins. Orogs usually serve as the elite warriors of orcish armies. They are extremely aggressive creatures and very warlike.

Revenant

Armor Class:	14
Movement:	90
Hit Dice:	12d12+3
No. of Attacks:	3
Damage/Attack:	2d8+8/2d8+8/2d8+8
Special Attacks:	Paralyze
Special Defenses:	Standard undead, can't be turned
Magic Resistance:	None
Fortitude Saving Throw:	10
Reflex Saving Throw:	8
Will Saving Throw:	12
Exp. Value:	3,000

Revenants are undead avengers who've returned from the grave to attack their murderers. They solely seek revenge against those who deprived them of life. Beware these creatures, as they are immune to turn undead. Usually alone when encountered, use the advantage of numbers to finish them off.

Shadow

	SHADOW	MASTER SHADOW
ARMOR CLASS:	13	15
MOVEMENT:	60	60
HIT DICE:	3d12	7d12
NO. OF ATTACKS:	1	2
DAMAGE/ATTACK:	0	0/0
SPECIAL ATTACKS:	Strength drain	Strength drain
SPECIAL DEFENSES:	Undead, incorporeal, +1 to hit, +2 vs. turning	Undead, incorporeal, +1 to hit, +4 vs. turning
MAGIC RESISTANCE:	None	None
FORTITUDE SAVING THROW:	+1	+2
REFLEX SAVING THROW:	+3	+4
WILL SAVING THROW:	+4	+5
EXP. VALUE:	750	1,000

Shadows are twisted, evil, undead creatures. They travel in loosely organized packs that freely roam ancient ruins, graveyards, and dungeons. They exist only to torment living creatures, and always attack them without hesitation.

The chilling touch of a shadow temporarily drains 1d6 points of Strength. Any character that is reduced to zero Strength as a result of this effect is killed. In addition, they are incorporeal, so that an attack that would normally hit a shadow has a 50 percent chance of missing. Fortunately, shadows do not show any advanced strategy, preferring to attack the closest opponent. Gang up on them and destroy them one at a time, using magic such as *magic missile* and *Melf's acid arrow* to wear them down.

Skeletons

	SKELETON	SKELETON KNIGHT	SKELETON LORD
ARMOR CLASS:	13	14	18
MOVEMENT:	60	60	60
HIT DICE:	1d12	2d12	6d10
ATTACKS:	Weapon	Weapon	Weapon
NO. OF ATTACKS:	1	2	2
DAMAGE/ATTACK:	Weapon	Weapon	Weapon
SPECIAL ATTACKS:	None	None	None
SPECIAL DEFENSES:	Standard undead	Standard undead	Standard undead
MAGIC RESISTANCE:	None	None	None
FORTITUDE SAVING THROW:	+0	+1	+4
REFLEX SAVING THROW:	+1	+2	+3
WILL SAVING THROW:	+2	+3	+4
EXP. VALUE:	100	500	1,200

Skeletons are mindless automatons that obey their evil masters. They are rarely armed with anything more than what was on them before they died. They attack until they are destroyed and generally attack in groups.

Skeletons receive a fairly high initiative bonus and often go first in combat. Move your party into combat with them while they're still at a distance (click on them as soon as you see them). This forces them to use their first turn moving to meet your party and not striking blows against them.

Like other undead, they are immune to mind-influencing effects such as poison, sleep, and paralysis. Furthermore,

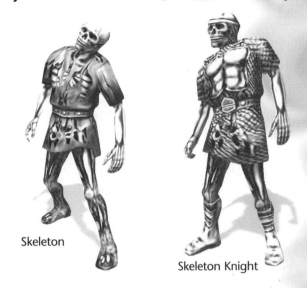

Skeleton

Skeleton Knight

because they are already dead and have no flesh, they take half damage from any piercing or slashing weapons. Fortunately, they are easily turned by clerics, and are vulnerable to warriors with blunt weapons such as clubs and hammers.

Spectre

	SPECTRE	MASTER SPECTRE
ARMOR CLASS:	15	17
MOVEMENT:	80, Flying: 160	80, Flying: 170
HIT DICE:	9d12	14d12
NO. OF ATTACKS:	1	2
DAMAGE/ATTACK:	1d8	2d6+1 2d6+1
SPECIAL ATTACKS:	Drain 2 levels	Drain 2 levels
SPECIAL DEFENSES:	Standard undead, incorporeal, +1 to hit, +4 vs. turning	Standard undead, incorporeal, +1 to hit, +6 vs. turning
MAGIC RESISTANCE:	None	None
FORTITUDE SAVING THROW:	+2	+3
REFLEX SAVING THROW:	+5	+6
WILL SAVING THROW:	+7	+8
EXP. VALUE:	1,650	12,000

Spectres appear as semitransparent beings. They are often dressed as they were when they died, giving you an eerie reminder that, if you are not careful, you're just a few touches away from joining their horrible existence.

Spectres inflict pain and damage in a number of insidious ways. A spectre's chilling touch drains energy from any living creature. If they are successful in an attack, in addition to the damage they inflict, they drain two life energy levels from any character that fails a Fortitude saving throw. They are incorporeal opponents, so half of the attacks that would normally hit them will miss instead. Attack them with magic as much as possible.

Wight

ARMOR CLASS:	15
MOVEMENT:	30
HIT DICE:	5d12
NO. OF ATTACKS:	2
DAMAGE/ATTACK:	1d4+1/1d4+1
SPECIAL ATTACKS:	Drain 1 level
SPECIAL DEFENSES:	Standard undead, +3 vs. turning
MAGIC RESISTANCE:	None
FORTITUDE SAVING THROW:	+1
REFLEX SAVING THROW:	+2
WILL SAVING THROW:	+5
EXP. VALUE:	413

Wights are dark undead whose appearance is a twisted reflection of the form they had in life. They seek to destroy all life, and do so mainly through hammering it with their fists. However, their most dangerous power is their ability to drain levels with their touch.

Like most undead they are immune to sleep, poison, paralysis, and stun. However, turn undead is sometimes effective against them. Fire and lightning magic is also useful. By the time you encounter them, you should have the tools you need to emerge victorious.

Wraith

ARMOR CLASS:	15
MOVEMENT:	60, Flying: 120
HIT DICE:	7d12
NO. OF ATTACKS:	1
DAMAGE/ATTACK:	1d4
SPECIAL ATTACKS:	Constitution drain
SPECIAL DEFENSES:	Standard undead, incorporeal, +1 to hit, +4 vs. turning
MAGIC RESISTANCE:	None
FORTITUDE SAVING THROW:	+1
REFLEX SAVING THROW:	+4
WILL SAVING THROW:	+6
EXP. VALUE:	825

The wraith is an undead spirit born of evil and darkness. The touch of a wraith does damage in two ways. First, the chilling effect of the touch inflicts 1–4 points of damage. Second, each hit drains 1d6 of Constitution points from the victim unless he or she makes a Fortitude save (DC 14). This lowers hit point totals as a result. The damage from the chill can be healed normally, but the Constitution points must be magically restored.

Wraiths are immune to normal weapons; a +1 or better weapon is required to damage them. Like most undead, wraiths are immune to sleep, charm, hold, death, poison, paralyzation, and cold-based spells. They are also incorporeal, so an attack that would normally hit them actually has a 50 percent chance of missing.

Zombie

	ZOMBIE	ANCIENT ZOMBIE	ZOMBIE LORD
ARMOR CLASS:	11	11	14
MOVEMENT:	60	60	80
HIT DICE:	2d12+3	4d12+4	9d12+3
NO. OF ATTACKS:	1	2	2
DAMAGE/ATTACK:	1d6+1	1d8+1/1d8+1	2d6+10/2d6+10
SPECIAL ATTACKS:	None	None	None
SPECIAL DEFENSES:	Standard undead	Standard undead, +2 vs. turning	Standard undead, +4 vs. turning
MAGIC RESISTANCE:	None	None	None
FORTITUDE SAVING THROW:	+0	+0	+2
REFLEX SAVING THROW:	-1	-1	+1
WILL SAVING THROW:	+3	+3	+6
EXP. VALUE:	150	900	2,000

Zombies are weak animated corpses. They shuffle slowly and awkwardly, as they are often decomposing and missing bones and flesh. They have no sense of strategy and always attempt to close on their nearest opponents and pummel them to death. They are easily turned or destroyed by clerics, and most strategies are equally effective at destroying them. Most of the time, just hitting them is the most efficient way to end their sorry unlives.

Chapter Three

Building an Effective Party

More than arsenals of magic weapons, piles of gold, and libraries of spells, your most potent weapon in the battle against evil is a good party. There are many ways to build a good party, and no one group of adventurers is "the best." However, you need to carefully craft a group of adventurers that can conquer any challenge. Most players will find that a balanced party suits their needs throughout the game. Others will find that a focused party better suits their style of play. This chapter will help you create your ideal party by giving you an inside look at the differences between the classes and by providing key strategies for building powerful characters.

Classes

A class is a character's profession. It determines a character's skills, feats learned, and role while adventuring. Different races are better suited to different classes, and each class relies on different ability scores. Understanding how to build an effective character of each class is a critical aspect of building a strong party.

Tip

You get bonuses and penalties for every two points placed into an ability score (so an ability score of 12 gives a bonus of +1, 14 gives +2, 16 gives +3, etc.). Maximize the effectiveness of your ability score points by raising your scores to even numbers if above 8 and lowering your scores to odd numbers if below 8.

Fighters

Fighters are the combat workhorses of the party. Their huge number of varied feats makes them equally effective at ranged and melee combat. Their flexibility allows players to change a fighter's role within a party to best meet the challenges.

> ### Tip
>
> If you have only a small number of combat characters in your party, at least one should be a fighter.

Special Abilities

Bonus Feats

Fighters gain a bonus feat every two levels, allowing them to quickly master ranged and melee weapons and pick up bonuses from saving throws, initiative checks, and more.

Feats

Feats are a fighter's greatest asset. They are gained on the following schedule:

LEVEL	FEAT(S) GAINED
1	Power Attack; Improved Critical
2	Lightning Reflexes
3	Combat Reflexes
4	Cleave
6	Iron Will; Blind Fighting
8	Run
9	Point Blank Shot
10	Improved Initiative
12	Great Fortitude; Precise Shot
14	Mobility
15	Skill Focus
16	Toughness

Fighters are generally the best at cutting their enemies to pieces.

Ability Scores

Three ability scores are important to fighters: Strength, Constitution, and Dexterity. All three should be at least 14. Take penalties in the other ability scores to free up points for your fighter's physical statistics. To maintain skill with both ranged and melee weapons, raise a fighter's Strength and Dexterity equally, then put whatever points are left into Constitution, which boosts hit points. Don't lower Wisdom below 10, or the fighter starts taking penalties to Will saves.

Races

Dwarves and half-orcs make excellent fighters because of their ability score bonuses. Which race you choose largely depends on whether you want to take a lot of damage (dwarves) or dish it out (half-orcs). Dwarves have lower movement rates, so they have more trouble closing to melee range quickly.

Elven fighters are very effective with ranged weapons because of their Dexterity bonus, but their Constitution penalty makes them less effective in the front lines. Humans are also less effective than other races as fighters, as fighters learn their most important feats very quickly without the human feat bonus.

Rangers are specialized fighters.

Ranger

Rangers get the bow feats (Point Blank Shot and Precise Shot) before any other fighting class, making them good archers near the beginning of the game. However, by level 8, fighters have as many, if not more, feats as Rangers. Rangers make up for this with their Favored Enemy ability, limited rogue skills, and divine spellcasting ability.

Tip

Because of their tracking skills, rangers notice things about their environments that other classes don't. This ability warns you about the types of enemies you'll face.

Rangers, like paladins, are a versatile class. In magic-heavy parties, they lend much-needed physical support while still being able to cast spells; while in a fighter-heavy group, their rogue skills and spellcasting are handy. If you anticipate strongly emphasizing either fighting or magic with your ranger, consider building a fighter or cleric instead.

Special Abilities

Favored Enemies

At levels 1, 5, 10, and 15, rangers gain a favored enemy. When fighting or using skills against that enemy, the ranger gets a bonus. This bonus can sometimes turn the tide of a close battle. A ranger receives favored enemies according to the following schedule:

Level	Favored Enemy
1	Orcs
5	Reptiles
10	Drow
15	Dragons

Rogue Skills

Like rogues, rangers learn the skills Hide, Move Silently, Search, and Spot. However, they may not find or remove traps. Still, their stealth skills make them effective scouts, and their Spot skill helps you find secret doors.

Divine Spells

Like paladins, rangers can cast divine spells starting at level 4. This lets them complement the party's clerics with healing and other magic.

Feats

Rangers gain feats according to the following schedule:

LEVEL	FEAT GAINED
1	Point Blank Shot
3	Mobility
6	Precise Shot
9	Improved Initiative
12	Great Fortitude
15	Run
18	Combat Reflexes

Ability Scores

A ranger's primary ability score is Dexterity. High Dexterity increases his or her effectiveness with a bow, which is what a ranger uses most often in combat. A ranger should also have a good Wisdom score to maximize magic abilities, and a high Constitution to help stay alive. Spread your remaining ability points between the physical statistics, but don't lower your Intelligence below about 6. Because rangers must be so well rounded, they rarely have individual ability scores above 14.

Races

Elves make excellent rangers. Their Dexterity bonus makes them excellent bow fighters, but their Constitution penalty means they should avoid being the primary target in combat. Their racial bonus to Listen, Search, and Spot skills also enhances their ranger skills. Humans

Tip

Don't pump up your ranger's physical statistics at the cost of Wisdom—build a fighter instead.

make good rangers as well. Their bonus feat helps them learn critical abilities such as Precise Shot quickly, and their skill bonus enhances the ranger's rogue skills nicely.

Barbarian

Barbarians are the best melee fighters in the game. Their feats and special abilities revolve around getting into close combat range quickly and doing as much damage as possible with as large a weapon as possible. They are less effective with ranged weapons than some other fighting classes, but their ability to take and deal damage is unmatched. If you need a dedicated melee fighter in your party, the barbarian is the way to go.

Tip

Barbarians should consider taking one multiclass level as a fighter early on to gain access to the Power Attack feat.

Special Abilities

Rage

Rage is a powerful barbarian ability that drastically increases Strength, Constitution, and hit points for a minor penalty to Armor Class. See the manual for details. Barbarians should use this skill as often as possible.

Barbarians of Various Races and Genders

Tip

The maximum length of a Rage is limited by Constitution. A high Constitution lets your barbarian Rage longer.

Fast Movement

A barbarian moves faster than other classes, allowing him or her to close to melee range quickly.

Feats

Barbarians gain feats according to the following schedule:

LEVEL	FEAT GAINED
1	Cleave
3	Run
6	Improved Initiative
9	Mobility
12	Improved Critical
15	Power Attack
18	Combat Reflexes

Ability Scores

A barbarian's primary statistic is Strength, which increases the chance to hit and the damage dealt with melee weapons. A high Constitution (at least 14) is critical, as it not only increases hit points, but increases Rage length. Dexterity can be left at around 10 or 12 because the Barbarian doesn't use ranged weapons and usually wears heavy armor that restricts movement. Don't neglect Wisdom completely, as Wisdom aids Will-saving throws.

Races

Half-orcs make the best barbarians because of their Strength bonus.

Tip

A barbarian almost never uses Intelligence or Charisma, so can get by with harsh penalties in these ability scores. Put those points into physical ability scores instead.

Tip

Consider a halfling barbarian. The size bonus offsets the Strength penalty, the Dexterity bonus makes them very hard to hit, and a Raging little guy is very amusing!

Their penalties to Intelligence and Charisma do not hamper a barbarian much. Dwarves also make excellent barbarians because their Constitution bonus helps them Rage longer.

A Paladin is a jack-of-all-trades!

Paladin

The paladin's combat skill and feats make him or her an effective melee fighter, and the limited divine magic makes a paladin a useful backup for the party's cleric. Furthermore, paladins' special abilities make them very hard to kill, making them excellent front-line characters.

Like rangers, paladins make great magic support for fighting parties and fighting support for magic parties. Their usefulness in a variety of situations makes them a welcome addition to any party.

Special Abilities

Lay on Hands

This skill lets the paladin heal a number of hit points equal to his or her Charisma modifier multiplied by their level. Any healing skills are welcome, and this is a fast and reliable way to heal a lot of points if your paladin has a high Charisma.

Smite Evil

This great ability allows a 2nd level or greater paladin to deal an extremely powerful attack to an evil foe once per day. This attack

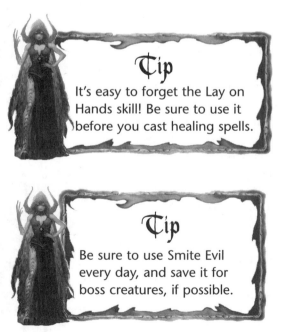

Tip

It's easy to forget the Lay on Hands skill! Be sure to use it before you cast healing spells.

Tip

Be sure to use Smite Evil every day, and save it for boss creatures, if possible.

has a greater chance to hit based
on the paladin's Charisma bonus
and does extra damage based on
the paladin's level.

Divine Grace

The paladin adds his or her
Charisma modifier to all saving
throws, protecting him or her
from many magical spells and other hazards.

Aura of Courage

Beginning at level 2, the paladin is immune to fear.

Turn Undead

At level 3, paladins can turn undead with the same effectiveness as a cleric two
character levels below the paladin's current level (so a 3rd level paladin turns
undead like a 1st level cleric). This ability is enhanced by a high Charisma. See the
section on clerics beginning on page 54 for a full description of turning undead.

Feats

Paladins gain feats according to the following schedule:

LEVEL	FEAT GAINED
1	Improved Critical
3	Power Attack
6	Iron Will
9	Combat Casting
12	Skill Focus
15	Blind Fighting
18	Great Fortitude

Ability Scores

Because paladins spend a lot of time locking swords with the enemy, their
primary ability scores are Strength and Constitution; both should be at least 14.
Charisma enhances the paladin's special abilities. Paladins should also have
decent Wisdom to enhance their magic abilities. Paladins can survive with low
Intelligence scores, but like rangers, they need well-rounded ability scores.

Races

Humans and half-elves make great paladins. Their lack of racial bonuses or
penalties nicely complements the paladin's "do everything well" nature, and

Prima's Official Strategy Guide

humans' bonus feat helps them get critical feats such as Power Attack quickly. Half-orcs and dwarves also make good fighting paladins, but their Charisma penalties mean they should focus more on their magic skills (powered by Wisdom) than their special abilities.

Monk

The monks are a unique melee class that rely more on Dexterity than Strength, fight primarily with their hands, earn extra attacks faster than other warriors, and have numerous unique special abilities. However, they have fewer hit points, don't use most magic weapons, and lose some of their special abilities from wearing armor. The monk is an interesting melee fighter, and can be very effective if used properly.

Monks can hit like no other.

Special Abilities

Wisdom and Class AC Bonuses

Because of long training, monks develop a "sixth sense" that helps them dodge blows. So, in addition to their Dexterity bonus, they add their Wisdom bonus to their AC (Armor Class). Monks also get an additional AC bonus as they advance in level. These AC bonuses are critical, because monks have fewer hit points than other fighting classes, and it's important that they don't get hit.

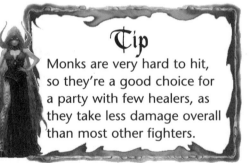

Tip
Monks are very hard to hit, so they're a good choice for a party with few healers, as they take less damage overall than most other fighters.

Unarmed Strike Bonus

A 1st level monk attacking unarmed does as much damage as a fighter with a short sword. At 4th level, he or she does as much damage as a longsword. At 8th level, he or she is the equal of a two-handed sword! Considering the other bonuses monks get for attacking without weapons, it rarely makes sense for them to use weapons.

Tip
All monks start the game equipped with a quarterstaff. Remove it immediately, as monks do as much damage with their hands from the start!

Limited Rogue Skills

The monk, like the rogue and ranger, learns the skills Hide and Move Silently.

Stunning Attack

The monk can stun an opponent for one round with the Stunning Attack. This can happen one opponent per day per character level.

Deflect Arrows

At 2nd level, monks gain the ability to deflect arrows by making a Reflex save. If the save succeeds, the damage is avoided.

> **Tip**
>
> In combat with several creatures, have your monk stun an opponent, then attack it with another character while the monk tries to stun a different enemy.

Fast Movement

Monks earn increasing speed bonuses starting at 3rd level, which help them close to melee range in combat quickly.

Still Mind

This 3rd level ability gives monks a +2 bonus against Enchantment spells.

Evasion and Improved Evasion

When monks make successful Reflex saves against magical effects such as *fireball* or dragon's breath, they take no damage, instead of half damage like most classes. At 9th level, monks take half damage even if they *fail* the save!

Wholeness of Body

At 7th level, monks gain the ability to cure twice their current level in hit points once per day.

Ki Strike

At 10th level and higher, the monk's unarmed attacks can damage creatures that can only be hurt by magical weapons.

Diamond Body

At 11th level, monks gain immunity to all forms of poison.

Diamond Soul

At 13th level, monks gain spell resistance equal to their level + 10. To affect a monk, sorcerers must roll the monk's spell resistance or higher on 1d20 + the spell caster's level.

Quivering Palm

A powerful melee ability gained at 15th level, Quivering Palm allows the monk to instantly kill an opponent he or she hits with an unarmed strike. A monk can use this ability only once a week, so save it for especially dangerous enemies.

Feats

Monks gain feats according to the following schedule:

LEVEL	FEAT GAINED
1	Combat Reflexes
3	Iron Will
6	Improved Critical
9	Run
12	Lightning Reflexes
15	Great Fortitude
18	Improved Initiative

Ability Scores

The monk's primary ability scores are Dexterity and Wisdom, and both should be at least 16. Bonuses from both these scores increase AC, which is crucial because monks usually don't wear armor. Put any remaining points into Strength, then Constitution. A monk can largely ignore Charisma and Intelligence.

Tip

Monks get more attacks than other warriors as they advance in levels. This makes half-orc monks, with their increased Strength damage bonuses, extremely punishing.

Races

Surprisingly, half-orcs and dwarves make great monks. (Never mind the odd image of a seven-foot tall half-orc or a stumpy dwarf jumping around and yelling like Bruce Lee.) Their ability score bonuses are critical to monks, who generally have to spread their ability score points very thin.

Rogue

Rogues are a critical part of any party. They alone can detect and disarm the many traps your party will encounter. They can also Hide and Move Silently, allowing them to scout ahead without being noticed. Finally, their skill with ranged weapons and ability to sneak attack makes them handy in combat as well. Every party should contain at least a multiclassed rogue, if only for the trap countering skills.

Rogues can detect and reveal the unknown.

Special Abilities

Rogue Skills

Rogues gain two critical skills that are not available to any other class: Open Locks and Disable Device. In addition, rogues rely heavily on the skills Search, Move Silently, and Hide. These skills are based on the following ability scores:

SKILL	ABILITY SCORE
Open Locks	Dexterity
Disable Device	Intelligence
Search	Intelligence
Move Silently	Dexterity
Hide	Dexterity

Sneak Attack

When a rogue flanks an enemy or attacks a foe that is not aware of his or her presence, the rogue deals additional damage depending on level. Use this in combat by engaging a foe with a fighter, then moving a rogue in to sneak attack from the side or from behind. This ability also works when shooting arrows at enemies who have not had a chance to act in combat. This ability does not work against undead and other enemies with no vital areas.

> **Tip**
>
> Note that all these skills are based on Dexterity and Intelligence. Make sure those ability scores are high.

Feats

Rogues gain feats according to the following schedule:

LEVEL	FEAT GAINED
1	Skill Focus
3	Improved Initiative
6	Mobility
9	Combat Reflexes
12	Toughness
15	Point Blank Shot
18	Lightning Reflexes

> **Tip**
>
> Rogues gain the Mobility feat very early. This lets them avoid the attacks of opportunity they draw when they move into combat to make sneak attacks. Be sure to capitalize on this!

53

Ability Scores

A rogue's unique skills are all based on Dexterity and Intelligence, so make these ability scores as high as possible. Dexterity increases a rogue's Armor Class and ability with a bow, so it should be at least 16. Intelligence increases the number of skill points a rogue has available, so it should be at least 14. Any leftover points should be split between Strength and Constitution.

Races

Halflings are especially well suited to be rogues. Their Dexterity bonus helps them stay out of trouble by boosting their AC and gives them bonuses to important rogue skills such as Open Locks and Hide. Halflings gain racial bonuses to the skills Move Silently and Listen, and their small size makes them harder to hit in combat and gives them a huge bonus to Hide checks. Humans theoretically make good rogues because of their skill bonuses, but halflings are better. Elves also make good rogues, and make especially good multiclass rogue/sorcerers and rogue/fighters.

Cleric

No party can do without a cleric. The cleric's ability to cast healing spells is critical throughout the entire game. Having a cleric significantly decreases the amount of time you spend resting and restoring. Also, clerics are capable in combat, and they have several enhancing spells that increase the effectiveness of the whole party.

Clerics of Various Races and Genders

Special Abilities

Divine Spells

The bread and butter of the cleric, divine spells allow them to heal party members, enhance their combat skills, and strike down their opponents. In *Pool of Radiance: RoMD*, clerics don't have to pray for spells ahead of time. They can cast a set number of spells of each level each day, and they can choose what spell to cast at any time. The most common reason to rest in the game is because the cleric is out of spells and needs to recharge.

Tip

A high Wisdom score enhances a cleric's effectiveness with divine magic.

Turn Undead

A cleric can draw upon his holy powers to turn undead or kill them outright. If they aren't killed instantly, they freeze in place, giving party members a free attack. Use this ability whenever you fight undead.

The number of times a cleric can turn undead is 3 + his or her Charisma modifier. Charisma increases the effectiveness of the turning.

Feats

Clerics gain feats according to the following schedule:

Level	Feat Gained
1	Extra Turning
3	Combat Casting
6	Skill Focus
9	Spell Penetration
12	Great Fortitude
15	Power Attack
18	Iron Will

Ability Scores

A cleric's most important ability score is Wisdom. It increases the number and power of divine spells the cleric can cast each day. It should be at least 16. Charisma is also important to clerics, as it improves their ability to turn undead. This score should be at least 14, as you face plenty of undead in *Pool of Radiance: RoMD*. Split your remaining points between your physical statistics. Constitution helps a cleric stay alive in combat, so focus on it, and don't lower Intelligence below 6, because you need some skill points in Concentration and Heal.

Races

Many races make good clerics. Humans and half-elves make great clerics because their ability scores are balanced across the board. Dwarves and half-orcs are more effective in combat than other clerics, but they need extra points in Charisma and Intelligence to make up for their penalties.

Sorcerer

Sorcerers are the only class in *Pool of Radiance: RoMD* with mastery of incredibly powerful arcane magic. They can cast spells that allow them to hit enemies from a distance with *magic missiles*, cripple them with *stinking clouds*, and devastate whole crowds of them with *fireball*. Despite a sorcerer's physical weakness, most parties will want to have one.

Special Abilities

Arcane Magic

Sorcerers have the innate power to cast arcane spells. Using magic is as natural to them as breathing or talking. Though they can choose to cast any spell at any time, they can only learn a limited number of spells of each spell level.

Sorcerers are the masters of arcane magic.

Feats

Sorcerers learn feats according to the following schedule:

Level	Feat Gained
1	Toughness
3	Spell Penetration
6	Combat Casting
9	Lightning Reflexes
12	Iron Will
15	Mobility
18	Improved Initiative

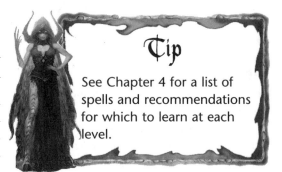

Tip

See Chapter 4 for a list of spells and recommendations for which to learn at each level.

Ability Scores

A sorcerer's skill with arcane magic is based on Charisma, so it should be a full 18 or close to it (at least 14). Having a high Constitution helps sorcerers stay alive a little longer and increases their chances of not being distracted when they are attacked while casting, as it grants a bonus to their Concentration checks. Dexterity and Wisdom are also useful to the sorcerer.

Races

Humans, half-elves, elves, and halflings all make good sorcerers. Halflings in particular have a number of bonuses to saving throws and Armor Class that helps them stay out of trouble in combat, but largely it's a question of which race you prefer.

Multiclassing

In the new D&D rules, characters can choose which class they wish to advance in when they gain enough experience points to advance a level. They can choose any class they wish, and it doesn't need to be the same one they've been advancing in before. The class abilities and restrictions of each of the character's classes combine to form the multiclass character's total abilities and restrictions. Multiclassing improves a character's versatility at the expense of focus.

While this can be useful at times, it is also a dangerous approach. Having multiclass characters in your party does increase the number of abilities you have access to. However, with the new rules, multiclass characters have much lower levels relative to their single class companions than multiclass characters did previously. A character with more than two classes ends up less focused than his or her companions.

Fortunately, having full 18 ability scores is not so important now as it was with the previous D&D rules. A character with several ability scores at 14 is nearly as capable as a more focused companion, and far more versatile. This is good news for multiclassed characters, who must effectively use numerous abilities.

> ### Tip
> Half-orcs and dwarves should never be sorcerers because of their Charisma penalties.

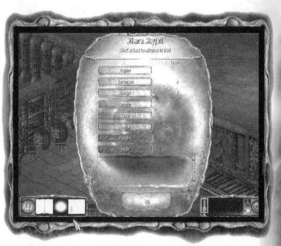

The level up screen allows you to choose what class to advance your characters in.

57

Naturally, some multiclass combinations work better than others. Here are some very useful multiclass combinations that you should consider:

Monk/Rogue

A rogue that starts a level as a monk gets a large advantage over his fellow rogues. Monks and rogues generally share high scores in Dexterity, Intelligence, and Wisdom, and monks even begin with rogue skills such as Move Silently and Hide. In addition, monks get a bonus to their Armor Class from their Wisdom scores, can stun enemies at 1st level, and have Evasion. These skills can make a rogue *very* hard to kill. Try this strategy: stun an opponent, then attack it to get the rogue's sneak attack bonus!

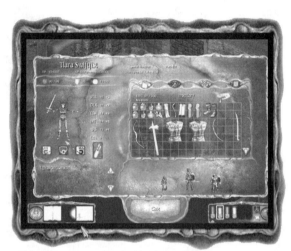

Character sheet of a half-elf monk/rogue

To create this character, make a human, half-elf, or halfling monk (other races suffer experience penalties) with relatively high Dexterity, Wisdom, and Intelligence scores. At 2nd level, become a rogue and don't look back. Avoid wearing armor so you continue to get your Wisdom Armor Class bonus. This isn't much of a loss, because most rogue skills are actually hampered by armor.

Rogue/Sorcerer

If a party wants to get additional magical power at the expense of rogue skills, the rogue/sorcerer is a useful compromise. This should not be the only sorcerer in your party, so be sure to learn spells that are different from those of the core sorcerer. This character should stay at the back of combat and use magic when possible and arrows anytime else.

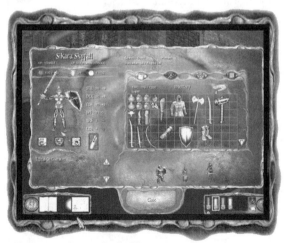

Character sheet of a halfling rogue/sorcerer

To create this character, make an elven or halfling rogue with very high Charisma and Dexterity. If this is your only rogue, make sure his Intelligence is high as well (a score of 12 should suffice). Advance two sorcerer levels for each rogue level until the rogue level is 4 or 5, then advance exclusively as a sorcerer.

Fighter/Rogue, Ranger/Rogue, or Barbarian/Rogue

This handy multiclass helps balance a party that is otherwise low in rogues. Plus, having a fighting character that can cause extra damage from sneak attacks is very useful. Have this character sneak attack as much as possible, either with ranged weapons before the enemies act in combat, or from behind. Barbarian/rogues can be especially useful because their Improved Initiative feat and increased movement rate lets them close in on foes and sneak attack them with powerful melee weapons at the start of combat. The focus should be fighting, but the rogue skills can often come in handy.

To build this character, create a human, half-elf, or halfling fighter, ranger, or barbarian with high physical stats, especially Dexterity, and a decent Intelligence score.

Note

Because rogues gain experience for disarming traps and opening locks, multiclass rogue characters tend to advance in levels faster than other characters. This is very useful with a rogue/sorcerer, as it allows access to high level spells quickly.

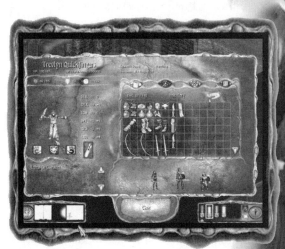

Character sheet of a human barbarian/rogue

59

Cleric/Fighter or Cleric/Barbarian

All parties should contain a cleric to heal wounded characters, but many will want to have a backup healer in case their cleric is incapacitated or runs out of spells. If your party doesn't have a ranger or paladin, the cleric/fighter or cleric/barbarian is the way to go.

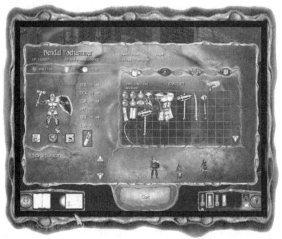

Character sheet of a dwarven cleric/fighter

To create this character, follow the rules for creating a fighter or barbarian, but be sure to keep the Wisdom score high. Create either a human, half-elf, or dwarven fighter or half-orc barbarian to avoid experience penalties. As a cleric, this character should focus on healing and enhancing spells, so there is no reason to take more than about 5 levels as a cleric, which gives access to 3rd level divine spells. Advance both classes equally until you are happy with the divine spells you can cast, then focus exclusively on the fighting class.

Building a Powerful Party

You now know how to build perfect characters. But what classes should you actually have in your party? What combinations work best in the game? It's best to have a diverse party with a good balance of fighting and magic skills. Have a couple characters who can fight well from a distance to support your melee characters. In general, a party must be able to adapt itself quickly and easily to any situation it encounters.

An experienced, powerful party in action.

However, there are many parties that can succeed. Here you'll find general guidelines on how to build a balanced party, some suggestions of variations that might suit your particular style of play, and a sample party that will work for most players throughout the entire game.

How to Build a Balanced Party

Here are the four recommended characters for a balanced party:

❖ A strong melee warrior. A barbarian, monk, or fighter is best.
❖ A second warrior. Any fighting class will do, but rangers and fighters work well in this role because of their skill with the bow.
❖ A rogue or multiclass rogue
❖ A cleric

It's a balanced party! A barbarian, monk, and fighter engage the enemy in melee combat while the cleric, rogue, and ranger engage from a distance.

You meet a powerful sorcerer near the beginning of the game, and you should definitely add him to your party. Your sixth party member can be whatever class you prefer, but will probably be a fighting class. Some of the best NPC party members are a fighter, a ranger, and a paladin. See Chapter 2 for a detailed description of all the NPCs who can join your party.

Remember that variety is your main priority here. You need a cleric, sorcerer, and rogue, or multiclass variations of them. Don't have more than one single-classed character of any class, as this hampers variety. Make sure that one or more of your fighting characters is a fighter or ranger with high Dexterity who can use a bow.

If you want a barbarian or monk in your party, create them as part of your first four characters. You will not meet any barbarians or monks in *Pool of Radiance: RoMD* who can join your party. Additionally, the only NPC rogue doesn't appear until late in the game. If having a rogue is important to you, include one in your initial party.

Party Variations

Following these suggestions, you'll have a party consisting of three fighting characters, a cleric, a rogue, and a sorcerer. This is a well-balanced, fighter-oriented party that will be equal to any challenge in the game. But depending on your style of play, you might consider one of the following variations:

Create an Extra Sorcerer

A major weakness of sorcerers is the limited number of spells they can learn. Creating an extra sorcerer gives your party access to a larger number and wider variety of spells than other parties.

This party has an extra sorcerer.

The game offers only one NPC sorcerer and one fighter/sorcerer. It isn't necessary to have more than one single-classed sorcerer, so consider replacing your rogue with a rogue/sorcerer. See the Multiclassing section beginning on page 57 for making a rogue/sorcerer.

Though this leaves you with a less effective rogue, your multiclass rogue/sorcerer should still be able to disarm most traps and open most locks. However, you may want to replace your long-range fighter with a fighter/rogue who can supplement your rogue/sorcerer.

Include a Backup Cleric

If none of the warriors in your party are paladins or rangers, or if you simply want more healing power, replace one of your warriors with a fighter/cleric or barbarian/cleric. This party should constantly be using its extra divine magic to heal and enhance itself during combat.

Despite their usefulness, don't keep too many healers in your party. One pure cleric and a paladin, ranger, or multiclass cleric is sufficient. Any more than that, and you won't have enough pure characters to be effective.

Sacrifice Magical Ability for More Fighters

If you think that the standard balanced party still has too many magic users for your taste, replace your cleric with a fighter/cleric or barbarian/cleric and multiclass your sorcerer into a rogue as soon as he joins your party. Fill the rest of your party with fighters, monks, paladins, rangers, and barbarians.

This party has a *severe* weakness when it comes to magic, but makes up for it with pure brute force. Bring at least one paladin or ranger in addition to your multiclass cleric so you have enough healing magic, but otherwise just wade into combat

This party of bruisers can kick butt.

and start hacking away! This is a strategically simple party to play, and it is incredibly satisfying to see your warriors crush their puny foes.

Sample Party

Four wet-behind-the-ears adventurers are in search of glory. Rallying to calls for help from New Phlan, this team of would-be heroes is inexperienced and poorly equipped. However, they are capable and strong, and with some luck and proper management from someone like yourself, they can grow to be some of the greatest champions in the Realms.

The four characters detailed here form the backbone of a strong, balanced party. Build them exactly as they are, or introduce some variations to suit your personal play style.

63

Grieg, Half-Orc Monk

Grieg's Characteristics

Race:	Half-Orc
Class:	Barbarian
Alignment:	Chaotic Good
STR:	18
DEX:	14
CON:	17
INT:	3
WIS:	11
CHR:	2

Grieg is the melee workhorse of the party. In any combat, his role is to rush his opponents and pummel them into submission. His physical ability scores (Strength, Constitution, and Dexterity) are all very high. In your party, you may choose to replace Grieg with a monk, fighter, or paladin. Those classes also make good melee specialists.

Bornan, Dwarven Fighter

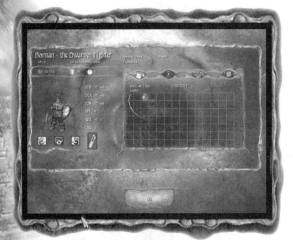

Bornan's Characteristics

Race:	Dwarf
Class:	Fighter
Alignment:	Neutral Good
STR:	17
DEX:	16
CON:	17
INT:	4
WIS:	10
CHR:	2

Bornan is an excellent all-around fighter, equally comfortable with a bow or battleaxe. He spends most of his time on the front lines with Grieg, but he's capable of quickly switching to a bow and turning his enemies into pincushions when the situation demands. As a fighter, he gains feats that make him capable at both melee and ranged combat. As a dwarf, he gains a natural resistance to poison and harmful magic.

Jandera Sunstar, Human Cleric

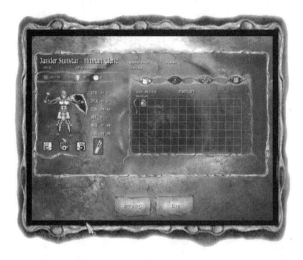

Jandera's Characteristics

Race:	Human
Class:	Cleric
Alignment:	Neutral Good
STR:	11
DEX:	10
CON:	14
INT:	3
WIS:	17
CHR:	14

A devoted priest of Lathander the Sun God, Jandera provides healing magic and divine support for the whole party. Her ability scores are balanced, with high Wisdom. Though clerics are effective both with magic and in combat, with Grieg and Bornan in the party, it is more important that Jandera focus on her magic. In most fights, Jandera stays back and casts spells or tries to turn undead. As a human, she gains balanced ability scores and bonus skills and feats that will serve her well.

Prospero, Halfling Rogue/Sorcerer

Prospero's Characteristics

Race:	Halfling
Class:	Rogue
Alignment:	Chaotic Good
STR:	10
DEX:	14
CON:	13
INT:	12
WIS:	10
CHR:	14

This party is thin in both rogue skills and arcane magic, and though Jarial will join very quickly, Prospero helps to fill both roles. His Charisma is high to assist his magic, his Dexterity is high to keep him alive and help his rogue skills, and his Intelligence is high to give him more points to put in those skills. He starts his quest as a rogue so that his initial skill points improve his rogue skills. As he adventures on, he will likely alternate advancing in his two classes until he has 4 or 5 levels as a rogue, then he will focus completely on improving his magic.

Begin the Adventure

Now you know how to build an effective party. The next chapter details the general strategies and combat mechanics within the game—which will prove helpful when you find your party surrounded!

Chapter four

General Combat Strategies and Game Mechanics

Adventuring

Fighting monsters is not the only thing that an adventuring party needs to know how to do well. While adventuring, a party explores abandoned crypts, encounters dangerous traps, and travels through treacherous wildlands. Simply tramping around can leave a party weak and unprepared when enemies do appear. Follow these guidelines, and your party will be ready for anything.

Resting

As you adventure, you'll note a tent icon that changes color between green, yellow, and red. This indicates how safe it is to rest in your current location. As a rule, when the icon turns green and your party is not at full strength, rest. There is no penalty for resting, and it's important to stay at full health.

As you adventure, note places where you can rest safely, so you can return to them easily. Nothing is worse than being hurt and in need of rest, but unable to remember where the nearest resting spot is.

The resting safety indicator

Exploring

When exploring, be ready for combat, avoid unnecessary damage, and find as much treasure as possible.

Always be ready for combat. Your characters should have their best armor and weapons equipped. As you find treasure and magic items, immediately equip them on characters that can use them. Keep the party together, and make sure that your rough and ready warriors are in front and your vulnerable magic users are in back.

The city of Myth Drannor contains more hazards than just monsters. Traps can tear an unprepared party down quickly. Have your rogue use the Search skill on every chest you find (it helps to hotkey it). You usually won't find anything, but always try anyway, in case a chest is trapped. If your rogue fails to disarm a trap, save your game, have most of the party stand back, and have a character with lots of hit points and good saving throws open or smash it.

Tip

Have the warrior with the highest initiative bonus lead the party. Often, you'll open a door and find monsters on the other side, immediately beginning combat. If your group leader acts last in the round, he or she may block the door. If the leader usually acts before your other characters, he or she can quickly clear the doorway. You can view each of your characters' initiative bonuses in the stats window of the character profile.

Monks and paladins are perfect for this. If the chest or door is locked, have your rogue repeatedly try to open it until he or she gets it. Otherwise, just smash it.

Explore a map thoroughly before advancing to the next. New maps often contain powerful monsters that can catch your party unprepared. More experience is the solution. Annihilating all monsters on every map guarantees your party's preparedness. Plus, it's easy to miss treasure if you don't take the time to look around. The maps at the end of this book point out the important locations and treasure troves. Glance through the overviews of each dungeon section to judge whether it is worth exploring fully.

Breakable Objects

Pool of Radiance: RoMD allows your characters to destroy objects such as tables and barrels. Always destroy objects that block passageways. You never know when you'll encounter enemies, and you don't want to have to move through bottlenecks during combat.

He is clearing the way for easy access.

Combat

The Combat Round

Combat is divided into rounds that you control. Regardless of how long a round takes you to complete, it equates to about six seconds in the game world. Every combatant can take an action in these six seconds. In a normal combat round, a character can take either a standard action or a full round action.

> **Tip**
>
> Don't destroy doors unless there is no other way through them. They make an easy barrier in combat, which can give your characters a breather to cast protection and healing magic.

A standard action allows you to do something and move a distance equal to your movement rate. You can move before or after taking your action. You can perform the following actions and move with a standard action:

- Make a single attack
- Cast a spell
- Use an inventory item, such as a scroll or a potion
- Use a special ability, such as turn undead
- Use a skill, such as Heal

Full round actions allow the character to move only five feet before or after the action, as they require far more time. Full round actions include either:

❧ Making a full attack
❧ Moving up to twice your movement rate or more

The Surprise Round

Before regular combat begins, the surprise round takes place. Only characters who are aware of their enemies can act, and each takes only a partial action (basically any standard action minus the move).

You see a + sign on the cursor if the action you are considering is a standard action and your character has not moved yet that round. Your character can move after the action.

Use the surprise round to position your characters for combat. Place your warriors in front to protect your spellcasters. If possible, block a doorway with warriors so monsters can't get through. Any warriors who don't need to move should fire a missile weapon. Any spellcasters who don't need to move should cast a spell.

Initiative and Being Flat-Footed

At the beginning of combat, all combatants make an initiative check, which is modified by the combatant's Dexterity bonus, the Improved Initiative feat, and some magic items. The results of this check determine the order of actions in combat. The character with the highest result acts first, the one with the second highest result acts second, and so on.

Tip

You can use magic items such as the Miner's Burnished Light Plate Mail and Fruhvogel's Pendant to enhance particular characters' initiative checks. Use these items to enhance your sorcerers, so they can cast area effect spells such as *fireball* before your warriors have engaged the enemy.

70

Before each character's first action (which does not include the surprise round) in a combat, that character is "flat-footed." A character is considered flat-footed anytime they are denied their Dexterity bonus to their AC, which can include the surprise round. A flat-footed character does not add his or her Dexterity bonus to Armor Class, cannot make attacks of opportunity, and can be sneak attacked by rogues from any direction. Take advantage of this with your own rogues by having them target enemies who haven't had a chance to act yet.

Attacking

There is a significant difference between a standard attack and a full attack. A character can move before or after making a standard attack but cannot make multiple attacks. To take advantage of higher-level characters' abilities to attack more than once in a round, position them close to enemies at the beginning of their actions. They can move about five feet to get closer to an enemy and still be able to complete multiple attacks.

For characters with Strength bonuses, melee attacks are the best way to cause damage quickly. These characters should generally close to melee range, especially against spellcasters or enemies with ranged weapons. Because casting spells draws attacks of opportunity if the spellcaster is within melee range, a barbarian can easily tear down even a powerful mage at close range. Don't let your warriors get too far from the rest of your party, however. Their biggest responsibility is to keep enemy warriors away from your spellcasters.

> ## Tip
>
> It is sometimes effective to delay a warrior's action and let the monster come to him, instead of rushing out to meet the monster. This allows the warrior to take a full attack next turn.

A gang of warriors surround an enemy mage.

71

Two feats that require some strategy in combat are Power Attack and Cleave. Power Attack increases damage at the cost of accuracy. It's most effective against enemies that have many hit points but low Armor Classes, such as cadaverous undead. If you have a weapon that doubles damage, the damage from a Power Attack is doubled as well. Try to inflict more than 100 points of damage in one hit!

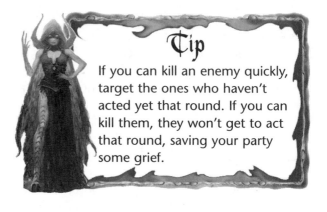

Tip

If you can kill an enemy quickly, target the ones who haven't acted yet that round. If you can kill them, they won't get to act that round, saving your party some grief.

Tip

One characteristic of weapons that is not visible in the game is their critical hit range and multiplier. Some magic weapons may have lower bonuses than others, but cause critical hits more often and inflict more damage when they do. Check Appendix A to find the critical hit range and multiplier of your weapons, and take this into account when equipping your characters.

Cleave lets warriors make an immediate attack against an adjacent foe if they kill a monster with their previous attack. This is an excellent way to get extra attacks in combat. Try to position your warriors next to multiple enemies to take advantage of Cleave. Note that Cleave is the first feat barbarians learn.

It is often to your advantage to use ranged weapons against monsters instead of rushing out to meet them. You can get a couple of extra attacks at a charging orc this way. It's especially important to keep monsters with special melee abilities (such as shadows and ghouls) at a distance as long as possible. In addition, ranged weapons are flexible, letting you attack the most deserving enemy, such as an enemy mage or a fighter with one hit point left.

Enemy Types

Every enemy you face can be divided into one of three basic types: melee, ranged weapon, and magic enemies. There are some variations and combinations, but this rule is generally true. Knowing what strategy to use against which enemy will vastly increase your chances of victory.

Tip

Ranged weapons are not as potent at lower levels in the newest D&D rules as they were in the previous rules. Your characters do not get as many bonus attacks per round with them, and they are not enhanced by Strength bonuses. However, once your warriors can make about three attacks in a round, ranged weapons become very worthwhile, as a character equipped with a bow does not have to close to melee range before making a full attack.

Tip

Don't wander very far afield during combat. There are often monsters nearby that don't know you're there. If you walk near them, they will join the combat, making the fight that much harder.

73

Melee Enemies

A selection of melee enemies

Melee enemies advance to close range very quickly. They are the simplest type of creature to face. Present a warrior or cleric of your own for them to attack, then hit them with your own melee weapons and assail them with spells and missiles if possible until they die.

Tip

You will quickly find yourself fighting creatures that are immune to normal weapons. Find magical weapons for all your characters quickly.

Tip

In underground areas, when combating enemies who have only melee attacks, position your melee warriors in a semicircle outside of a door. The enemies will walk toward the melee fighters in your party one by one through the doorway and into the range of your melee weapons. This prevents having to face multiple melee enemies from different directions simultaneously, and prevents monsters from reaching your spellcasters in back. It also lets you move any character into the room regardless of initiative order.

Ranged Weapon Enemies

Enemies with missile weapons easily attack your weakest characters, such as your sorcerers. Force them to put down their bows by closing to melee range with them as quickly as possible. They are also great targets for area effect spells such as *fireball*. This technique quickly reduces them to ashes while minimizing the chance of hitting any of your own characters.

An orc uses a ranged weapon to keep the party at bay.

Tip

Focus your efforts! Kill enemies one at a time instead of spreading out your attacks. Four enemies with one hit point each can attack your party four times, but two enemies with full hit points can attack only twice. Minimize the number of times your characters are attacked by focusing your attacks.

Lizardfolk geomancers make formidable adversaries.

Magic-Using Enemies

Kill magic users first. Especially at high levels, magic-using creatures can inflict serious hurt on your party with spells such as *fireball* and *lightning bolt*. If one of your warriors can close to melee range with a mage, then every attempted spell cast gives your warrior an attack of opportunity. Otherwise, focus your ranged and magic attacks on mages until they're toast.

Magic

Nothing can turn the tide of a battle faster than magic. Magic lets your characters blast, burn, and trap their opponents, bless themselves with divine grace, and generally tilt the odds in their favor.

Tip

When you know you'll be facing a mage, spread your characters out before combat to make it harder for mages to target your entire party with a single spell.

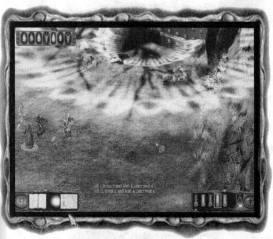

The power of magic

Tip

Having sorcerers attack from the back ranks with weak ranged weapons is almost useless. Exhaust your magic quickly then rest to restore it.

The Rules of Magic

The first rule of magic is to use it! Your clerics and sorcerers can use only a certain number of spells of each level before they must stop and rest. As a result, many players rely on their warriors in combat and only start casting spells when things get desperate. This approach is very wasteful. It's easy to find safe places to rest in *Pool of Radiance: RoMD* (just watch for the tent icon to turn fully green), and there is no penalty for doing so.

The second rule of magic is to remember to use it *before* you get in a bad situation. Both sorcerers and clerics have useful "prep" magic that can give a party a huge edge in a fight. Make frequent use of spells such as *bless*, *prayer*, *haste*, *bull's strength*, and *improved invisibility*.

The final rule of magic is never to cast spells within melee range of an enemy, as it gets a free attack on your character! Keep your sorcerers well away from enemies, and try to keep your clerics out of melee unless you clearly outmatch your foes. You never know when a party member will need a quick healing spell, and you don't want some monster disrupting your cleric's concentration during the casting.

Divine Magic

Clerics draw upon faith in their gods to cast divine spells. Most divine magic enhances characters' abilities, protects them from certain kinds of harm, or heals them when they're hurt. Some divine spells impair enemies with conditions such as blindness, silence, or paralysis. A few even inflict direct damage.

> ## Tip
>
> If monsters close in on your magic users, move them away from the monsters before casting any spells. The monsters will get an attack of opportunity, but they won't interrupt the spell.

> ## Tip
>
> *Magic missile* and *sleep* are the most effective spells for 1st or 2nd level characters. They are widely applicable to many combat situations when starting out.

A cleric healing an injured party member

Most often, clerics are used to heal party members with curing spells, but their other spells are worth trying. Here are some suggestions for using some of the best divine spells:

Bull's Strength

This spell enhances a character's ability score. It lasts *one hour per level of the character*. Cast *bull's strength* on your barbarian after resting, and you'll likely have to rest again before the spell expires. In the meantime, your barbarian has a bonus to hit and damage!

77

Bless, Prayer, and Protection from Evil

Cast these spells before entering any difficult combat. Their effects are subtle (see the game manual for specifics), but they are easy to cast and could mean the difference between victory and defeat.

Hold Person

This spell works on most humanoids, such as orcs and orogs, and instantly paralyzes them, removing them from combat until you're ready to strike them down. Use this against mages whenever possible.

A blessed party

Searing Light and Flame Strike

Both of these spells inflict direct damage. *Searing light* is especially effective against undead, and clerics learn it at relatively low levels. Although they don't match the damage or versatility of arcane attack spells, these spells are powerful ways for clerics to hit distant opponents, such as mages.

Arcane Magic

Arcane magic is the realm of sorcerers. It is flashy, direct, and immensely damaging. Many arcane spells, such as *cone of cold* and *fireball*, directly damage your party's opponents. Other spells protect the party, turn opponents to your side temporarily, or help remove the effects of harmful magic.

Use your sorcerers as artillery units. Their ability to inflict damage on many enemies at once is their primary power, and they can also turn the tide of a battle against a single powerful foe. Here are some of the most useful arcane spells:

Sleep

Sleep is a very useful spell for low-level parties, as it can incapacitate large groups of weak monsters. It's especially useful against orcs. Sleeping creatures are very vulnerable to attack, but focus on their awake companions when you can kill them quickly. Unfortunately, *sleep* is completely ineffective against higher level monsters, so don't expect to rely on it forever.

78

Magic Missile

This spell is an absolute staple that you get at the very beginning of the game. It grows in power as your sorcerer progresses up levels. It also inflicts damage to enemies who are resistant to certain types of magic, such as fire or poison. Use it until it is exhausted, then rest.

A sorcerer puts the smack down with a *magic missile*.

Fireball

Arcane magic gets really powerful at 3rd level. *Fireball* inflicts severe damage against many opponents at once. Make sure your own party members aren't in the blast area (you'll see the affected area before you cast this spell), and then burn your foes to the ground!

Set up the kill, then blast the opposition with *fireball*.

Haste

This awesome spell imbues a single character with exceptional speed. Hasted characters can take an extra partial action on their turn, meaning an extra attack for warriors or an extra spell for casters. In addition, they gain a +4 speed bonus to their AC, making them *very* tough to hit!

They speed off with great *haste*.

Confusion

Confusion is possibly the game's best spell. It works on any opponents other than undead or constructs, and if they fail their saving throw, they are completely incapacitated for the rest of combat. It's like an area effect *hold person*. Later in the game, when you face large groups of drow and cult warriors, *confusion* is almost a necessity to survive.

Chain Lightning

The problem with *lightning* and *fireball* is that sometimes you damage your own party members as well. Not so with *chain lightning*, which lets you individually target each opponent. It also does much more damage than the 3rd level attack spells.

Other Spells

Other great spells include *cone of cold* and *halt undead*. Learn them as soon as you can and unleash their power frequently!

Status Ailments

A surprising number of things can go wrong with your characters. They can be poisoned, paralyzed, knocked unconscious, and much more. These conditions are all

severely detrimental and should be reversed as soon as possible. Each has a different effect and way to remove it. If you're not sure how to get a character hale and hearty again, refer to this section for the appropriate cure.

Afraid

Effect: Fear causes your characters to quiver in their boots instead of taking action during battle. Sissy adventurers have a great deal of trouble getting the job done, and should be cured immediately.

Cause: The most common causes are the cause fear and fear spells, but some powerful creatures cause fear by their presence alone!

Cure: The spells *remove fear* and *dispel magic* will help you out here.

Blind

Effect: A blind character suffers a 50 percent chance to miss in combat, loses any Dexterity bonus to AC, moves at half movement rate, and suffers a –4 penalty on most Strength and Dexterity based skills. All enemies get a +4 bonus to hit a blind character.

Cause: The *blindness* spell blinds characters.

Cure: A *remove blindness* or *dispel magic* spell restores a character's sight.

Charmed or Dominated

Effect: A charmed or dominated character loses control of his or her actions, and is under the influence of the enemy. This character will turn against his or her companions. Remove this as soon as possible!

Cause: The spells *charm*, *dominate person*, and *mass suggestion* can allow enemies to control your characters

Cure: Cast *dispel magic* to remove charm or domination.

Confused

Effect: Confused characters stand around not doing anything. Like paralyzed characters, they are very vulnerable.

Cause: Not surprisingly, the *confusion* spell confuses characters. Often, your own sorcerers confuse your characters!

Cure: Either cast *dispel magic* on the victim or win the combat without that character.

Cursed

Effect: Curses are incredibly crippling. A cursed character has a -4 penalty to all attack rolls, skill checks, and saving throws.

Cause: The *bestow curse* spell is the only way to become cursed.

Cure: For once, *dispel magic* won't work. A cleric must cast *remove curse* on the victim. Otherwise, a curse is permanent!

Paralyzed

Effect: Paralyzed characters cannot move or take action of any kind. They are extremely vulnerable to all types of attack.

Cause: The most common cause of paralysis is a hold spell, such as *hold person* or *hold monster*. Ghouls and ghasts paralyze with mere touch!

Cure: The first way to cure paralysis is to reverse what caused it. If paralyzed by poison, use one of the divine spells against poison. If held by magic, cast *dispel magic*. The second way is to cast *remove paralysis*, which negates all types of paralysis, including magical paralysis. The *freedom of movement* spell also counteracts paralysis.

Poisoned

Effect: Poison can have a variety of effects, ranging from damage over time to paralysis.

Cause: The *poison* spell reduces a character's Constitution. Dark nagas can spit vile poison at their foes from a great distance.

Cure: A variety of divine spells affect poison. *Delay poison*, *neutralize poison*, and *hold poison* all counter the effects of poison.

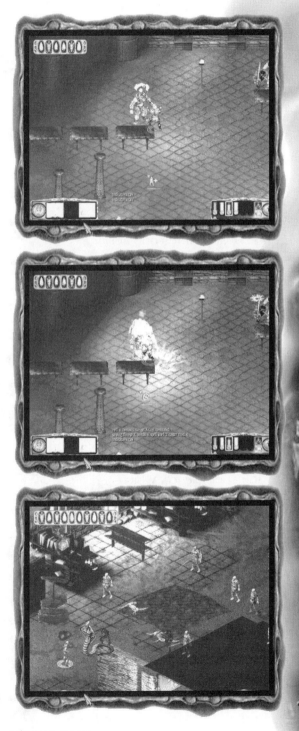

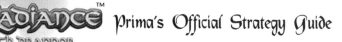

Reduced Ability Score

Effect: Reduced ability scores temporarily impair all skills and actions based on that ability score. For example, a fighter with reduced Strength causes much less damage in battle.

Cause: The *poison* spell reduces Constitution, and shadows and wraiths can reduce Strength with their touch alone!

Cure: Rest restores one ability score point per day. The divine spell *restoration* immediately restores reduced ability scores. Keep an eye out for *restoration* wands and potions.

Silenced

Effect: A silenced character cannot cast spells.

Cause: This condition is caused by the spell *silence*, which, incidentally, is a great way to shut down enemy spellcasters.

Cure: Cast *dispel magic* to remove silence.

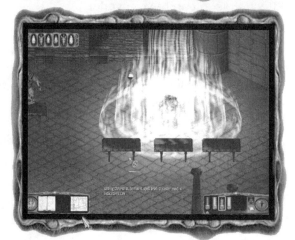

Slowed

Effect: Slowed characters take only a partial action each turn, and they suffer -2 to all combat rolls. This is no big deal for mages, but it's crippling to warriors.

Cause: The *slow* spell slows your characters.

Cure: Cast *haste* or *dispel magic* on the victim to correct this condition.

PART TWO
The Walkthrough

Chapter five

Stillwater Ruins

Here the adventure begins. Stillwater Ruins is populated with weak undead and orcs and features a couple simple quests to acquaint you with the game. Observant explorers will find a number of nice trinkets scattered around. Later in the game, you return to find Stillwater Ruins inhabited by stronger roaming monsters.

Quick Overview

The first thing your party should do after killing the orcs looting the corpses of Athan's group is to find the Fountain of Healing immediately to the east of your initial position. Return there to heal and rest if anyone is hurt.

You also meet some welcome friends in this dangerous land. A halfling named Nottle needs rescuing, and he helps your party find a pair of elves. These friends know only a little of what is happening in Myth Drannor, but they are still a valuable information source. Return to the Stillwater Shrine often throughout the game to receive new information about quests and the happenings in Myth Drannor.

Note that some groups of roaming monsters are not specifically mentioned in this walkthrough. Stillwater Ruins at night is particularly dangerous, as that's when the undead come out.

87

Dungeon Master's Notes

⬆ ⬇ Staircases leading up or down

1 The party is unceremoniously dropped into Myth Drannor at this location, right in the middle of a pair of orcs looting what's left of Athan's group. These orcs aren't hard to kill, since your party has the jump on them. You then find some pieces of Athan's journal where he describes his efforts to restore the Mythal. The orcs are carrying a light healing salve and a battleaxe.

The remains of Athan's party don't indicate whether he survived or not. However, there are a few bodies strewn around, so the odds are against his survival.

2 Three zombies guard a fountain that heals whomever drinks from it, making it a great center of operations once you clear the area. The zombies also guard a chest, which is locked and trapped. A hardwood key in a nearby barrel unlocks the chest. The chest contains a light healing salve and two scrolls of *remove paralysis*.

3 Here the party finds the halfling merchant Nottle under attack by two zombies. After they rescue him, Nottle teaches the party a Word of Power to help them visit a pair of his friends. He also sells them gear and lets them rest by his caravan.

4 There are two orcs on the west side of this bridge. The orcs carry a Suit of *Leather Armor +1*.

5 While exploring various dungeons, the party finds doors that lead up to this cave entrance. You can return to any passage leading from this cave at any time, making it a useful tool for navigating the game's dungeons.

> ## Tip
>
> When you find a doorway that leads to this cave, take a moment to sell your extra gear and talk to Faeril and Beriand.

6 After learning the Word of Power from Nottle, the party can enter this stump to speak with Faeril and Beriand, two elves who can tell you something of Athan and help you with the next portion of your quest. They teach the party a Word of Power to enter the Dwarven Dungeons and offer rumors of challenges the party may face. In addition, Beriand will heal party members whenever they visit. If your characters can find his staff, "*Deathbane*" (which he lost to orcs), Beriand can raise fallen characters from the dead. Faeril and Beriand offer other news as the party progresses.

After the party has freed the Shrine of Mystra in the Nightingale Court, revisit Faeril and Beriand. Faeril offers to join the party at this point, or the party can elect to take a token of Mystra back to the shrine.

After the party has completed the Elven Catacombs, Faeril and Beriand are captured by the scarred mages. The party can follow them through a portal to a stronghold in the northern region of the Second Cellar of the Elven Catacombs. See Chapter 17 for details.

89

7 This lookout is also the end of a drawbridge. The drawbridge is currently up, but the party can lower it from location 17 in the Windrider Glade (see Chapter 14 for details). From then on, they can move between the two areas at will.

8 A chest is here, packed with loot. Unfortunately, opening it summons two skeletons that immediately attack. The chest contains an *Amulet of Constitution* and a *Ring of Protection* +1.

9 The three orcs here pose a tough challenge, so characters should be 2nd level before facing them. Rest before and after the fight. These orcs declare their allegiance to an orc named "Zud," denouncing the orcs that follow a chief named "Mol." Behind them is a rock that, when smashed, allows the party to get into the orc camp.

10 This camp is guarded by one orc and a leader. They protect a trapped chest that contains a *Ring of Protection* +1 and a *Warhammer* +1.

11 There are two orcs here. One patrols the bridge and will pepper the party with arrows. Walk past to the south and climb the stairs to the east, to close to melee range with this orc without attracting its attention. Otherwise, the party faces a ranged weapon fight. The orc carries a *Longbow* +1 and a *Quiver of Arrows* +1. The other orc is located on the landing up the stairs to the overpass.

If you walk down here, out of arrow range, the fight is a lot easier.

12 Use the patch of healing moss here to get a quick boost before the fight in location 13.

13 The entrance to the Dwarven Dungeons is guarded by two orc leaders and sealed with a glyph. The party must learn the Word of Power from Beriand (at location 6) to enter the dungeon. The orcs carry a two-handed hammer.

The entrance to the Dwarven Dungeons lies ahead.

14 Once the party has entered the Elven Catacombs and returned to the Stillwater Shrine in the stump to see Beriand and Faeril, you find four orogs facing off against four lizardfolk. They are arguing about something called "it," and the party gets stuck in the middle of a fight. When the monsters are dead, the party finds *Deathspike, Spear of Skewering*, on the lizardfolk. This powerful weapon turns the tide of the battle in favor of your party later on in the game. The orogs drop a *Longbow + 3*.

Chapter Six

The Main Halls (The Dwarven Dungeons, Level 3)

Welcome to the first major area of the game. The Dwarven Dungeons, once the primary home of the Dwarves of Myth Drannor, are a massive thoroughfare of homes and hallways, filled with secret doors and hidden treasures. After the fall of Myth Drannor, powerful creatures such as phaerrim and alhoon repopulated the dungeons, taking control of a large block of rooms and holding it against attack from other invaders. These inhabitants have been cleared out by the Cult of the Dragon (and Pelendralaar, of course), and now only undead and other scavengers remain. The 3rd level of the Dwarven Dungeons is filled with orcs and several varieties of undead. This is also where you'll find your first truly powerful magical items. Entering as 2nd level novices, your characters rise to about 4th level if they finish clearing this level.

Quick Overview

The Great Hall

This is the first zone the party must cleanse of evil. Zud, a powerful orc chieftain, rules it. Defeating him is difficult, but the reward is great: Beriand's *Deathbane* staff! Also of note is the *Dwarven Great Warhammer of Death*, which will make the undead fights through the rest of the dungeon *much* easier.

Turgild's Square

The battle between the orcs and zombies continues into this region, where your party faces more groups of both. The party also meets an important ghost named Elena, and Jarial, the first character who can join the quest. Jarial can help you overthrow Mol, a formidable orc chief who has set up camp in the area. Keep an eye out for the *Massive Club*, a humble but powerful weapon.

The Rhonglyn Room

This mysterious area is crawling with undead. Its central location, the Rhonglyn Room, features prominently in your quest to come. Related to the room is the lock of ice, a magical block of rooms to the south, whose secret the party must uncover. North of the Rhonglyn Room itself, the party finds a dwarven tavern, long since overrun by orcs, with a hidden secret that is well worth investigating!

Central Ruins

These once-beautiful halls have been ransacked by orcs and undead in their fight against each other. Now several groups of skeletons and zombies wander about, set on ambushing any orcs that return to collect materials for their fortresses. There is no treasure of note, just a little gold. Clearing it out is not really worth the effort, but you need to pass through it on your way to Apothecary Row.

Lizardfolk Row

Once a bustling district of the dwarven city, this region harbors a number of secrets. While exploring, the party uncovers a clandestine group of lizardfolk, fights a powerful zombie lord, and discovers a bizarre burial ritual. This is an excellent area to find powerful magical gear, and wise parties will explore it thoroughly.

Bedlam Prison

A small area on its own, Bedlam Prison hides a mysterious wanderer whom the party can help or hinder. Adventurers brave enough to venture into the prison's catacombs can set an ancient spirit to rest at last.

Dwarven Tombs

Filled with restless dwarven dead, the Dwarven Tombs are not for the faint of heart. There are significant rewards for those who brave their horrors, however, and they don't call you "adventurers" for nothing. Before the tombs are finally clear, you will have uncovered the relics of the ancient dwarves and faced your most formidable foes yet: the master shadows.

Grand Avenue

North of the Stone Flower Halls, you find Grand Avenue, a short strip inhabited by several parties of tough undead. It's well worth clearing out, and at the end of a trail of gold, you find a powerful new type of enemy hiding a powerful weapon.

Avenue of Smiths

The final destination of the 3rd level of the Dwarven Dungeon, the Avenue of Smiths houses a hidden collector of amulets, hints of encounters to come, and answers about the mysterious foes that are the reason you came to Myth Drannor in the first place. When you are finished here, you will be ready to climb to the next level of the dungeons to continue your quest.

Dungeon Master's Notes

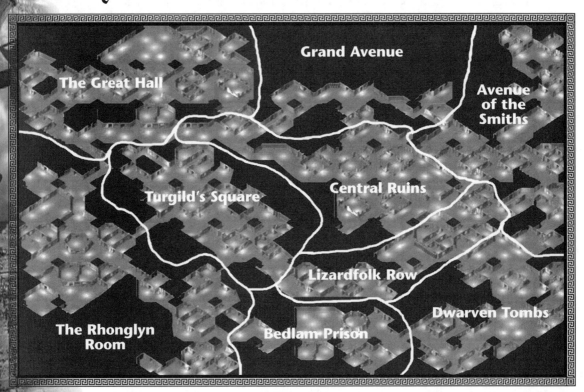

The 3rd level of the Dwarven Dungeons, the Main Halls

The Great Hall

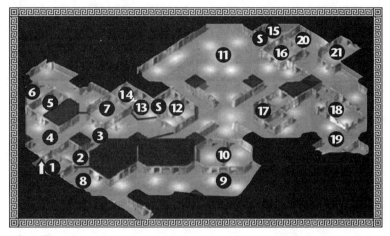

⬆ ⬇ Staircases leading up or down   Ⓢ Secret door

❶ The party enters the dungeons to find a pair of orcs pawing over a pile of dead bodies, supervised by a 2HD orc leader, in the shadows near the southeast door. The Key of the Dead is on the table and the Key of the Living, a *Shortsword* +1, and a *Sling* +2 in the chest. The Key of the Dead opens the northeastern door in this room. The Key of the Living opens the southeastern door.

❷ Four skeletons lie in wait in this hallway.

❸ The party comes across a group of three zombies here.

❹ Behind this barricade are two skeletons and two zombies. They block the entrance to a library. There is gold in the two wells to the southwest and in the fountain.

❺ On the far side of the library, a fight rages between some orcs and undead. Two orcs and one orc leader fight three zombies. The victors attack the party. The orcs carry a *Longspear* +1.

❻ The six skeletons in this room rise two at a time to attack when the party approaches. The chest they guard contains a *Battleaxe* +1 and two *potions of restoration*. This room is a safe place to rest after the battle.

❼ In this room, two orcs and an orc leader are at a standoff with a wraith—the undead form of the body on the table, who guards the body and the chest behind it. Take on the orcs first to get them out of the way. If you attack the wraith first, the orcs wait until the battle is over, then try to take down the party—

they want the treasure in the chest but are afraid of the wraith. Neither the orcs nor the wraith will initiate combat unless the party gets too close to the treasure chest. The orcs carry a *potion of speed* and some gold, and the chest behind the table contains a suit of *Leather Armor +3*, a suit of *chainmail*, a *Longsword +1*, and the Ancient Dwarven Chest Key, which you need to open the chest in location 14.

8 After opening the door that requires the Key of the Living, the party is attacked by four orcs in this hallway.

9 The crossroads sign states that the Great Hall is to the north and Turgild's Square is to the south.

> ## Tip
>
> As your party clears out networks of rooms in the dungeons, they become safe to rest in. Some networks are small, perhaps only a single room, while some are larger, such as the Great Hall and the surrounding chambers (see location 11). By proceeding carefully, you can always make safe resting places and avoid having to backtrack to heal up and restore your spellcasting capacity.

> ## Tip
>
> The wraith is a tough foe. He is vulnerable only to magic weapons and spells. On top of that, he is incorporeal, so 50 percent of all attacks that would normally hit him actually miss! Keep attacking with all your fighters and pepper him with spells. *Magic missile* and *burning hands* are particularly effective.

10 These rooms house some of chief Zud's orcs. There are three orcs in each of these two rooms, for a total of six.

11 The Great Hall is the new home of chief Zud. This is the same chief Zud that the party might have heard the orcs in the northeast corner of Stillwater speaking about. One orc shaman and one orc witch doctor join him in battle. This is the first tough fight the party faces.

Zud and his minions carry a *Wand of Cold*, a *Wand of Healing*, and two *potions of neutralize poison*. The chests on the back wall hold only gold. When you finish off Zud, you find a Crude Pot Metal Key clutched in his fist. This key opens Zud's personal treasure chest found in location 17.

12 Three orcs lurk in each of these three rooms, for a total of nine. There is a secret door in the northwest room.

13 Both coffins here contain a ghoul, a formidable foe for a party of 2nd level characters. There is a secret door to the northwest.

14 This secret room contains a deadly ghast. Inside his coffin are two *Dwarven Ceremonial Daggers*. He guards a chest that requires the Ancient Dwarven Chest Key (found in location 7) to unlock. It contains the Pale Blue Key (for use much later at location 124), 200 GP, two *potions of restoration*, and the *Dwarven Great Warhammer of Death*.

15 The secret door into this room is trapped with *shocking grasp*.

16 This is the orcs' treasure room. Each of the two locked chests contains a *Large Shield +1* and 100 GP.

Tip

If this battle is too tough, skip forward to location 28, rescue Jarial, and then return to this location.

Tip

Quickly send two warriors into melee range of the orc shaman and the orc witch doctor. This causes the orcs to stop casting spells and switch to melee attacks. Their spells can be crippling, and this strategy minimizes the number of spells they can safely cast. This strategy is effective against virtually all spellcasters, especially those you meet early on.

Note

Due to its immense power against undead, the *Dwarven Great Warhammer of Death* is one of the best weapons to use throughout the Dwarven Dungeons.

17 The two orc leaders in this room guard a small treasure room to the south; they carry a *Scimitar* +1. Inside the treasure room are two chests. The left chest contains some minor scrolls, potions, and *Gauntlets of Dexterity*. The right chest is locked with the Crude Pot Metal Key (found in location 11), and contains Beriand's staff: *Deathbane*. Returning the staff to Beriand in his shelter in the west of Stillwater nets the party a tidy experience points award.

Tip

Locked chests and doors that don't require a specific key can be picked open by a rogue or simply smashed. Rogues can uncover secret doors, find dangerous traps, and pick locks, and they gain experience for doing each of these things, so let your rogue try first. Make sure that your party leader is equipped with a melee weapon, as many things can be broken, and switching weapons or characters slows down your party's adventuring.

18 Two orcs and one orc leader are here. The leader carries a *Great Warhammer* +1.

19 One of the coffins here contains a *Quiver of Arrows* +1.

20 On the floor, find an Iron Key that opens the door to location 21.

21 This room is the Tomb of Onglore and Inglore, and it requires the Iron Key from location 20 to open. Onglore and Inglore, two extra-tough ghasts, are difficult opponents. Their coffins contain gold, an *Amulet of Strength*, and *Onglore's Amulet of War*, which is one of the best amulets in Myth Drannor.

98

Turgild's Square

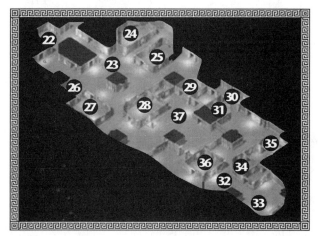

⬆ ⬇   Staircases leading up or down

22 Three zombies attack the party here.

23 After defeating the four orcs guarding these fountains, the party is approached by Elena, a ghost who wishes nothing but to see the fountains of Turgild's Square restored. She teaches your characters the Echoing Word and tells them that they will find others to help them in their quest. After you defeat the Lifespring Guardian in the Deep Halls, the fountains here grant special boons. The Well of Wisdom in the north grants one character a bonus Wisdom point, the Well of Beauty in the west grants one character a bonus Charisma point, the Well of Endurance adds three to a character's total hit points, and the Well of Rest revitalizes the entire party.

24 Two skeletons and two zombies guard a trapped, locked chest in this room. Additionally, the chest is blocked by a dwarven spire, which the party must lower. In the chest are the Ancient Rusted Iron Key (see locations 93 and 94) and a *Dagger* +3. A mysterious note, written by someone trying to protect the Dwarven Tombs, is among the other treasure.

25 One of the barrels in this room holds a scroll of *harm* and the *Fists of Ranman*, a great item that enhances the damage monks deal out. Watch out for the fountain, as two zombies attack if you investigate it.

26 Both these trapped chests are guarded by two orcs and contain some gold and a *Longbow* +1.

27 Three orcs hide in this room; they reinforce the fight with the two in the outer chamber if you don't quickly finish them off.

99

28 In this room, the party meets Jarial, a sorcerer whose true love encased him in stone. He tells amusing stories about the inhabitants of the dungeon, and he's waiting for someone who can solve the riddle that keeps him imprisoned. The answer to his riddle is "ring," and the party can solve it by equipping a character with a ring, then smashing the stone. Jarial is a great addition to the group. Reference Chapter 2 for a brief description about the strengths he adds to a party. One of the bookcases in the room holds useful healing treasures.

29 The bodies in this room hold a note naming their killer: Mol.

30 Four orcs watch this hallway. They guard the treasure in location 31. A couple of short bows and a *Quiver of Arrows +1* are on some shelves in the hallway. And look for the Rogue's Fountain farther to the south and east. It casts *cat's grace* on any who drink from it.

31 The chest in this room full of junk is trapped and locked with the Hidden Chest Key, carried by the orcs in location 33. It contains two *Bucklers +1*, a *Wand of Charm Monster*, and gold.

32 Six orcs have set up camp here. The large number of orcs around here indicates that the party is getting close to a leader.

33 The orcs in this party are some of Mol's most trusted troops. There are two orc leaders, one orc witch doctor, and one orc shaman. Try to take out the shaman first, before he starts casting *hold person* spells. These orcs carry a *Massive Club +3* (double damage) and the Hidden Chest Key (see location 31). This club is one of the most powerful weapons in all of the Dwarven Dungeons.

34 By sneaking around to the south, you can ambush Mol in his lair in this location. The orcs in this room are Mol's elite guards, and this will be a tough fight. Mol himself is joined by one orc shaman and two orc leaders. Mol and his minions carry an *Orcish Lead Mace*, a *Longbow +2*, a *Quiver of Arrows +2*, two *Chain Shirts +1*, a *Ring of Cold*, and the Undead Cell Key (see location 36). The *Orcish Lead Mace* is massive and hard to wield, but it does big damage when it hits.

35 More of Mol's orcs live in this room: two orcs and one orc leader.

36 The door to this chamber is locked with the Undead Cell Key, which is carried by Mol in location 34. Inside, three zombies pick over the corpses of several lizardfolk and a human mage. Find a pair of *Magician's Boots* and a couple of short swords on the ground after defeating the zombies.

37 One ghoul, two zombies, and two skeletons roam this hallway.

The Rhonglyn Room

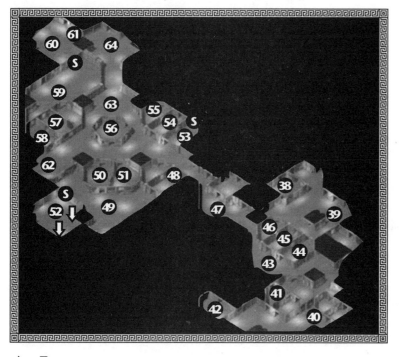

⬆ ⬇ Staircases leading up or down   ⑤ Secret door

38 Trekking to the south, enter a hall, once richly furnished but now gone to ruin. In a room full of pillars, find four zombies.

39 Four zombies lurk in this hallway.

40 Drinking from the Keg of Shielding here gives a *shield of faith* to every character who drinks from it.

41 These three rooms grow progressively colder. In each of the first two rooms, two zombies attack. In the deepest, coldest room, you find three wells. Smash the wells to break the lock of ice on the door at location 42. A party of orcs tried to do just that, but some cold attack killed them all. Each well releases a *cone of cold* toward the center of the room when smashed, so have most of the party stand back while one character stands to the side of a fountain and breaks it.

42 After breaking the lock of ice, you can get into this room. One shadow attacks when the party invades his home. Inside, find two trapped and locked chests, which contain sorcerer scrolls of *Melf's acid arrow* and *protection from evil* plus a *Wand of Chain Lightning*.

101

43 Two skeletons and a skeleton knight guard the locked door leading to the next location. Smash the door to gain entry.

44 Three skeletons and a skeleton knight lurk in this room.

45 Two zombies have ransacked this room, creating a terrible mess. Two cleric scrolls, along with a few gold coins, are on the ground.

46 A ghast, a ghoul, and a zombie attack the party in this room. Behind them is a locked and trapped chest that contains a *Wand of Melf's Acid Arrow* and a suit of *Reptilian Scale Mail*.

47 Traveling up this corridor, the party is attacked by several weak groups of undead: a group of two zombies, a group of three skeletons, and another group of two zombies.

48 The next few rooms house groups of skeletons of various types. This room contains five skeletons. All the undead here guard the entrances to the Deep Halls in location 52. *Turn undead* is extremely useful here.

49 The seven skeletons and one skeleton elder in this region attack the party two or three at a time. They drop several useful weapons, including a *Scimitar* +1, two *Short Swords* +1, two *Longswords* +1, and a *Dagger* +2.

50 The door to this room is locked. Four skeletons and a skeleton elder attack the party here.

51 The most powerful undead of the region live in this room: three skeleton knights. Defeating them yields a *Battleaxe* +2 and a couple of standard issue battleaxes. The chest in this room has a deadly *shocking grasp* trap on it, so have a rogue disarm it rather than having a character set it off and die immediately.

Inside the chest is a handful of gold, the Black Skeleton Key, a *Wand of Magic Missiles*, and a mysterious note regarding the entrance to the Deep Halls.

52 Here are the spires referred to in the mysterious note from location 51. You'll also find a secret door, locked with the Black Skeleton Key (which is also in location 51). Inside the room, two sets of stairs lead down to the Deep Halls. The northern stairs connect to location 1 in that level, and the southern stairs connect to location 2. These small, isolated sections of the Deep Halls do not link to the rest of the level.

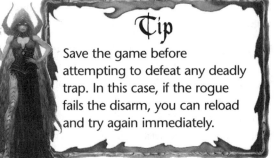

Tip

Save the game before attempting to defeat any deadly trap. In this case, if the rogue fails the disarm, you can reload and try again immediately.

53 Three zombies occupy this room. A secret door leads back to Turgild's Square on the northeast wall.

54 This locked chest contains two healing potions.

55 The party finds a mysterious mage leading two skeletons and two skeleton knights in this room. Could this be one of the scarred mages Athan spoke of? Be sure to attack him right away, before he can cast his powerful spells. The party also finds a scroll of *lighting bolt*, a *Wand of Resurrection*, and a *dagger*.

> ## Tip
>
> Take the northern stairs first and explore the rooms below, then take the southern stairs and explore the rooms there. These stairs are the only way to get to some useful treasure.

56 The doors to the Rhonglyn Room are frozen over, but they can be smashed down. Inside are five pedestals covered with ice. Once the ice is broken, the room can be used to warp between levels of the Dwarven Dungeons. To free the room, the party must break the ice in the Rhonglyn Room in the Deep Halls. There is a Rhonglyn Room on each level of the Dwarven Dungeons. See Chapters 7, 8, and 9 for details.

57 This dwarven inn has been taken over by orcs, and the party faces a single orc immediately upon entering. Two more orcs lurk in the room to the east. After the orcs are dead, this room is a good place to rest.

58 A barrel in this room gives the character who drinks from it Constitution +1 permanently. Keep an eye out for these "Tavern Barrels." They're scattered around various dungeon and catacomb levels throughout the game.

59 Seven very inhospitable orcs take offense at the party's exploration of this area. They are rearranging the furniture and removing several heavy treasure chests that mostly contain mundane gear. The chest in the back requires the Wrought Iron Key to open, which can be found in location 60, and contains a *Warhammer +2*. There is a Fountain of Restoration in the northeast region of this room but use it wisely: it has only two sips left.

60 This is the Tavern of Health. It has remained hidden behind a secret door for years. Characters can draw two potions of power from one of the kegs in the back and two healing salves from another, but moving near either keg summons a shadow and a zombie. You'll also find two *Small Shields +1* and the Wrought Iron Key on a table.

103

61 Each of these barrels gives the character who drinks from it a bonus to an ability score.

62 A quiet circle of spires here has a pile of Orog bodies inside it. If the party enters the circle of spires, a shadow attacks. He carries a *Wand of Restoration* and some gold.

63 As the party leaves (or enters) the Rhonglyn Room area, four zombies attack here.

64 A Fountain of Healing is nestled in the shadows here.

Which barrel provides which ability score bonus? Here's the key: 1 = Charisma, 2 = Constitution, 3 = Strength, 4 = Intelligence, 5 = Dexterity, 6 = Wisdom.

Central Ruins

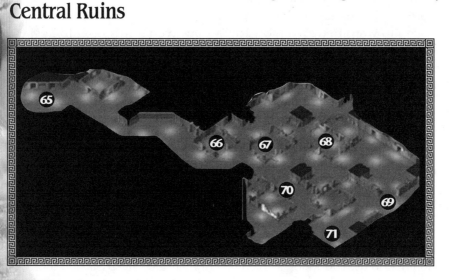

⬆ ⬇   Staircases leading up or down

65 Two zombies attack as the party walks down this road.

66 Here you find a zombie and a skeleton knight.

67 Four skeletons lurk here.

68 Fight the two skeleton knights and three skeletons.

69 This is a major crossroads for this level; use the sign to help orient yourself. Some zombies, generally in groups of two, shamble west of the sign.

70 One ghoul and two zombies are here.

71 This area contains two zombies.

Lizardfolk Row

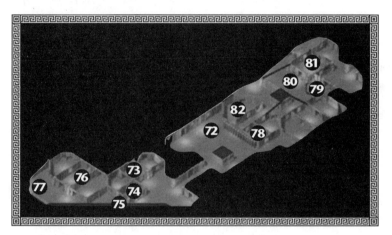

⬆ ⬇   Staircases leading up or down

This area has been overrun by lizardfolk in their attempt to establish a foothold on this level of the Dwarven Dungeons. They are valiant fighters, so prepare your party well.

72 A Keg of Health is to the north and three skeletons and two zombies are to the southeast.

73 Within this room, the party finds a locked chest with a minor trap. Inside is a suit of *Studded Leather +2* and *Boots of Health*. A nearby bookcase holds a sorcerer scroll of *bull's strength*.

74 Outside this room, it appears that someone has swept away any footprints, indicating a nearby secret stronghold. Inside the room is a locked chest, filled with three ordinary *short swords*. Could someone be offering a decoy treasure chest? The keg in the chamber to the northwest contains a few sips of healing juice.

75 These screens can be smashed, opening the way into the lizardfolk lair.

76 This series of rooms is the center of operations for the lizardfolk lair. Two lizardfolk guard the door to the first room and two more lizardfolk guard the first room itself. The second room is guarded by two lizardfolk leaders, and the third room is the home of the lizardfolk chief and a lizardfolk shaman. The chief is carrying the Brass "L" Key. The lair contains two chests, both armed with acid traps. The first requires the Brass "L" Key to open and contains the Brass "R" Key, a *Greatsword +2*, and a *Large Shield +2*. The second chest requires the Brass "R" Key to open and contains a *Greataxe +2* and a *potion of neutralize poison*.

77 These bookcases hold useful potions.

78 This mysterious block of rooms contains piles of dead bodies. The most powerful looking corpses are arranged with single gold pieces over their heads. This is a mystery to the party.

79 After following the trail of bodies to its end, the party finds a small library, which has useful potions on the shelves. A screen appears to have been knocked out of the west wall. The party can walk through this opening to location 80.

80 You find a sick lizardfolk here. He tries to warn the party of something but succumbs to his illness shortly before two ghouls burst out of a door to the north and attack.

81 This ghoul's lair is filled with more bodies. The body of one lizardfolk has useful treasures: a *Ghoulstopper Amulet*, a *Handaxe +3*, and a *Large Shield +1*. A barrel contains a *Wand of Resurrection* and a *potion of neutralize poison*.

82 This room is ruled by a solitary zombie lord. A pedestal in the center of the room releases damaging clouds of fire. The chest in the room has a powerful fire trap on it and contains a *Greatsword of Fire* and a *Staff of Harm +3*.

Tip

Be careful, because the zombie lord hits for a *lot* of damage. If your characters rush him, they'll take damage from the pedestal. Instead, try to position your party so that the zombie lord stops in the middle of the room, taking damage from the clouds of fire. Destroy the stone marker to stop the flames.

Bedlam Prison

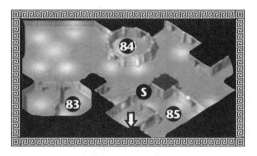

Note

The best way to reach Bedlam Prison and the Dwarven Tombs is through Turgild's Square, then past the lock of ice in the south. These areas are optional, so if you would rather skip them, jump to the Grand Avenue section, starting at location 103.

⇧ ⇩   Staircases leading up or down

S   Secret door

83   The hallways leading up to this room appear to be swept clean, and the reason why becomes immediately clear upon meeting Geb, a solo ormyrr. He is a member of the Sharpstick clan, and he's been searching for the mythical "magical thing" that all ormyrr believe will grant them magical powers. Sadly, if the "magical thing" exists, it is not in Myth Drannor. However, Geb will give the party a *Wand of Cone of Cold* that he has found if the characters are friendly. Geb is an incredibly tough opponent if you choose to fight him. If you talk to him, you earn points for later when you find his tribe.

84   This circular cell contains six weakened orcs (each has only one or two hit points) that have been imprisoned by Geb. If the party enters the cell, the orcs cower in the corner. If you get too close, they try to defend themselves.

85   Hidden behind a secret door in this room is a message from the jailer of Bedlam, entreating people to not take keys into the dungeons below. However, the jailer has been dead for years, so what's he going to do about it? Descend the stairs to the dungeon, which places you at location 5 in the Deep Halls. The room also contains two chests. One contains a healing potion, a *Ring of Constitution*, and a *Wand of Restoration*. The other holds a *Ring of Protection* +1 and a *Great Warhammer* +1.

Dwarven Tombs

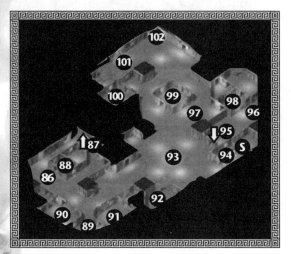

⬆ ⬇ Staircases leading up or down   **S** Secret door

86 This chest is locked and trapped. It contains two *potions of restoration*.

87 This doorway leads to a cave in Stillwater, right next to Faeril and Beriand's tree. This is a good time to return the *Deathbane* staff if you haven't done so already.

88 The coffin in this room contains treasure, but it also releases a *fear* spell and some undead. Those who want the *Wand of Resurrection*, *Half Plate +1*, and two *potions of neutralize poison* have to fight a shadow and a zombie.

89 A sizable group of undead lurks here: a ghoul, two skeletons, and two zombies.

90 This rooms holds four orc ghouls—ultimate symbols of the orcs' failure to ward off the undead. Your party should be tough enough to handle them by now. The only treasure is a pair of wine casks that cast magical effects on characters who drink from them. Be careful of the central fountain, as touching it causes the orc ghouls to attack.

91 Two ghouls guard some scrolls and a *Wand of Restoration*. The fountain here contains poison.

92 Two shadows guard the chests in this room. The trick here is to lock the creatures in the cells before going after the treasure. Both chests are locked and trapped with gas that drains Constitution, so if you can't disarm them, you'll have to cast *restoration* on any afflicted characters. The west chest contains two *harm* scrolls and a small skull head, and the east chest contains two *heal* scrolls and a small skull head. The skull heads, called "idolons," will be useful much later.

93 This is the central dwarven tomb. If party members touch a stone marker in the center of a circle of stones here, they hear the voices of a dwarven funeral party. If you have the Ancient Rusted Iron Key from location 24, the party will be transported into the tomb itself, below, in the Deep Halls. These tombs can also be entered at location 95. Without the key, only flickering memories come to mind.

94 This is an ancient tomb. Two seemingly empty coffins lie on the ground. The party can lower three dwarven spires to the northeast. Lowering the left or right spires releases a ghoul from one of the coffins. Lowering the middle spire releases a master shadow. Each of the ghouls has a *Ritual Battleaxe of Blessing*. Behind the spire, a secret door leads to a short passage. The door at the end of the passage is locked with the Ancient Rusted Iron Key, which can be found in a chest in location 24.

95 A ghast guards the stairs in this room that lead down to the Dwarven Tombs in the Deep Halls, location 7. There is useful treasure in this room as well, including some gems and a *Dwarven Ceremonial Staff*.

96 After breaking down the wall, the party finds this well. It's guarded by a master shadow, a formidable adversary. The well contains a *Necklace of the Dead*.

97 Three skeletons and a skeleton knight patrol here. A halberd and an *Ancient Dwarven Shield of Protection* +1 lie on the ground. By carefully timing your movements, you can avoid the monsters and pick up the treasures.

Note

The Dwarven Tombs are an optional area. They are filled with undead, and you can find a *Serpent Ring* in them. Turn to Chapter 8, location 7 for details.

98 These three rooms house numerous undead: three zombies in the first room, three more zombies in the northwest room, and two ghouls in the northeast room. They guard a number of sorcerer scrolls, a *Longspear* +1, a suit of *Ringmail* +2, and a *Ring of Intelligence*.

99 This room contains a useful dagger for sorcerers: a *Blunted Dagger of Armor*.

100 This room is haunted by a powerful master shadow and his three zombie minions. The chest to the east contains only a few gold pieces, but the western chest contains *Boots of Wisdom* and a pair of cleric scrolls. This chest is trapped.

101 Here a ghast and a ghoul lie in wait. These chests are empty.

102 Don't be tricked by the name of this "Fountain of Restoration." It drains Constitution from any character who drinks from it. Fortunately, there's a *potion of restoration* in a nearby barrel.

Grand Avenue

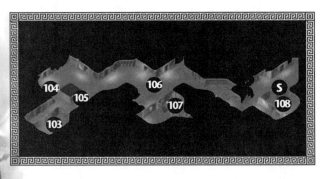

⬆ ⬇ Staircases leading up or down **S** Secret door

103 Five orcs have made this room their home. They have hidden their greatest treasure in a trapped and locked chest. Unfortunately, their "greatest treasure" is only an ordinary *greataxe* and an ordinary *great warhammer*. It is also safe to rest here.

104 Five more orcs block this hallway.

105 This unassuming bookcase houses a *Wand of Resurrection* and a *potion of neutralize poison*, a vital tool for the trials ahead.

106 Grand Avenue is filled with undead. In these hallways, the party encounters two groups of skeletons, each consisting of a skeleton knight and two skeletons.

107 This room appears empty, but a great deal of archery equipment lies on the shelves on the east side of the room, including two *Quivers of Arrows +1*.

108 A secret door is on the north side of this room, and a suit of armor indicates that this area was once inhabited by a derro, an evil species of underground dwarves. Now it is home to a ghoul, a skeleton lord, and two ancient zombies. A Fountain of Healing stands in the center of the room, and two trapped, locked chests contain a miner's adventuring gear. Inside the first is a *Miner's Great Hammer*, and the second contains *Miner's Burnished Light Plate of Protections* and a *Miner's Ward of Invulnerability*.

109 A trail of gold pieces leads into the lair of three orogs. They are stronger than the orcs the party has faced so far. A chest in the back of their lair contains a *Club +4*, a notably powerful weapon that is especially useful against skeletons.

Avenue of Smiths

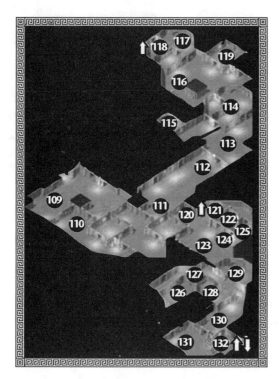

⬆ ⬇   Staircases leading up or down

110 This fountain is currently inoperative, but it will work after the party restores a pumping station later in their quest. Fountains such as this are the home of a water spirit named Plinshree. For details about Plinshree, refer to location 3 in the Glim Gardens, Chapter 13.

111 Four zombies block this passageway.

112 Two skeletons and two ghouls attack as the party approaches this doorway.

113 A large group of undead occupy this area: three skeletons, one skeleton knight, one zombie, and one zombie lord. Stay close to the door and polish off the skeletons before moving farther into the room to take on the zombies.

114 These three rooms now house undead. The first room contains three zombies, the second contains a ghoul and a zombie, while the third contains a skeleton and two zombies. In these rooms you'll find a *Wand of Neutralize Poison* and a *potion of speed*. The door behind a bed in the third room is easy to miss.

115 This mining equipment room is filled with ordinary weapons. It's safe to rest here.

116 The barrels to the west in this location hold *potions of restoration* and a scroll of *remove paralysis*. To the east, you will discover the fate of Jarial's lover and a pair of *snakeskin boots*.

117 This room holds the Fountain of Worship and the Well of Worship. If a character drinks from the Fountain of Worship, a master shadow is summoned. If

111

a character drinks from the Well of Worship, he or she is knocked unconscious and loses 1 point of Wisdom and 1 point of Constitution, plus all characters in the party gain 750 experience, and another master shadow is summoned.

118 The door to this room is locked and the party needs to lockpick to open it. Come to this room from the staircase in location 38 in the Halls of Light. Inside the room the party finds the lockpick and a *Dagger +1*.

119 Perhaps the party has heard Faeril and Beriand talk about a reclusive amulet collector. They were talking about Preybelish. He hides here behind a magically sealed door. If a party member is wearing *Onglore's Amulet of War*, retrieved from location 21 (or *Kluusar's Bloodstone Amulet, Theodore's Token of Luck*, or *Tyr's Locket of Justice*), Preybelish will ask about it, then instruct

> ## Note
> It's up to you whether to drink from the Well of Worship. Later in the game, 750 experience points will not be significant. However, early in the game that XP may be enough to push your characters up to the next level, giving them a significant edge for the next few levels.

the group to come back. When the party returns, if they insult Preybelish, he will open the door and attack. For Preybelish to acknowledge you when you return, you have to move on to location 117 or back to 113. Alternately, learn the Word of Venom at the Shrine of Mystra in Nightingale Court. This automatically opens the door when you approach it. Preybelish is a dark naga, and his room is filled with darkness. When he is defeated, the darkness is dispelled and the party is free to loot his treasure. He has been hoarding the Wizard's Torc (necessary to enter the Catacombs, later in the game), a *Necklace of Protection +3*, an *Amulet of Protection +2*, an *Amulet of Protection from Paralysis +1*, and a *Medallion of Defense*.

120 A shadow, a skeleton knight, a skeleton, and an ancient zombie attack the party here.

121 The chest in this room is trapped and locked. It holds a *potion of strength*, *Ringmail +4*, and the Pale Green Key (for use at location 124). The bed in this room can be searched; it contains a Silver Key and the *Jeweled Dwarven Dagger—Orckiller +1*. The door to the southeast requires the Silver Key to open.

122 A couple of the barrels in this room hold a *Ring of Strength* and a *Ring of Wisdom*.

123 A shadow, two skeleton knights, and a skeleton lurk in this corner of the room.

124 The locked door into this room can be opened with the Pale Green Key, found in location 121. The barrels hold a *Ring of Charisma* and a *Ring of Intelligence*. The door to the northeast is locked with the Pale Blue Key, found in location 14.

125 The Fountain of the Earth is in this room. A character who drinks from the fountain is rewarded with +4 Constitution and +8 total hit points, but takes a -2 penalty to Charisma and a -1 penalty to Dexterity. A *Wand of Fireball* is on the shelf in the back of this room.

126 Heading toward the final destination on this level, the party happens upon a fight between two ghouls, two lizardfolk ghouls, and two orc ghouls. Party members gain experience for any they kill, and the ghouls are weak from fighting each other, so this is a good opportunity earn experience. The open chest in the back of the room is empty.

127 Two locked and trapped chests are here. The left chest contains a *Ring of Brute Strength*, and the right chest contains *Boots of Withering Beauty*. When you touch either chest, a shadow appears and attacks.

128 A single skeleton lord loiters in the hallway here. When he notices you, his buddies, three skeleton knights, join the combat. The room contains some gold, but the chests are empty.

129 A skeleton lord, an ancient zombie, a skeleton elder, and a zombie inhabit this room.

130 Two skeleton lords, two skeleton knights, a skeleton elder, and a skeleton guard the entrance to the room to the south.

131 Answers at last! This room is home to a high-level scarred mage and his undead minions: two zombies and two ancient zombies. All attack the party on sight. When they are defeated, the party finds a potion, a scroll, and a note on the mage, revealing their enemies in Myth Drannor as the Cult of the Dragon.

132 In this final room, a flight of stairs lead up to location 1 of the Halls of Stone and a flight of stairs lead down to location 42 of the Deep Halls.

Tip

The scarred mage can cast high-level spells such as *fireball* and *lightning bolt* that can hit multiple characters at once, so spread your characters out to minimize the number that can be hit with each spell. Most importantly, move a warrior into close melee range of the mage immediately to make it harder for him to cast spells. Once he is neutralized, the rest of the battle is very straightforward.

Chapter Seven

Halls of Stone (The Dwarven Dungeons, Level 2)

The 2nd level of the Dwarven Dungeons, Halls of Stone, is harder than the 3rd level, with much more powerful monsters and traps. However, it is notably smaller and easier to navigate. Three factions contest ownership of the Halls of Stone: the undead, a tribe of lizardfolk, and a large group of orogs. To fully explore this level, your party must face, and defeat, all of them.

Quick Overview

Undead Infestation

Like most of the 3rd level of the Dwarven Dungeons, the south section of the Halls of Light is crawling with undead, and it even contains the source of the foul legions. To the southwest, you also find a cult mage torturing Emmeric, a hardy fighter who will join your party if you rescue him. When you reach the stairs to the Deep Halls at location 20, choose whether to go to the bottom level or to continue exploring the Halls of Stone. The Halls of Stone contain numerous treasures and plentiful experience, but none are critical to escaping the Dwarven Dungeons.

Lizardfolk Lair

The lizardfolk in the northwest portion of these halls swear allegiance to Malgi Hi, and they are a thorn in the side of the cult mages. However, this does not make them your allies, and they will attack on sight! The *Marshbane Dagger* is especially handy here, helping your party reach the heart of the lizardfolk camp. Within, the party finds another dried up dwarven channel and a room that was once very special to a long-dead pair of lovers.

Orog Stronghold

A large number of orogs has set up camp in this area of dungeon, putting up defenses against the hordes of undead in the south. They protect many treasures, including several weapons and an important key. In the back of this stronghold is a magical forge said to be able to turn mundane weapons into magical ones!

Dungeon Master's Notes

Undead Infestation

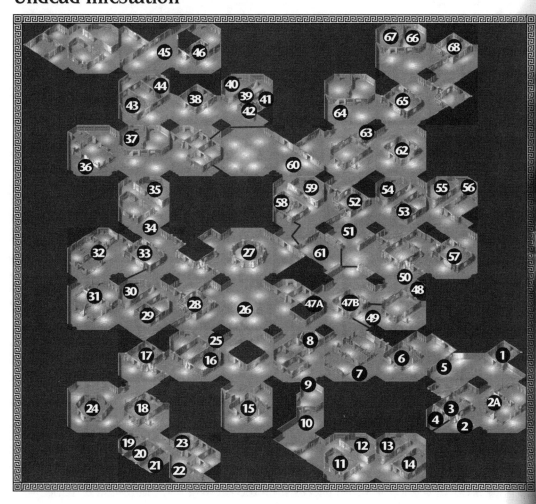

1 When you climb the stairs in Dwarven Dungeon Level 3, location 132, you arrive at this entrance staircase.

2 The door here is trapped with poison (a poison dart trap, actually). The second chest in the room has another poison dart trap and contains some gold.

2A Find the *Dagger of Defense* here, stuck in a shelf near some ruins.

3 A row of fountains lines the northwest wall of this room. The middle fountain grants protection from poison, which comes in handy in the next room.

4 This room contains a permanent *cloudkill* spell. Drinking from the middle fountain in location 3 allows characters to enter the cloud without harm. The first chest contains *Pureblade*, and the second chest contains gold.

5 A *shocking grasp* trap guards the door to this room. In addition, the door is locked, but it can be picked or smashed. The room on other side has four skeleton knights and three ancient zombies.

6 This room contains a Channel of Earthborn Wind, which is currently inactive. After you restore the channels on the 4th level of the Dwarven Dungeons at location 19, breathing the enchanted wind here gives each party member 400 XP.

7 Six ancient zombies carry a Vial of Naga Blood.

8 Two ancient zombies, two skeleton knights, and one skeleton lord attack the party here. A *potion of serious healing* is found here as well. Disarm another poison dart–trapped door before entering this location.

> ## Tip
>
> Adventurers need to keep all the Vials of Naga Blood with them as they progress through this level. Return to location 6 after successfully clearing level 3, the Main Halls.

9 This door is trapped with *burning hands*.

10 This large room contains two ancient zombies, a skeleton lord, and four skeleton knights. Attentive adventurers also can find 55 GP here. The door to the south east is trapped.

11 The three chests in this room are all locked and cannot be picked or broken open. If the characters leave the Halls of Stone and return, they will find the chests opened and the room filled with three orc rogues. The orcs carry the room's treasure: *Hextor's Cruelty*, *Hextor's Might*, and *Hextor's Vengeance*.

12 This door is sealed with the Glyph of Song. The Singing Word is located in a scroll in the Ancient Tomb, location 24. This room contains waterbells that are useful to your party later in the adventure.

13 This door is sealed with the Glyph of Song. Refer to location 12 for information.

14 Upon opening the chest in this room, the characters are attacked by four shadows and one master shadow. This is a very difficult battle, and you may wish to return after you have cleared the rest of the level and upgraded your magical gear. The monsters possess an idolon and the *Wings of Diabolicus*. The chest contains a small amount of gold.

15 Four skeleton knights, one skeleton lord, and three skeleton elders guard an empty fountain known as Fountain Macabre. Pour four Vials of Naga Blood into the fountain to be rewarded with the *Ring of Naga's Kiss*. The four Vials of Naga Blood can be found in the Halls of Stone in locations 7, 32, 55, and 67.

16 Three dead elven clerics lie on the floor in this room. They have a large shield that the party can use later in the enchanted forge. Two skeleton knights, two skeleton elders, and a skeleton lord await your party here.

17 This is a scribe's room. The locked gate in the center of the room can be picked or smashed. There is a note on a table regarding the threat of the lizardfolk, and a second note regarding the Nightmare Gate. There is gold in the back of the room.

18 Two skeleton knights, two skeleton elders, and a cult mage threaten an anonymous fighter in this room. When your party enters, the fighter draws a hidden dagger and attacks! If your party helps him, you learn that his name is Emmeric, and he will join you. Emmeric has useful information about Athan's band, including the news that Athan is still alive. Open the chest to receive two *salves of serious healing* and *Chainmail + 2*.

19 The chest here is trapped with the stabbing projectile trap and contains gold.

20 The stairs here lead to location 11 in the Deep Halls, the 4th level of the Dwarven Dungeon.

21 A note refers to a "weapon in a bookcase upstairs" (location 23) that will be very helpful against lizardfolk.

22 Two skeleton lords, two ancient zombies, and two zombies attack the party. Nearby is a chest containing a *salve of serious healing* and a scroll of *shield* (level 5).

23 These stairs go up to the Halls of Light, the 1st level of the Dwarven Dungeon, to location 1. Climb the stairs and search the room to find a *Marshbane Dagger* in a shelf. Beware of the door to the south, as it is trapped with *cloudkill*.

117

24 This is the Rhonglyn Room on the 2nd level. Like the room on the 3rd level, it is completely frozen over and unusable. After the ice is broken on the 4th level, it can be used to travel between the levels of the dungeon and the Hall of Wizards.

25 Two skeleton lords, two ancient zombies, and two skeleton elders attack the party.

26 In the center of this courtyard is a spinning spire. After solving the puzzle of the Orrery Planets, the party can use this spire to transport around Myth Drannor. Rangers can find signs of enemy movement by investigating tracks in this area as well.

27 Undead constantly enter through this Nightmare Gate portal, and it can't be sealed without the Word of Constriction. The room initially contains a skeleton lord, three ancient zombies, and three skeleton knights. During the battle, another skeleton knight and a skeleton lord step out of the gate. It is possible for your party to quickly enter, loot the chest, get out, and close the door without knowing the word. The trapped chest holds *Tyr's Locket of Justice*.

28 Three skeleton knights, one skeleton lord, and two ancient zombies attack the party. The chest contains *Boghurst's Putrefication*—a unique dagger.

29 This room holds a scroll of *dispel magic*.

30 Three skeleton knights and four ancient zombies attack. They have a *potion of serious healing*.

31 Four shadows attack from the ruins.

32 Four dead lizardfolk litter the floor here. When the party approaches, four shadows appear, then after two rounds of combat, four more shadows appear from the south. The first chest in this area holds *Chainmail +3* and *Boots of Mobility*. The second chest holds a *Vial of Naga Blood*.

33 Three ghouls and two ghasts attack.

Lizardfolk Lair

34 Five lizardfolk scavengers and a lizardfolk faith healer guard this gateway to the lizardfolk lair. They tell the party to go back, as it is the realm of "Malgi Hi". They carry the *Twilight Guardian*.

35 This library holds three lizardfolk scavengers, a lizardfolk faith healer, and a lizardfolk taskmaster. The bookcases and the chest each hold a scroll of *chill touch* and a scroll of *spiritual weapon*.

36 These ruins provide few hiding spots for the lizardfolk taskmaster and four lizardfolk scavengers lurking here.

37 Three lizardfolk scavengers and two lizardfolk faith healers guard this room. They carry a *salve of serious healing* and a scroll of *shield*. Consider resting here before moving on.

38 The party encounters a lizardfolk taskmaster, two lizardfolk, three lizardfolk scavengers, and a lizardfolk faith healer. The chest on the room's right is trapped and contains gemstones of little value and an idolon. Both chests are trapped with *poison spit* but only one contains gold. Be sure to pick up the *Veil of Vanity Ring* dropped by the lizardfolk.

39 Two lizardfolk taskmasters and two lizardfolk faith healers attack in this hallway.

40 This room contains a pair of evil books, which Beriand spoke of. Before you pick up the books, one book instructs you to burn them at the Pyre of Silence in the Deep Halls, in location 47.

41 The initials "G + E" are carved on a table in this room. The door to the south requires the Delicate Pewter Key, which can be found at location 63, in the orog stronghold. This is the trysting room of Elena and Garras, two long-dead lovers that your characters will learn more about as they continue to explore the dungeons.

42 This room contains Garras' equipment, left for him by Elena. The chest contains a *Shortbow* +2, a *Quiver of Arrows* +1, and *Elena's Pewter Locket*.

43 Four lizardfolk scavengers and a lizardfolk taskmaster make this room home. On the stool is a scroll of *dispel magic*.

44 This room holds another Channel of Earthborn Wind. If your characters touch it, they are attacked by two lizardfolk scavengers, a lizardfolk, a lizardfolk warrior, and a lizardfolk faith healer as they leave the room. After the channels are restored on the 4th level of the Dwarven Dungeons, location 19, breathing the enchanted wind here grants 2,400 experience to the party (400 XP to each party member).

45 Four lizardfolk, two lizardfolk scavengers, two lizardfolk faith healers, and a lizardfolk taskmaster attack the party here. The Glyph of Water on the floor near the door to the northwest seals it tightly shut. It can be opened only with the Splashing Word. Speak to Plinshree in the Glim-Gardens to receive the Splashing Word, which grants access to all doors sealed with the Glyph of Water. The lizardfolk carry a healing salve and a scroll of *shield*.

46 The Brewer's Key is required to open the door to this room. The stairs lead up to location 75 of the Halls of Light, which, incidentally, is where the party will find the Brewer's Key.

Orog Stronghold

47A Use this room to get to the Halls of Light (location 26, Chapter 9). Look for the rope ladder.

47B Two orogs fight a gang of undead here. A skeleton knight and three ancient zombies are poised to fight. The orogs call out to your party for healing. If your party heals them and helps them defeat the undead, they will return to assist later, in location 49.

48 The first chest here holds a *Sling* +2. The second chest holds a *Warhammer* +2. Saving the best for last, the third chest holds the *Sacred Vestments*.

49 As the party members leave through this room, they are attacked by two ghasts, a ghoul, and three ancient zombies. The orogs from location 46 will assist against the undead if the party spared them.

50 This entryway is littered with screens that the orogs have positioned to hamper the advance of the undead to the south. The party encounters an undead assault party here, consisting of two skeleton elders and three ancient zombies.

51 Five orogs and an orog guardsman protect the entrance to the orog stronghold. They carry *Libertas*, a magical spear.

52 The chest in this room contains a scroll of *bull's strength*, a healing potion, and a healing salve. The other chest has some gold.

53 Three orogs and two orog healers guard a chest. The chest contains some gold.

54 Here the party finds the third Channel of Earthborn Wind. After the channels are restored on the 4th level of the Dwarven Dungeons, location 19, breathing the enchanted wind here grants 2,400 XP (400 XP to each member).

55 The barrels in the hallway spout *burning hands*, so step cautiously. This room contains a *Vial of Naga Blood*.

56 The chest here contains a suit of *Leather Armor* +2.

57 These stairs lead up to the top level of the Dwarven Dungeon, the Halls of Light, location 47. The Halls of Light are a more challenging area than levels 2 or

4, so clear the rest of the dungeon before venturing up. The stairs are guarded by two orog healers and four orogs. They carry a suit of *Full Plate +2*.

58 A ghast and three ancient zombies have infiltrated the stronghold here. Upon defeating them, the party will be attacked by the two orogs and one orog veteran, who were waiting in location 59 preparing to kill the undead.

59 The door to this room is locked. The orogs within open it after your party kills the undead in location 58. There are two orogs and an orog veteran, and they have the *Hammer of Martel* and a *salve of critical healing*. Two lizardfolk taskmasters and a lizardfolk warrior await if your party explores farther to the north. After defeating all enemies, the party finds two *salves of critical healing*.

60 This open room is home to three orogs, two orog hunters, an orog healer, and an orog veteran.

61 Two orogs, two orog hunters, and an orog healer attack here. They carry only gold.

62 One orog healer, one orog guardsman, and three orogs gather around this fountain. There is a useless pair of *Waterlogged Boots* in the bottom of the fountain.

63 The party finds the Delicate Pewter Key on a bed in this room. There is also a note from Elena to her lover Garras. The key can be used in Elena and Garras' old trysting room in the lizardfolk lair, location 41.

64 Two orog hunters and three orogs patrol this area. There is a chapel in the room behind them, to the north.

65 Four orogs and two orog healers protect this room. The words "To Moradin, the Soul Forger, our Protector and Shield" are engraved above the door.

66 This magical foundry is infested with undead. This first room contains five skeleton elders. They have the Foundry Key that opens the door to the west. There are three large shields on the walls of the room. Placing three large shields in the foundry returns one *Large Shield +3*. Make as many *magical shields* for your party as you can.

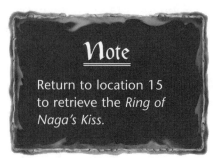

67 The second room of the foundry houses five more skeleton elders. There are two battleaxes on the walls. Placing three battleaxes in the foundry returns one *Battleaxe +3*. One can be found in a room northeast of 64. Another can be found in the room east of 37. Additionally, the chest in the back of the room contains a *Vial of Naga Blood*.

> ## Note
> Return to location 15 to retrieve the *Ring of Naga's Kiss*.

68 The stairs in this room lead up to location 56 in the Halls of Light.

Chapter Eight

The Deep Halls
(The Dwarven Dungeon, Level 4)

This level of the Dwarven Dungeons is more of a "no man's land" than the other levels. Because it is so far from the sun, many undead have holed up here, and unaligned bands of various creatures roam from place to place. The Cult of the Dragon has a small stronghold here, including a torture chamber, and lizardfolk have been making their way into this level from their base camp in the Nightingale Court.

The first 10 locations (1–10) are areas that are only accessible from the Main Halls of the Dwarven Dungeons. Read on and the way to access these rooms will become clear. From the cult stronghold in the Halls of Stone, your party enters this level of the dungeon starting in location 11. If you enter from the stairs down in location 132 of the Main Halls, you start in location 44.

Quick Overview

Lower Tombs

These small tombs contain a couple minor treasures and are easy to explore.

Bedlam Prison

Bedlam Prison was once a holding cell for the worst of Myth Drannor's dwarves. It seems the Lockmaster of the prison is not resting peacefully, though, and his spectre roams the empty cells.

123

Dwarven Tombs

These mysterious tombs are partially designed as a trap to snare unwary travelers who venture into the Dwarven Tombs hoping to find treasure. Overcome the enemies that greet you immediately upon arriving, claim some small treasures, and return to your quest on the level above.

Cult Stronghold

It seems the Cult of the Dragon has a presence on every level of the Dwarven Dungeons, and this small stronghold is their home in the Deep Halls. There is a prominent holding cell here and a couple of ransacked treasure rooms. Of far more importance is the Rhonglyn Room, which you can finally free from Borea's ice. Use it immediately to travel to the Hall of Wizards and hear what Caalenfaire has to say.

Southern Dungeons

The Southern Dungeons house a mixture of orogs and undead, but also contain two major landmarks: the Well of the Earthborn Wind and the Sharpstick Room. Both are worth a visit.

Tombs

The tombs in the Deep Halls are full of useful treasure left on the bodies of the deceased as mementos of their life. However, don't feel bad about looting the tombs of heroes. They no longer need their gear, and their spirits would be far more comfortable with you using it to right wrongs in the world than with it languishing for eternity. Explore these tombs thoroughly.

Middle Dungeons: Orog Territory

This region is where most of the orogs on this level have set up their base. They battle lizardfolk to the north and undead to the south. They don't understand the importance of some of the treasures hidden right under their noses, so this area is well worth exploring thoroughly, especially if you plan to fight the Lifespring Guardian in the Northern Dungeons.

Northern Dungeons

This area of the dungeon has two major features: the Lifespring Guardian and a lizardfolk complex. The Lifespring Guardian is the culmination of a very useful quest. Definitely invest the time to defeat him and return to the Lifesprings in the

Main Halls for your reward. Since you can use the Rhonglyn Room to reach the first level of the dungeon, the lizardfolk complex is mostly optional. You don't need to take the stairs here, but the complex does hold a useful monk weapon, and one of the doors sealed with the Splashing Word.

Cult Inner Sanctum

After learning the Word of the Dragon in the Halls of Light (see Chapter 9), force your way into the Cult Inner Sanctum on this level. Inside you learn an important word of passage!

The Lost Waterbells

After exploring the Cult Inner Sanctum, you know the Splashing Word. With this word, you can open the doors sealed with the Glyph of Water, gaining access to the treasures—and dangers—behind them. The treasures relate to Plinshree, a naiad that the party can meet in a fountain in the Glim-Gardens after they have restored the water system.

Dungeon Master's Notes

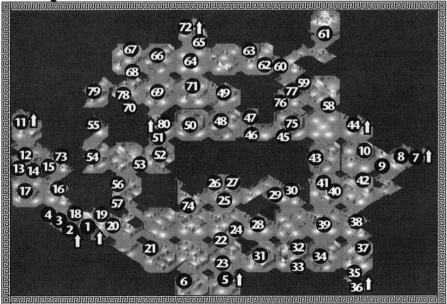

⇑ ⇓   Staircases leading up or down

Lower Tombs

1 The staircase in this room leads to the northern staircase in the room at location 52 of the 3rd level of the Dwarven Dungeons. Find the *Winter Blade* and the Blood Moon Key in a barrel hare.

2 The stairs in this room lead to the southern stairs in the room at location 52 of the 3rd level of the Dwarven Dungeons. The room is full of coffins, but is otherwise unoccupied.

3 Two skeletons and a wraith attack when you enter this room. The door to the northwest requires the Blood Moon Key, found in location 1 of the Deep Halls.

> **Tip**
>
> Walk back up these stairs after you have the Blood Moon Key and take the other staircase down, which puts you in location 2. Finish exploring locations 2, 3, and 4, then continue exploring the Main Halls.

4 This room is the Tomb of Aeseder, Planeswalker, and brother of Kluusar. His brother has left a gift in his tomb which your party can take: *Kluusar's Bloodstone Amulet*.

Bedlam Prison

5 This room contains the staircase to the depths of Bedlam Prison. The stairs here lead up to location 85 on the 3rd level of the Dwarven Dungeons. Find the *Blade of Larceny* and a *Quiver of Arrows of Speed* here.

6 After exploring most of the prison cells, your party finds the Lockmaster of Bedlam spectre here and a pair of *Dymon's Dutiful Gloves*.

> **Tip**
>
> When your characters are low level, a spectre is a powerful foe. Equip your party with magical weapons and pepper the spectre with magical attacks as much as possible, as it can't avoid them with *incorporeality*. Any clerics should focus on healing and combat instead of turning, which is unlikely to be effective.

Dwarven Tombs

7 This is where the party enters the Dwarven Tombs, and where it leaves the Tombs as well. There is only one entrance in or out.

9 Two zombies and two skeletons attack your party as soon as they arrive in this hall. Three ghouls and two more zombies await you.

10 Two skeletons and a wraith attack when you enter this tomb. The chest in this room contains a *Serpent's Ring*. From here, your party needs to return to the stairs in location 7 to continue exploring the Main Halls.

Cult Stronghold

11 These are the stairs that lead from location 20 in the Halls of Stone.

12 This cult treasure room is full of treasure chests, but low on treasure. Various chests in the room contain gold, and one locked chest contains *Milla's Blessing*. The door to the southeast is locked tight, and the door to the southwest is trapped with *shocking grasp*.

13 Five orogs, an orog guardsman, and an orog healer guard the entrance to the cult treasure room you just left. Though they are surprised to see your party, they react quickly and attack. They carry only gold.

14 This room is marked with the Rune of Dumathoin, and the party can hear cult members interrogating a prisoner within.

15 If you've made it as far as the 1st level of the Dwarven Dungeon, then you'll find a cult soldier, a cult mage, and three orog guardsmen interrogating Nottle here! Nottle will distract them, allowing you to act first. When the monsters are defeated, Nottle tells you to find the Key of Dumathoin to open his cage (find the key in the 1st level of the Dwarven Dungeons at location 36). After you free him, he tells you about a couple of significant treasures in appreciation for his freedom. He then returns to his wagon.

The door to the north is sealed by the Cult of the Dragon and requires the Word of the Dragon to open. Your party finds it in the Halls of Light after they have exited the dungeons and returned.

16 This cult treasure room has been almost completely ransacked. The one remaining locked chest holds some gold. Two orc guardsmen and three orc healers lurk just outside the west door.

17 This is the Rhonglyn Room on level 4, but unlike the other levels, the ice is weaker here, allowing you to break it and free the room from its spell. Breaking the ice reveals *Borea's Blood*, a useful dagger that casts *cone of cold*.

The Rhonglyn Room is essentially a magical elevator, allowing the party to quickly move between levels of the dungeon. Each level is color coded. Level 1 is purple, level 2 is green, level 3 is yellow, level 4 is red, and the Hall of Wizards is blue.

18 Three orog healers and two orog guardsmen protect the entrance to the Cult Stronghold.

Southern Dungeons

19 This room holds the Well of the Earthborn Wind. If the party has the Ruby of Earthborn Wind, drop it into the well to reactivate the Channels of Earthborn Wind on level 2 of the dungeons, the Halls of Stone. Find the ruby in location 32.

Tip

At this time, go to the Hall of Wizards to meet with Caalenfaire.

20 Two orog hunters, an orog guardsman, and an orog patrol here, and they attack on sight. Beware of the door to the south that separates locations 20 and 21, as it is trapped with *poison vent*.

21 One orog healer, two orog guardsmen, and three orogs hide in this room. They have a *scroll of shield* and a healing salve. There is an idolon in the cupboard.

22 Two orogs, an orog hunter, and two orog healers attack here.

23 Four ancient zombies lurk here.

24 This is the entrance to the Sharpstick Room. It used to be the home of a group of ormyrr (which you meet in location 86 in the Halls of Light). Now it is overrun with powerful orcs. Find *Thundergrip* gauntlets and a *Jaws of Malice* Shortbow here. The door leading to location 25 is trapped.

25 A horde of orcs dwells in the Sharpstick Room. To clear the room, you must fight two orcs, two orc witch doctors, six orc leaders, three orc shamans, and one orc chief.

26 The chest contains a *Shortbow +3*.

27 Find a *Small Shield +2* and *Theodore's Token of Luck* here.

Tombs

28 A group of orogs fights undead from the tombs in this room. Four orogs and one orog hunter face two ancient zombies. Smash the chest for enchanted boots known as *Lenore's Sanctuary*.

29 Four arraccats nest here.

30 Deep in the arraccat lair is a chest that contains *Gauntlets of Ogre Power* and a note describing a planned tomb raid of an elven warrior named Faldis.

31 This is the Tomb of Faldis. He writes of his magic shield and how it served him well; find it in a hidden chamber in the back of his tomb. The shield, *Faldis's Defender*, is an excellent shield because of the initiative bonus it grants.

32 A skeleton lord and six skeleton elders haunt this room. It's the tomb of the wizard who summoned the Earthborn Wind, and you find the Earthborn Ruby in this room. The wizard's spirit implores them to return it to the well in location 19.

33 Three ghasts and a ghoul attack here. They carry a scroll and healing potions.

34 Three ghouls and three ancient zombies search for prey here.

35 Three ghouls and two ghasts guard the doorway to the south. They carry a healing potion.

36 The door to this room is barred from the south. Your party can get to this room from location 3 in the Sullymarsh on the overland after they have escaped the dungeon.

37 Three ancient zombies, a ghast, and a ghoul attack here.

38 Four ghouls and a ghast play with the remains in the coffin in the center of the room. The coffin contains the remains of Garras, Elena's lover. By arranging the remains in a peaceful state, the party earns the gratitude of Garras's spirit, who will later assist against the Lifespring Guardian.

39 Four ancient zombies and two ghasts attack the party here.

40 This room is completely empty.

41 Two ghouls and three ancient zombies hide in this room.

42 Two wraiths and two zombies protect some gemstones, an idolon, and the *Runic Shield +2*.

43 Four ancient zombies lurk here.

44 This room contains a stairway that leads up to location 132 in the Main Halls, the 3rd level of the Dwarven Dungeons. That room also contains the first staircase you found leading up to the Halls of Stone, so you have finally come full circle.

Middle Dungeons: Orog Territory

45 This door is sealed with the Glyph of Water. Return after you have learned the Splashing Word to open this door.

46 Four orogs and an orog guardsman guard the room to the north. They carry a healing potion. The door to the north is also trapped with a *poison vent* spell.

47 Here is the Pyre of Silence where you can finally burn all of the evil books you've been carrying (found in location 40 in the Halls of Stone and location 49 in the Halls of Light). Each book burned is worth experience. Some books wail, others plead, some even try to deceive with promises of goodly power. All are evil and should be burned to destroy their power.

48 Two orog guardsmen and three orogs guard the mysterious crypt to the north.

49 This room contains Elena's corpse. Like Garras's corpse in location 38, Elena's corpse has been disturbed. Return her to a normal state of rest, and her spirit will assist in the battle against the Lifespring Guardian.

50 Two orogs, two orog healers, and an orog guardsman dwell here. They only carry gold.

51 One orog healer, one orog guardsman, and three orogs guard three empty chests in this corner of the dungeon.

52 These rooms are mysteriously empty of enemies. The northern room has a *Quiver of Arrows* +1 in a barrel.

53 The well here is dry, but it seems someone has rested here recently. If there is a rogue in your party, he or she will find a note from Athan, who describes killing the nearby monsters and tells his companions to follow him up the stairs to the north.

54 Three orogs train with bows here, and an orog healer is around to cure them in case of mishap. Two orog guardsmen lurk outside the northern door.

55 Two skeleton lords and two shadows guard this room. What's more, when the party opens the chest, three additional shadows attack. The undead guard has a very potent weapon: the *Mountain Fist*.

56 There is a *Crimson Brooch* in the rightmost coffin in this room.

57 A group of orogs fights zombies here. Two orogs, an orog healer, two orog guardsmen, and an orog hunter are demolishing three ancient zombies.

58 Two ancient zombies and four ghouls attack here.

59 This door is trapped with *poison spit*.

Northern Dungeons

60 This door is sealed with the Glyph of Enigma, and requires the Echoing Word to open, which you learn from Elena in location 23 of the Main Halls.

61 Here you find the Lifespring Guardian, a powerful golem! If you arranged either Garras's or Elena's corpse at locations 38 and 49, one or both of their spirits will join the party in battle. When the Guardian is defeated, the Lifespring wells in the Main Halls will be activated, and Garras's and Elena's spirits will finally be freed. Use the Lifespring wells to get several useful benefits (see Chapter 6, location 23).

62 Two lizardfolk taskmasters and two lizardfolk faith healers patrol the entrance to the lizardfolk complex here.

63 A lizardfolk taskmaster, a lizardfolk faith healer, and three lizardfolk scavengers make their home in this room.

Tip

The Guardian is a very powerful foe. He hits several times per round for huge amounts of damage, and he is resistant to all magic. Have your fighting characters gang up on the Guardian while your magic users stay back and help with healing magic and salves. Save your game first, as it's easy to lose a character in this fight!

64 This is a massive lizardfolk infirmary. One faith healer is working with three injured lizardfolk. Chances are, they're about to get more injured. There is a *Blade of Venom* under the smith's table by the fire.

65 The door to this room is locked with the Soot Coated Key, found in location 69.

66 Two lizardfolk taskmasters, two lizardfolk faith healers, and two lizardfolk scavengers attack the party here.

67 Five lizardfolk faith healers guard some of the lizardfolk treasure. Their stash contains the *Luther's Protector*, a powerful monk weapon, and a *Ring of Cloudy Mind*.

68 A lizardfolk taskmaster, a lizardfolk faith healer, and three lizardfolk scavengers attack the party here, but they only carry a little gold.

69 Here you find the leader of this complex, a lizardfolk warrior. He is supported by a lizardfolk taskmaster, and three lizardfolk faith healers. They have the Soot Coated Key and a healing potion.

70 This door is sealed with the Glyph of Water and requires the Splashing Word to open.

71 A lizardfolk taskmaster and four lizardfolk faith healers attack the party here. They have some minor scrolls and potions.

72 This stairway leads up to location 74 in the Halls of Light, right in the middle of an extensive lizardfolk base.

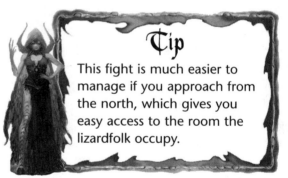

Tip

This fight is much easier to manage if you approach from the north, which gives you easy access to the room the lizardfolk occupy.

Cult Inner Sanctum

73 After opening the sealed door, the party must defeat a cult quartermaster, two cult soldiers elite, and two cult mages. They guard a portal to location 74.

74 Four arraccats killed all the cultists in the inner sanctum and now attack your party. The Splashing Word is written on a scroll on the ground. A portal here returns the party to location 73.

The Lost Waterbells

75 Three spectres attack when you open the sealed door.

76 Two sets of two master shadows and a shadow ruthlessly assault you here. They fight viciously to protect their treasure, one of Plinshree's waterbells.

77 There is nothing but an empty chest in this room.

78 Three shambling ghasts and a spectre attack as soon as your party opens this door.

79 Two master spectres haunt this room. The metal chest contains another of Plinshree's waterbells.

80 This staircase leads down to the Lizardfolk Tunnel, which connects to a lizardfolk camp in the Nightingale Court (see Chapter 11), but the party cannot exit this way yet.

Note

You will have a good opportunity to explore the tunnel thoroughly in Chapter 11. Leave it be for now.

Chapter Nine

Halls of Light
(The Dwarven Dungeons, Level 1)

Welcome to the hospitality suites of the Dwarven Dungeons, now overrun with the nastiest enemies you've seen yet. The monsters in the Halls of Light are a significantly tougher than the ones you've been facing on levels 2 and 4, but if you've been thorough, you should be ready. In exploring this level you'll come across hostile orogs, an established tribe of lizardfolk, a fortified Cult Stronghold, and an ancient Dwarven Brewery. Useful treasures and clues about your quest abound, and when you reach the end, you'll step out under the sun again at last.

Quick Overview

Dwarven Brewery

As it is in many cultures today, brewing was of critical importance to the dwarves of Myth Drannor and was overseen by their Brewmaster, who held a position of great respect. Recently, the brewery was overwhelmed by undead from the Halls of Stone, who desecrated the once-holy grounds. While clearing the undead from the brewery, you find the greatest treasures of the last dwarven Brewmaster.

Cult Stronghold

Explore the Cult Stronghold in two forays. First, break into it early, even if you're not ready to face the monsters within, to get the Word of Constriction. However, the rest of the stronghold is very difficult, and you must explore and gain a great deal of strength to defeat it. You earn the legendary *Helm Cleaver* here, and it's also the best place to learn the Cult's Word of the Dragon, which is useful in the Deep Halls.

Cult Orogs

A cult mage has enslaved a group of orogs and turned them against your party. It's a clever ploy, but it won't be effective against a prepared party, and you should have little trouble clearing out the whole nest. Upon clearing this section, you learn some interesting news about Nottle, making this a worthwhile venture.

Peaceful Orog Camp

Unlike the enslaved orogs in the southeast of the dungeon, these orogs are not initially hostile to the party. Under siege by lizardfolk, they have more important battles to fight. If you are honorable and do not attack without cause, you can explore this area, rest, and gain a few good treasures without the threat of battle. Enjoy this moment of calm, as it will be the last for a long time.

Lizardfolk Outpost

This extensive compound is crawling with lizardfolk. They have been antagonizing the honorable orogs to the east, and they now stand in the way of your quest. Before you conquer them all, you will face two new powerful opponents: stone lizardfolk and the lizardfolk warlord. They guard powerful magic treasures, so defeating them brings no small reward.

Orc Territory

Don't be misled by the fact that the occupants of this area are orcs. These are not the same weak, easily-defeated orcs you faced at the entrance to the Dwarven Dungeons. These orcs are sergeants, shamans, warlocks, and even captains. However, you should be strong enough to face them by now. They guard your final reward: the Seal of Mythanthor and safe passage to the light of the surface again.

Dungeon Master's Notes
Cult Stronghold

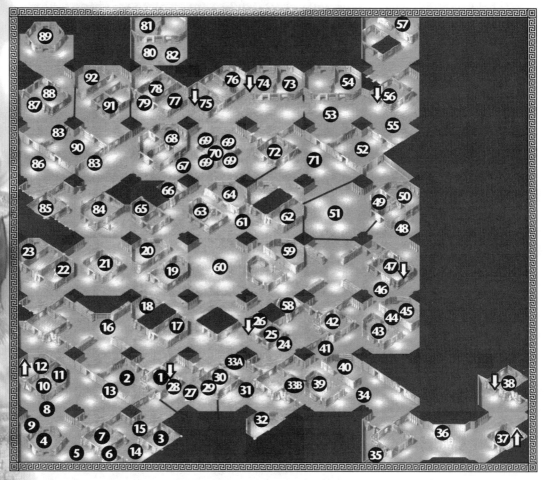

⬆ ⬇   Staircases leading up or down

1 The stairs in this room originate in location 23 in the Halls of Stone. The party enters this library meeting room to find it unoccupied. Search the bookcases to find a *Marshbane Dagger*, a useful tool against lizardfolk.

2 A skeleton lord, two skeleton knights, and four ancient zombies gather about a rancid fountain. This can be a tough fight for low-level parties, but the treasure in the next room is worth the effort.

3 This long-unused classroom contains a skeleton, three ancient zombies, and three skeleton lords. This is a very difficult battle for low-level parties, but fighting it now saves a lot of backtracking later. When the undead have fallen, pick up the Word of Constriction from the table. This word can be used to close the Nightmare Gate portal in the Halls of Stone, location 27.

Dwarven Brewery

4 This is the Rhonglyn Room. If you unlocked it on level 4, you can use it to travel between the levels of the dungeon.

5 Four skeleton lords guard this courtyard. They carry gold.

6 More undead attack the party here: a skeleton lord and three skeleton elders.

7 Two master wraiths and a wraith appear when the party walks into this room. They carry a healing salve and a healing potion, as well as a *Small Shield* +2 and a *Pike* +2.

The Rhonglyn Room allows you to link between levels of the Dwarven Dungeons.

8 The two skeleton lords and three skeleton elders here carry nothing but gold.

9 Four ancient zombies attack the party here.

10 Three dead orcs lie on the ground in this beer cellar. The orcs once controlled the brewery, but they've been driven north by the undead. These three didn't make it.

Tip

Use as much magic as possible against strong incorporeal undead such as master wraiths. They can be very hard to kill with weapons. The cleric spell *searing light* is especially effective when it hits.

11 The five ancient zombies in this room carry gold.

⑫ The door to this room is locked from the other side. The stairs within the room lead to location 8 in the Windrider Glade, but you can't get there from here.

⑬ The Dwarven Brewmaster speaks when you open this chest, instructing you to find the *Onyx of the Richest Wort* "in the throat of one of our children."

⑭ Many ancient zombies lie on the floor here. Seven rise when you go near the chests to the south. The two chests, both trapped with poison darts, contain a couple of healing salves and various scrolls, including a *scroll of dispel magic*.

Tip

What would a Brewmaster consider his children? See all the kegs scattered about?

⑮ The Stronghold Key, found in location 31, is required here, but walking through the room at location 1, gets you to the other side of this door without the key.

⑯ Following a ghast south, the party is ambushed by five ghasts. They have a scroll and a healing salve.

⑰ Three dead orogs litter the floor of this room. Their weapons are scattered about, as if they saw a lot of use before these orogs were overwhelmed by undead.

⑱ Two specters—powerful, incorporeal undead—guard this chest. Inside, you find the *Sword of Marshbane*.

⑲ Three skeleton knights, two ancient zombies, and two skeleton lords guard this room. The undead carry *Soul Biter*, which allows characters to duplicate the draining effect of undead such as wraiths and spectres.

⑳ This room was once heavily protected but has been broken into. The chest was particularly reinforced, but all of its traps have been defeated. The only sign of the thief is an "N," Nottle's sign.

㉑ This door has the dwarven mark of brewing on the door. Inside is the heart of the brewery. As if sensing its ancient importance, four skeleton lords stand guard within. Defeat them, then turn the tap on the glowing keg to reveal the *Onyx of the Richest Wort*.

㉒ Four ancient zombies and a shambling ghast attack.

㉓ This room contains the preserved body of a dwarven warrior. Four ghasts and a shambling ghast attack as you enter the room. This is the body of the Dwarven Brewmaster, and in this room, you find his weapon: the *Brewmaster's Cudgel*.

138

Cult Stronghold Revisited

24 Five ghasts roam this hallway.

25 This small entry room is empty.

26 A ladder here leads down to a cluster of isolated rooms on level 2, location 47A.

27 When the party exits the Dwarven Dungeons and returns to this location, four orogs will parley with them here. It is important to return, as these orogs will teach you the Word of the Dragon, which is required to open doors that have been sealed by the Cult of the Dragon. The doors to this stronghold and the door at location 15 in the Deep Halls are among them. This meeting can occur in two places: here, and location 33B.

28 This door is trapped with a *poison vent* spell.

29 This door is sealed by a glyph placed by Cult of the Dragon. The Word of the Dragon is required to break the glyph.

30 This room is the Cult's furnace. Unfortunately, there is no treasure here.

31 Four cult soldiers, two cult mages, and a cult archmage await when your party bursts into the room. When the cult members are defeated, some orogs offer the Duel of Champions to determine who gets to keep the *Helm Cleaver*.

32 This is the site of the Duel of Champions. One of your characters must face an orog champion. He is a strong fighter who hits frequently and can inflict severe damage quickly. When he is defeated, the orogs tell you that the leaders of the Cult of the Dragon hide below an elven castle. They also honorably hand over the *Helm Cleaver*. Also find the *Gloves of Archmage* here.

> **Tip**
> This ladder is the only access to a series of rooms where there's a nice treasure, the *Sword of Firebrand*. Take a moment from your exploration to take the ladder and retrieve it.

> **Tip**
> The cult mages are dangerous opponents, so have warrior characters close to melee range with them as soon as possible. Save your game before beginning the Duel of Champions!

139

33A This is the stronghold's meeting room. The wooden chest contains 400 gold, two *potions of full healing*, and the Stronghold Key. The metal chest contains an idolon and a scroll. Neither chest is trapped or locked.

33B Parley with the orogs who teach you the Word of the Dragon here or in location 26.

> ## Tip
>
> Choose a strong fighter to face the orog champion. Alternatively, if you have the *Staff of Harm*, have a ranger, paladin, or cleric use it to reduce him to 1 hit point immediately, then finish him off in melee or with a spell such as *inflict wounds*.

Cult Orogs

34 Three orog hunters, an orog veteran, two orogs, and two orog guardsmen make this room their home. They carry a paltry sum of gold.

35 This secret door provides an alternate route to the southeast corner of the dungeon as well as a safe place to rest.

36 In this expansive hall, you find the cult mage who has enslaved the nearby orogs and turned them against your party. He has bodyguards, so you face a cult mage, two orog hunters, two orog guardsmen, and two orogs. The cult mage has the Key of Dumathoin and a *Wand of Magic Missiles*. Unfortunately, news of his demise travels slowly, and most of the orogs under his command will still attack your party on sight.

37 The two orog veterans in this room parley with your party. If your characters say they killed the mage, the orogs will give the party information, including some hints about the Key of Dumathoin and the news that the Cult recently kidnapped Nottle! One orog is a follower of Shar (a goddess of the Realms), and if your party insults her, the orogs will attack. The stairs in this room lead to the House of Gems Tower, level 1, location 1.

> ## Tip
>
> To exit the Dwarven Dungeons, lay siege to the House of Gems Tower and claim the arm for yourself. The Room of Words is in the tower. That's where the Cult of the Dragon has taken the skeletal arm that wears the *Ring of Calling*.

38 Four skeleton lords and two skeleton knights have fortified this room against the nearby orogs. The chest on the left contains gold. The chest on the right is trapped with *shocking grasp* and contains a *Topaz Band*. The stairs here lead to Dwarven Dungeons level 3, location 118.

39 An orog veteran, an orog guardsman, and two orog hunters attack your party here. They carry a simple scroll and healing potion, but the real treasure, *Fruhvogel's Pendant*, is in the chest they guard.

40 The orog veteran and three orog healers here carry a small amount of gold.

41 These two orog guardsmen carry the useful Cold Brass Key in addition to a standard healing potion.

42 These two orogs have taken advantage of the ancient taproom they've been assigned to guard and are now completely drunk. They're no match for you in their present state.

43 This library has long since been evacuated.

44 This door is trapped with a poison dart.

45 This is the resting room for the orogs enslaved by the Cult. It's empty when your party finds it; barricade it and rest in peace and quiet.

46 Three orogs, an orog veteran, two orog guardsmen, and two orog healers guard this highway. They carry a second Cold Brass Key (the first can be found in location 41) and some minor treasure.

47 These stairs go down to location 57 on the 2nd level of the Dwarven Dungeons. Three wraiths attack when you open the door to the northeast. The chest contains the *Inferno Knife*.

Peaceful Orog Camp

48 These two orogs do not attack the party. They are the guards for an orog camp that is fighting lizardfolk for territory. All the orogs in this area are nonhostile (unless your party attacks first).

49 There is an evil book in this room that an orog implores you to take. As with the other evil books, burn it in the Pyre of Silence in the Deep Halls, location 47.

50 Approach the door to this room cautiously because it's trapped. The chest in this room contains the *Girdle of Serenity*, an excellent suit of armor, especially for rogues.

51 More orogs roam peacefully. They have thoroughly barricaded the area.

52 This is an orog barracks.

141

53 As you enter this courtyard, you walk into the middle of a fight between the resident orogs and a party of lizardfolk consisting of a lizardfolk taskmaster and three lizardfolk warriors. The orogs have repaired the barricade where they broke through, so you can see the lizardfolk camp, but you cannot reach it yet.

54 These rooms are empty, except for a chest in the back with a little gold.

55 Faeril's voice speaks as you walk by here. She warns your party not to drink from the nearby fountain and tells you that the nearby orogs are friendly. Both pieces of advice are sound.

56 The stairs in this room lead to the 2nd level of the Dwarven Dungeon, location 69.

> # Note
> This encounter (location 53) only occurs if you pass this area after having defeated the cult mages in the Room of Words.

57 This is the Tomb of Arms-Captain Hachaam Selorn, a heroic elf. His sword has been taken long ago, but your party can find it in the bottom of the Elven Catacombs (see Chapter 19 for details). When they return it to the tomb, you learn the word to break the Glyph of the Moon. You need it to unseal a door at location 4 in the Castle Passage where you'll fight the Demon Rivener and gain a mighty treasure. See Chapter 21 for details.

Lizardfolk Outpost

58 Open the chest in this small room, and two spectres immediately attack. The chest contains gold, the *Halberd of Vigilance*, and a suit of *Leather Armor +3*.

59 Three lizardfolk scavengers, two lizardfolk warriors, and a lizardfolk taskmaster occupy this room.

60 When you approach the pedestal in the center of this area, your party is beset by two lizardfolk taskmasters, four lizardfolk, and two lizardfolk warriors.

61 The lizardfolk here speak protectively of "water," referring to the Fountain of Life Beriand spoke of. You must defeat the two lizardfolk healers, two lizardfolk warriors, and a lizardfolk taskmaster to continue through lizardfolk territory.

62 Three lizardfolk warriors and a lizardfolk faith healer live in this room.

63 A lizardfolk taskmaster, a lizardfolk faith healer, and two lizardfolk warriors search this library.

64 This chest is trapped with *chill touch* and contains small gemstones and an idolon.

65 The tables in this room hold a *scroll of haste* and a *scroll of protection from evil.*

66 This is the chess room that Brewmaster Durlin used to play in. The barrel in the center of the room contains the Gloves of Courage.

67 Two lizardfolk warriors and two lizardfolk taskmasters carry a paltry amount of gold.

68 Yet more lizardfolk antagonize the party here. The squad is composed of a lizardfolk faith healer, two lizardfolk scavengers, and two lizardfolk taskmasters. They carry a healing potion.

69 All four doors into this room are guarded with *poison spit* traps.

70 This is the lizardfolk camp's center of power. The lizardfolk here invoke the name of "Malgi Hi" as they rush into battle. The party must face two lizardfolk healers, a lizardfolk faith healer, a lizardfolk taskmaster, a lizardfolk, and two stone lizardfolk.

71 Once the leaders of the camp are defeated, clean out the rest of the lizardfolk in the area. This room contains a lizardfolk healer, three lizardfolk scavengers, a lizardfolk warrior, and a lizardfolk taskmaster.

72 This room is full of dead orogs, likely soon to be eaten by the lizardfolk.

> ## Tip
> This room is the heart of the lizardfolk camp, and the trapped doors make movement in battle difficult. Sneak around the room and have a rogue disable all the traps before entering the room.

> ## Tip
> Watch out for the stone lizardfolk! They are especially strong and durable, as well as being completely immune to magic. Double-team them with warriors if possible.

143

73 This lizardfolk barracks is home to three injured lizardfolk, a lizardfolk faith healer, and a lizardfolk healer.

74 The lizardfolk infirmary is guarded by only a lizardfolk faith healer and three injured lizardfolk. The chests contain healing scrolls, salves, and a Soot Coated Key, which can be used in the Deep Halls, location 65. The stairs in this room lead to location 72 of the Deep Halls.

75 Three lizardfolk scavengers, two lizardfolk healers, and a lizardfolk warlord guard a suit of *Windswept Armor* and the Brewer's Key. The Brewer's Key opens the door in the room at location 46 on the 2nd level of the dungeon. The stairs in this room lead to that very same location.

76 A note from Brewmaster Durlin here tells about a treasure he left in a room where he once played chess with an old friend. He is referring to location 66.

77 Two lizardfolk warriors, two lizardfolk scavengers, and a lizardfolk healer make this room their home. You find two blank books with arcane symbols on the tables here, but they are worthless.

78 A secret door is here.

79 A Sigil of Warding protects the northwest wall from something on the opposite side. Clearly someone wanted whatever is on the other side locked away. Explore to find that the wall is a secret door.

80 Many dead skeletons are scattered about here, killed by whatever was locked away so long ago.

81 The gold in a chest in this room has likely been left untouched for centuries. Find *Leraja's Spear* here.

82 As the party leaves the area, three arraccats and a guard arraccat suddenly attack!

The arraccats attack, but they won't last long against *fireball*.

Orc Territory

83 The Small Platinum Key required to open this door can be found in location 89.

84 Two orc sergeants and an orc warlock face a patrol of invading undead consisting of three ancient zombies, two skeleton knights, and a skeleton lord.

85 One poor orc is cut down by five ancient zombies as the party enters this room. Avenge his death and find a small amount of gold. The door just to the north has a *shocking grasp* trap.

86 A homeless group of ormyrr greets your party in peace here. They ask you to clear the Sharpstick Room, their former home, of the orcs that have taken over. The Sharpstick Room is in the Deep Halls, location 24. If you've already cleared the room, the ormyrr prepare to move back home; they'll be gone the next time you return to this area. Return to the Sharpstick Room and the ormyrr will trade with you there.

87 This door is trapped with a poison dart.

88 Three orc shamans and an orc warlock attack the party here.

89 Two orcs, three orc sergeants, two orc shamans, and a orc captain are investigating the Seal of Mythanthor. They carry a Small Platinum Key, a healing salve, and *Gloves of Steadiness*. If you have the *Ring of Calling*, you can use the Seal of Mythanthor to warp to location 1 in the City Heights.

Note

Though these arraccats were frightening enough to convince the old inhabitants of the dungeon to lock them away, your party is made of sterner stuff. Show them no mercy.

90 Four orc sergeants, four orcs, a orc shaman, and a orc witch doctor guard this room. They carry gold.

91 Two orc shamans and four orc sergeants attack the party here.

92 An orc witch doctor, an orc shaman, an orc warlock, and three orc sergeants guard the orcs' treasure room. The wooden chest holds gold. The metal chest is trapped with *burning hands* and holds a *Quiver of Arrows +2*, the *Hammer of Splintering*, and a Small Platinum Key.

Lighting bolt can terrify even the most formidable enemy.

Chapter Ten

The Speculum Grounds (Myth Drannor)

At last your party has conquered the inhabitants of the Dwarven Dungeons and stepped once more into sunlight. But your adventure is far from over. Now the majority of the city of Myth Drannor stands open to you, and the monsters that populate it are the most powerful you've faced yet.

The Speculum, where the Hall of Wizards stands, was the center of knowledge in old Myth Drannor. You spoke to Caalenfaire here before. It was quickly abandoned for more defensible positions during the fall of Myth Drannor, so it did not see as much fighting as other areas of the city. That and the magic protections on the building have kept it relatively unscathed over the centuries. However, the grounds around the Speculum have fallen into ruin, like the rest of the city, and are now occupied by roaming orcs, gargoyles, and undead.

Quick Overview

There are a few straggling groups of monsters in the Speculum Grounds, but nothing is really essential here right now. While you are here, visit the Orrery, clear the monsters from Ualair's Circle, visit Caalenfaire again, and open the door into the orc camp in the Dwarven Dungeons. When you finish here, travel to Nightingale Court to the west to continue your quest. Later, you will travel to Sullymarsh and eventually reach Windrider Glade from a different direction.

Dungeon Master's Notes

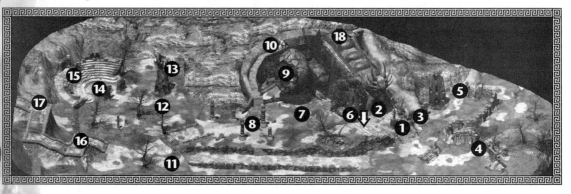

⬆ ⬇   Staircases leading up or down

❶ This is where the party appears after using the *Seal of Mythanthor* to escape from the Dwarven Dungeons. The party can use the statue of Mythanthor here to travel back to location 89 of the Halls of Light.

❷ This is the entrance to the Speculum. Four orcs, two orc sergeants, and two orc witch doctors guard it. They carry a potion and a salve of healing, some gold, and a suit of *Chainmail* +3. They left the key to the door in the lock, so the party is now free to come and go from the Speculum. If you enter the hall, you are rewarded with a new message from Caalenfaire and his companion Volun.

These orcs now understand the strength of the 3rd level spell *lightning bolt*.

❸ Two ancient zombies, three ghasts, and a shambling ghast guard this magically-sealed gate. The gate opens after you rescue the baelnorn from the Cult in the catacombs. See Chapter 20 for details.

❹ This is the entrance to what was once the House of Omberdawn. Now it is known as Sullymarsh. This gate leads to location 1 in the marsh.

5 This winding pathway leads up to Windrider Glade.

6 If your party can squeeze together, this is one of the few small places where resting can be done safely.

Tip

Don't travel to Windrider Glade just yet. There are other areas to visit first.

7 This plain is a battlefield, and the party is attacked by two orcs, an orc shaman, an orc witch doctor, four orc sergeants, and three arraccats. The chest to the north of this area contains two *potions of full healing* and a *Dagger +2*.

8 Four orc sergeants, three orcs, and an orc warlock guard this staircase.

9 This is the Orrery. You'll learn more about it when you find Harldain, but essentially it's a large machine that models the movement of the planets. Some of the colored stones that represent the planets are missing, so it isn't operational when the party first finds it. When it's finally complete, it can be used to warp between any of the spinning spires in Myth Drannor.

10 A margoyle gloats over the corpse of a lizardfolk. The corpse once owned a *Bow of Accuracy*, and your party finds it here.

11 Five orc sergeants and an orc witch doctor guard the west end of the roadway that runs along the bottom of the Speculum Grounds. There is also a patch of healing blueglow moss here.

12 Orcs have taken over this ruined tower. Your characters must fight an orc witch doctor, two orcs, an orc shaman, four orc sergeants, and an orc captain to pass. The captain carries some gold and a healing potion.

13 These five gargoyles have been preparing to assault the orcs the party just destroyed. Hoping to make short work of the weakened victors, these gargoyles are in for a surprise.

14 This is Ualair's Circle. The amphitheater has long since fallen to ruin, and there is little of interest here now. This circle is also a long-lost entrance to the Elven Catacombs, which the party will be able to open when they complete the broken Wizard's Torc they took from Preybelish in location 119 of the 3rd level of the Dwarven Dungeons (see Chapter 6).

15 Two gargoyles and two margoyles loiter around this door. Once they are defeated, the party finds a sorcerer's scroll and a healing potion. The door at the top of the amphitheater is barred from the other side, but the party can open it from location 8 on the 1st level of the Elven Catacombs. See Chapter 16.

149

16 Two margoyles guard the base of this staircase.

17 This path is the entrance to Nightingale Court, location 1.

18 After you have completed the Elven Catacombs, you return here to complete a portion of your quest. See Chapter 20 for details.

Tip

When first exploring the Speculum Grounds, take this pathway to Nightingale Court before exploring the rest of Myth Drannor.

Chapter Eleven

Nightingale Court (Myth Drannor)

Of all the Myth Drannor sections, Nightingale Court was hit hardest during the fall of the city. Once, many large, important structures stood on all sides of the court, but all were destroyed during the war. Over the centuries, erosion and vegetation have consumed the ruins, and now only the memory of the once-majestic structures remains.

For many years after the war, the only inhabitant of the ruined court was the spirit of Anorrweyn Evensong, head priestess of the Shrine of Mystra, who was killed when the temple fell. Time has not been kind, and the scavengers and beasts who dwell in Nightingale Court weaken her each year. Today, she is little more than a voice on the wind, and it is uncertain if anything can restore her benevolent presence.

Quick Overview

Nightingale Court

Nightingale Court is the center of lizardfolk power in Myth Drannor, and you'll encounter many territorial fights between the lizardfolk and the encroaching gargoyles.

The spiritual leader of the lizardfolk, a twisted sorcerer named Malgi Hi, also dwells here. He is the one who sent the lizardfolk into the Dwarven Dungeons on their quest for magical trinkets, and it is he who creates the powerful stone lizardfolk. A madman by all accounts, he is a potent magic user and always surrounded by his adoring minions.

You also find a spawn pool corrupting an ancient Shrine of Mystra. Free the shrine from the influence of the spawn pool to begin the process of restoring Anorrweyn Evensong. You return here several times during your quest.

Then walk back through the Speculum Grounds to Sullymarsh in the east.

151

Lizardfolk Tunnel

The short Lizardfolk Tunnel leads into the depths of the Deep Halls. This is an excellent opportunity to return to the Dwarven Dungeon and finish some old quests. In particular, you can now trade with the ormyrr in the Sharpstick Room at location 25 of the 4th level of the Dwarven Dungeons (make sure you killed all the orcs first), burn any evil books you're carrying on the Pyre of Silence at location 47, and open the door at location 80 that requires the Word of the Dragon. Once you have explored that room, you can open doors sealed with the Glyph of Water (at locations 70 and 45 and find the treasures within. See Chapter 8 for details on all of these tasks.

Dungeon Master's Notes
Nightingale Court

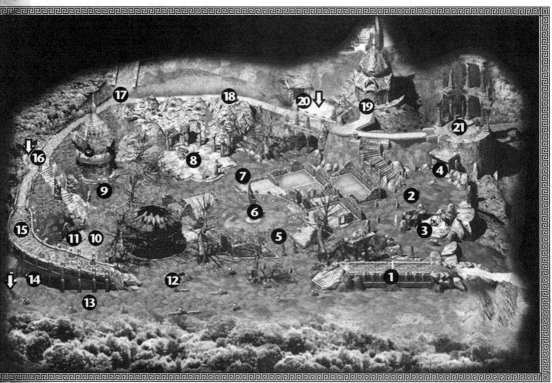

⬆ ⬇   Staircases leading up or down

1 As soon as the party enters Nightingale Court, a lizardfolk taskmaster, a lizardfolk faith healer, and three lizardfolk warriors attack. They carry gold. The pathway to the east leads to location 17 of the Speculum Grounds (Chapter 10).

2 As the characters enter this camp, a human voice calls out and threatens them with his lizardfolk allies. At last, you've found the enigmatic Malgi Hi, leader of the lizardfolk! In this camp, you face four stone lizardfolk, a lizardfolk faith healer, a lizardfolk taskmaster, three lizardfolk warriors, and Malgi Hi himself. The stone lizardfolk carry a *Wand of Hold Person*, while Malgi Hi holds a *potion of full healing*, and a scroll of *finger of death*.

3 Free the orange planet from this statue, and it flies back to the Orrery in the Speculum Grounds. The chest in the south of this clearing contains gold, and the chest to the north contains a *Ring of Relinquishment*. This is one of the few places to rest in the area.

4 Unbar this door to open the path into the Lizardfolk Tunnel, which starts in location 22 of this chapter. The tunnel leads into the Deep Halls of the Dwarven Dungeons.

5 Lizardfolk attack when the party enters this clearing. The group consists of two lizardfolk faith healers, a lizardfolk taskmaster, two lizardfolk warriors, and two lizardfolk scavengers. They carry gold and a healing potion. (See Tip at the top of the next page.)

Tip

Malgi Hi is a powerful spellcaster, so move a single warrior within melee range of him as soon as possible. This keeps him from casting too many spells. Attack with only one warrior, as the rest are needed to face the stone lizardfolk attacking from the north. This is a tough fight, so use all your tricks here. Items that cast *cone of cold*, such as *Borea's Blood* or the *Winter Blade*, are especially useful at clearing the battlefield.

Tip

There are a couple treasures in the tunnel, but more importantly, this is a good opportunity to finish some quests in the Deep Halls that you couldn't complete before. Take the tunnel for now, and see the Quick Overview for a suggestion of quests to complete.

153

6 Near the column in the center of this clearing, you hear the Whispering Wind, also known as the Ear of Myth Drannor. The wind hears sounds from all over Myth Drannor, and it gives you hints about where to find certain items in the ancient city. It talks for only a short time, but you can ask it more questions if you return later.

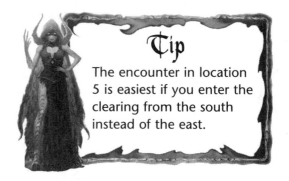

Tip

The encounter in location 5 is easiest if you enter the clearing from the south instead of the east.

7 Three stone lizardfolk and a lizardfolk geomancer attack the party here.

8 This is the ruined temple of Mystra. You'll return here multiple times, and different things occur here depending on what you have accomplished.

When you first arrive here, you find that dark nagas have taken over the temple. A spawn pool from the Pool of Radiance further corrupts the area. The nagas speak of silencing a voice that was constantly "whining to Mystra," but if you call out to Mystra, the voice responds. At this, the nagas attack. Defeat them and smash their idol to break their hold on the temple and banish the spawn pool. The chest here contains a *Sling +3*, an idolon, and a suit of *Leather Armor +3*. As the party walks away, the voice calls out, "Where are the faithful of Mystra?"

When the characters return with a symbol of Mystra, found in Stillwater Shrine after your party has returned and spoken to Faeril and Beriand, they can place it upon the altar to summon the spirit of Anorrweyn Evensong, the voice they heard before. Anorrweyn lives in the past and can't talk for long, but she tells the party of a Baelnorn

Tip

These three dark nagas are a difficult fight. If you have it, use *confusion* to remove one or more of them from the battle. Otherwise, try to eliminate them one at a time to reduce the number of foes you face. Although easy to hit, they have a lot of hit points, so save your game first!

named Miroden Silverblade who might be able to help them restore the Mythal. She teaches them the Word of Necessity, which will allow the party to find him in the Elven Catacombs (see Chapter 19). She also asks the party to find her skull to help anchor her more firmly in the present (found in Chapter 16, location 89).

When you return with her skull, Anorrweyn begs you to find Miroden Silverblade, the Baelnorn. After you have spoken to her, Anorrweyn bids you go to speak to Harldain about creating a new gem of the weave. See Chapter 20 for details.

9 Find a patch of healing moss on the ground here.

10 Lizardfolk are fighting with gargoyles over the idol here. Three lizardfolk taskmasters and a lizardfolk warlord face off against two gargoyles.

11 This giant stone head is where you can finally cash in on the strange "idolons" you've been collecting. The statue spits out a magic ring for each idolon the party feeds to it. The statue randomly dispenses one of the following rings for each idolon: *Beckon of Kelemvor, Bone of Myrkul, Breath of Kossuth, Bright Bane of Mellifleur, Cegilune's Perfume, Feather of Shar, Gears of Grumbar, Gong of Tyr, Gorgol's Asylum, Lens of Oghma, Oberon's Airy Lash, Olidammara's Whisper, Ring of Battening, Ring of Whiskers, Talona's Lashing Tongue, The Tremble Ring, Torm's Tiny Circlet, Touch of Cyric, Turabin's Cleansing Trinket,* and *Whip-Ring of Loviatar.* Additionally, if you return idolons to the ioun oracle (the giant stone head) after you have begun exploring the Lower Keep in the Catacombs, you can find five more powerful rings. They are: *Arknor's Vile Voice, Fist of Saint Cuthbert, Garras' Keen Sight, Misery's Embrace,* and *Stillness of Dawn.* The oracle then reverts to the first list of rings.

12 Four lizardfolk warriors are gathered around a dead gargoyle here. They carry the *Obsidian Edge* dagger.

13 A lizardfolk warrior fights a losing battle here against two margoyles and three gargoyles. They set aside their differences to attack you.

14 This door is barred from the other side. You eventually can open it from location 90 in the Elven Catacombs Level 4 (The Prisons).

15 Two margoyles and a gargoyle fight against a lizardfolk faith healer, a lizardfolk taskmaster, a lizardfolk warlord, and two lizardfolk scavengers here. Simply pick off the weakened combatants one by one.

16 This is the entrance to a tomb for the Knights of Myth Drannor. It is now home to a family of five arraccats. Once the arraccats lie dead, loot the tomb. You find a *Small Shield +3,* a *Light Mace +3,* and *Roderick's Walking Stick* in a chest near the center of the room.

17 Two lizardfolk warriors, two lizardfolk faith healers, and a lizardfolk taskmaster guard this collapsed passageway. They carry no treasure.

18 Two lizardfolk warriors, two lizardfolk faith healers, and a lizardfolk warlord patrol this section of the walkway. They carry gold.

19 This majestic tower is now a hollowed ruin. Despite its poor condition, however, it is better off than most buildings in this district. The party finds it defensible enough to rest here safely.

20 This doorway is locked from the other side and overgrown with grass. The party can open it from location 2 in the Castle Passage.

21 The spinning spire here is part of the city-wide Orrery.

Lizardfolk Tunnel

22 Upon entering the tunnel here, you hear the hiss of lizardfolk warriors to the north. The doorway here connects to location 4 in Nightingale Court.

23 A lizardfolk taskmaster, a lizardfolk faith healer, and three lizardfolk warriors live here. They have no treasure.

24 The staircase here connects to location 80 in the Deep Halls.

25 Arriving in this passageway, the party is ambushed by two lizardfolk warriors, two lizardfolk scavengers, and two lizardfolk faith healers. They have a *Silverleaf Rod* and a *Silverleaf Hatchet*.

Note

The above encounter takes place if you have left the dungeon before arriving here. If you approach this location before exiting the dungeons, you find a different encounter with three lizardfolk scavengers, a lizardfolk warrior, and a lizardfolk faith healer. They have no treasure.

Chapter Twelve

Sullymarsh (Myth Drannor)

In the days of Myth Drannor's glory, Sullymarsh was a public park that featured a magnificent lake nourished by the city's elaborate water system. Over the centuries following the fall of the city and the collapse of the water system, the lake reverted to its natural form: a swamp.

Sullymarsh is now home to packs of ormyrr, who are not hindered by the wet ground, and who are strong enough to fend off the roaming packs of predators. However, like the rest of the city, evil has spread to Sullymarsh and corrupted the once-peaceful ormyrr into something more sinister.

Quick Overview

Go north to clear an entrance to the bottom level of the Dwarven Dungeons. Opening pathways such as this one makes moving throughout the city much easier.

To the east is a group of ormyrr, led by its self-appointed king, Pujik. The Ormyrr have set up camp by a spawn pool from the Pool of Radiance. Be careful; there is evil afoot here. Visit the ormyrr several times to reveal the evil and put it to rest.

When you are finished, follow the winding walkways north to the Glim-Gardens.

157

Dungeon Master's Notes

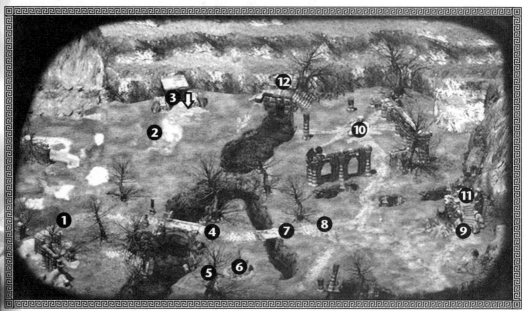

⬆ ⬇   Staircases leading up or down

❶ Immediately upon entering Sullymarsh, your party is attacked by a gargoyle leader and four gargoyles. They carry a *Cerulean Ring*. The gateway here leads back to location 4 of the Speculum Grounds in the west.

❷ Two shambling ghasts, two skeleton lords, and two skeleton knights venture out of the depths of the Dwarven Dungeons and attack you here. They carry only gold.

❸ This door is barred on the outer side. Removing the bar opens a path to location 36 of the Deep Halls.

❹ A voice speaks of the legend of the bridge and how Hachaam Selorn held back the marauding hordes here. It tells your party of his wondrous sword, the *Baneblade Faervian*, and laments its loss to the scavengers of the city.

❺ Two ancient zombies and three shambling ghasts attack the party here.

❻ Like the other spires of the city, this one is a part of the Orrery.

❼ A gargoyle leader and two gargoyles attack here.

8 The party comes across two ormyrr here. They are not initially hostile, but they defend themselves when you attack. If they aren't killed here, they join a later fight, making it more difficult.

9 This is the spawn pool where the ormyrr king, Pujik, has set up camp. He and his court are suspicious of your party, but they're willing to let you prove yourself by eliminating a band of rogue ormyrr to the north who have been driven mad by greed. When you have performed the task, the following events occur: When your party returns, the king shows his true colors. Kya Mordrayn is exerting magical control over him and his tribe through his axe, and she commands that you must die! When Pujik falls, his axe shatters, and Kya's hold on Sullymarsh is broken.

The spawn pool withers in defeat. The tribe hoards a *Longspear +3* and a *Small Shield +2*.

Once Pujik is dead, two ormyrrs approach and offer to trade with the party. They sell *Quivers of Arrows +3*, *salve of critical healing*, a *Longbow +2*, a *Sling +3*, and a *Longspear +3*.

> ## Tip
>
> Ormyrr are extremely powerful melee fighters who get five attacks per round. Thin their numbers, or this large group quickly takes down your characters. They bunch up, so hit many of them at once with spells such as *fireball* and *cone of cold*. While your magic users pummel them with sorcery, have your warriors gang up on one ormyrr at a time.

10 The mad ormyrr tribe live among several skeletons of their kind. Unlike the others, these three ormyrr attack the party on sight. They carry a *Handaxe +3*.

11 A mysterious green stone is attached to the end of a wooden pole here. Breaking the pole releases the stone, and it flies back to the Orrery in the Speculum Grounds.

12 This path leads north to location 1 in the Glim-Gardens.

These renegade ormyrr aren't too happy to see your party.

159

Chapter Thirteen

The Glim-Gardens (Myth Drannor)

In the days of Myth Drannor, this region held a grand mansion with majestic gardens that magically healed the spirits and bodies of weary travelers. The mansion and its surrounding structures were destroyed during the fall of Myth Drannor. In the centuries since, creatures have carried off the loose stones to barricade their homes, and what was left has been covered by vegetation. The once benevolent gardens were forever twisted, and their gifts now come with a sinister price.

Quick Overview

The Glim-Gardens are full of minor quests of interest to the party. None are required to restore Myth Drannor, but all promise adventure and make the path ahead easier to walk.

When exploring the ruins of the mansion, a section of ground gives out below you, dropping you into a basement. Overrun with undead, the basement also holds numerous treasures, including the Stone Mouth, which allows you to communicate with talkative gargoyles.

To the northeast is the tomb of a wight and a frozen paladin under its curse. To the southeast is the Thirsty Ground, which is all that remains of the fabled gardens. When you have finished your explorations, travel west to Windrider Glade.

Dungeon Master's Notes

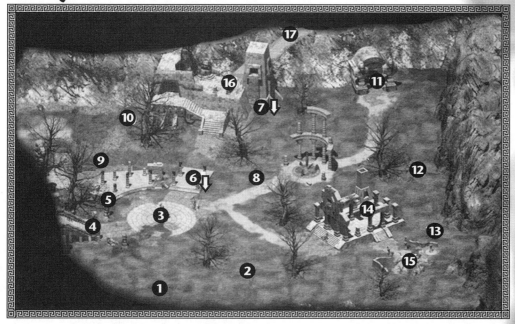

⬆ ⬇   Staircases leading up or down

The Glim-Gardens

1 This pathway leads to location 4 in Sullymarsh (see Chapter 12).

2 Gargoyles and undead fight on the grass here. Three margoyles and two gargoyles face a ghoul, two ghasts, and a shambling ghast. The winner takes a healing potion and gold.

3 This fountain will be active after the party restores the pump house in the courtyard of the House of Gems (see Chapter 15). Once it is active, you meet Plinshree, a water naiad who asks for your help retrieving her waterbells.

These bells are behind the doors sealed with the Glyph of Water in locations 45 and 70 in the Deep Halls (see Chapter 8) and location 45 in the Halls of Stone (see Chapter 7). Plinshree trades treasures to the party for each waterbell they restore. For the first bell,

> ## Note
>
> Plinshree can be met for the first time at any of the city wells, not just the one in the Glim-Gardens. The party must revive the pump house to meet her.

161

Prima's Official Strategy Guide

she gives a *Necklace of Odoacer*. For the second bell, she gives a *Ring of Calming*. For the third bell, she gives a *Dagger of Ritual*, and if you visit Plinshree after defeating Pelendralaar (see Chapter 23), she will give you a rare item called the *Jewel of Sammaster*. Another of Plinshree's fountains lies in location 110 in the Main Halls of the Dwarven Dungeon.

4 These stairs lead to location 2 in the Windrider Glade (see Chapter 14).

5 Three ghouls and three shambling ghasts attack the party here.

6 As you step onto this pedestal, the ground gives way, dropping you into the basement of the mansion. All characters take 10 points of damage and wind up in location 18 of the Ancient Tomb.

7 After fighting through the Ancient Tomb and opening the doors sealed with the Glyph of Song in the Halls of Stone, the party emerges in the Glim-Gardens at this door. Four shambling ghasts immediately attack.

8 A huge group of skeletons practices ancient military drills here, but breaks formation to attack the party. Your party must defeat five skeleton knights and five skeleton lords. Your enemies hold a healing potion.

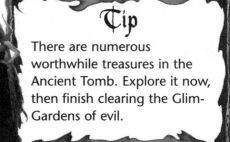

Tip

There are numerous worthwhile treasures in the Ancient Tomb. Explore it now, then finish clearing the Glim-Gardens of evil.

9 A shambling ghast, two skeleton lords, and three ancient zombies lurk behind the ruins of the stone amphitheater.

10 Find a patch of blueglow healing moss here.

11 Two skeleton lords and four ghasts block the doorway to this tomb. Inside, the party finds the preserved body of Eadred, the paladin. His voice informs the party that he is held by the final spell of a defeated wight. He and his lord, Hachaam Selorn, defeated the wight, but

Tip

Area spells such as *fireball* and *lightning bolt* are especially useful here, as is turning undead.

Hachaam was caught by the spell and frozen. To free his lord, Eadred took the spell upon himself and has been in the tomb ever since. If a character grasps the sword, Eadred is set free and joins the party. But, bear in mind that the character who grasps the sword takes Eadred's place. At any time, Eadred can grasp the sword again and free whomever sacrificed their freedom for his. He wears *Chainmail +2* and *Gauntlets of Dexterity*.

12 An orc warlock and two orc sergeants have mastered the art of controlling undead and now command a group of four ancient zombies and two shambling ghasts, which they immediately turn upon the party.

13 These four shambling ghasts, like many undead, are drawn to the Thirsty Ground to the south. To reach it, the party must defeat them.

14 Six ghasts dwell on this ruined structure, and they attack the party with gusto.

15 This is the Thirsty Ground. It is all that remains of the grand gardens that once surrounded the mansions. It can still heal travelers, but it's cursed with an insatiable thirst for blood. It can cast *restoration*, *remove curse*, and *resurrection*, but drains hit points in payment. It steals 21 HP for the Blood Lesson and the Blood Blessing. For Fiona's Kiss, it takes away all but 1 HP.

16 Three margoyles and a gargoyle have taken refuge in what remains of this structure, and they attack the party to protect it.

17 This walkway leads north to location 1 of the House of Gems Courtyard (see Chapter 15).

> **Tip**
>
> Follow this path after you have explored the Windrider Glade and returned to Stillwater.

Ancient Tomb

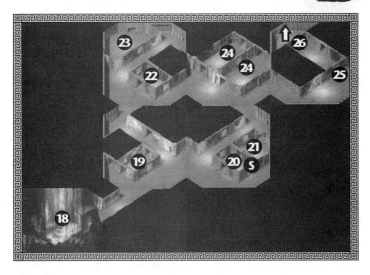

⬆ ⬇ Staircases leading up or down   **S** Secret door

18 This is the beginning of the Ancient Tomb, where the party lands after falling through the ground in location 6.

19 Powerful undead attack as soon as the party opens the door to this room. It takes everything the party has to defeat the two ghasts, two master shadows, and the spectre. The chest the undead guard is trapped with a *cone of cold* spell. It contains the *Necklace of Safe Footfalls*, which allows you to navigate the trapruns in Chapter 18 with greater ease, and the Stone Mouth, which allows the party to communicate with gargoyles.

20 A dark naga makes this room home. The party has faced worse before, so the dark naga should go down with little trouble. It guards two chests. The one on the left is trapped with *poison spit* and contains *Gauntlets of Ogre Size* and *Boots of the Tortoise*. The right chest is also trapped with *poison spit* and contains *Alaric's Charm*. The wall in the northeast of this room is a secret door.

21 In this hidden room, the party finds the treasures of Jelde Asturien, Priest of Lathander the Morninglord. The chest contains the *Blade of Destruction* and a suit of *Arcane Mail*.

22 The entrance to this room, if there ever was one, has long since been destroyed in the fighting for Myth Drannor and the general decay of the city.

Tip

The *Arcane Mail* is one of the best suits of armor in Myth Drannor because it does not impair arcane spellcasting, making it perfect for sorcerers, especially multiclass sorcerer warriors. Of course, a robed sorcerer in platemail appears as a very formidable adversary to any onlooker.

23 Four skeleton lords, the weakest creatures in the Ancient Tomb, attack the party here. The chest is open but must be smashed to retrieve an idolon.

24 One of the two rooms here is filled with blinding light, the other filled with stifling darkness. The light appears to be coming from a chest, and if the party closes the chest, the light is dispelled and a master spectre attacks from the second room. Defeating the master spectre breaks the spell of darkness in the second room, allowing the party to retrieve the Singing Word scroll from a table.

25 This door is sealed with the Glyph of Song. Find the Singing Word, which unlocks it, on a table in location 24.

26 This doorway leads to location 13 in the Halls of Stone (see Chapter 7). After entering this door, the party stands near a doorway leading back to location 25 in the Ancient Tomb.

Chapter fourteen

Windrider Glade (Myth Drannor)

The Windrider Glade is set on a raised platform in the center of the city, equidistant from Castle Cormanthor, the House of Gems, and the Speculum. In the old days of Myth Drannor, it was a public park dedicated to peace and diversity of religion, and it housed many shrines, with the Temple of Shaundakul being the greatest. But during the war, its central location made the Windrider Glade one of the most fiercely contested zones in the city. Destructive magic unleashed in battle toppled spires, razed buildings, and shattered walkways.

Only the Temple of Shaundakul has withstood the ravages of time, and only because it is watched by a long line of guardian naga protectors. Recently, the Pool of Radiance's corrupting influence has invaded the glade, and despite the efforts of its protectors, it has become a haven for the corrupt and unclean. But with some effort from those pure at heart, some of its former glory can be restored.

Quick Overview

Immediately upon entering the Windrider Glade, you are met by Odelinde, whom Caalenfaire told you to seek out. She requests your assistance in retaking her shrine, which has been invaded by orcs. Help her, and she will assist you in your quest. She knows much about Myth Drannor and can tell many useful tales.

You can open a locked doorway to the Halls of Light, and a group of gargoyles will challenge you for a significant treasure if you have the Stone Mouth and can understand their language.

Finally, to the northwest is a drawbridge that allows easy access to Faeril and Beriand, who may know something of the ethereal voice you heard at the Shrine of Mystra in Nightingale Court. When you have met with them again, travel east to the House of Gems through the Glim-Gardens.

Dungeon Master's Notes

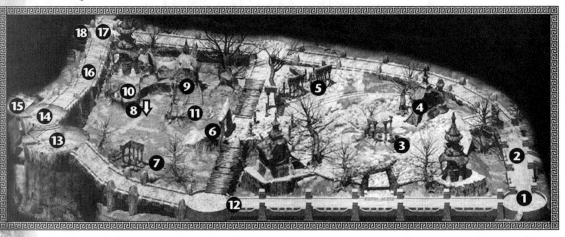

⬆ ⬇ Staircases leading up or down

1 The winding pathway to the south here leads to location 5 of the Speculum Grounds (see Chapter 10).

2 Odelinde the guardian naga meets the party here. She tells the party how her shrine has been taken over by orcs, and how the spawn pool that erupted near the shrine sapped her strength, preventing her from freeing the shrine. She beseeches the party to help her. The path to the east here leads to location 4 of the Glim-Gardens.

3 This is the Temple of Shaundakul. It has been overrun by an orog guardsman, two orogs, two orc sergeants, an orc captain, an orc shaman, and an orc warlock. They carry a *Scimitar +2* and a scroll of *bull's strength*. When they are defeated and the party destroys the idol on the altar, the spawn pool's link to the area is destroyed, and it retreats to the Pool of Radiance. Odelinde, in thanks, heals and rests the party. She has useful tales about the history of the city, and tells the party about the Mythal and how it was corrupted. She also puts a name to the voice the party heard at the Shrine of Mystra in Nightingale Court (see Chapter 11, location 8), telling them it was Anorrweyn Evensong, Priestess of Mystra. She suggests the party go to Harldain in the House of Gems to the northeast for more help. She, like Beriand, knows numerous tales of the surrounding area.

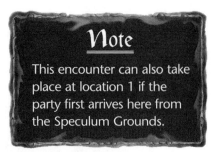

Note

This encounter can also take place at location 1 if the party first arrives here from the Speculum Grounds.

4 An orc captain and two orc warlocks guard this chest. It contains an idolon and the Firemeet Ceremonial Key, which you use in location 8.

5 Two orc sergeants, an orog healer, and three orog guardsmen attack the party here.

6 Two gargoyle leaders and two gargoyles have set up a blockade on these steps, but they're no match for the party.

7 A huge group of gargoyles are fighting to repel three ancient zombies from their territory. There are seven gargoyles and a margoyle. After a few rounds, two more gargoyles join in. When all enemies are defeated, the party finds a *Jeweled Dagger +2*.

8 This locked door requires the Firemeet Ceremonial Key, found in location 4. It leads to location 12 in the Halls of Light (see Chapter 9). From this side, the party can open the door that was locked to them before.

9 Three margoyles await the party at the top of the steps of this structure. Neither chest here contains anything useful. However, there is gold on the ground nearby.

10 This spire, like the other spires in Myth Drannor, is part of the Elven Orrery, which lets the party travel quickly around Myth Drannor after it is repaired.

11 Two more margoyles attack the party here. They carry *Ricimer's Barrier*.

12 Two skeleton lords and two shambling ghasts block this walkway.

13 The group of gargoyles here speaks if the party has the Stone Mouth (found at location 19 of the Glim-Gardens, in the Ancient Tomb; see Chapter 13). They ask the party if they are the great ones who have caused so much carnage in the city. If the characters say they are, the gargoyles mention that the Tusk-Lord will be pleased, then offer a tribute in a box that requires a Twisted Iron Key. The box contains a red stone that, when released, flies away to the Orrery device in the Speculum Grounds.

14 The Tusk-Lord the gargoyles mentioned confronts you here. He respects your party's power, but plans to take it for himself by defeating all of you. When he falls, the party finds the Twisted Iron Key on his corpse.

15 This walkway leads to Castle Cormanthor. However, the drawbridge is raised, so the party cannot pass.

16 Two margoyles and two gargoyles attack here.

17 Attempting to read this marred sign triggers magic that lowers the drawbridge to Stillwater, allowing the party to return and speak to Faeril and Beriand again. It connects to location 7 in Stillwater (see Chapter 5).

18 The walkway in this direction is broken. The party will have to find another way to Castle Cormanthor.

Chapter Fifteen

The House of Gems (Myth Drannor)

The House of Gems was once the great meeting hall of Myth Drannor's dwarves. Many of the city's nonmagical systems, such as the massive waterworks and lighting systems, were controlled and maintained from within the House of Gems. Due to its solid dwarven construction and massive size, most of the keep survived the fall of Myth Drannor, though the grounds around it have deteriorated.

Due to the deadly traps and mechanical protections in the House of Gems, it has avoided defilement from Myth Drannor's newer inhabitants. Recently, the Cult of the Dragon has taken control of the Room of Words on the top floor of the tower, where the dwarves once stored all the Words of Power to the many protective glyphs around the city.

Quick Overview

The House of Gems Round Tower

Your party first enters the round tower from within the Halls of Light in the Dwarven Dungeons. The cult mages inside have the skeletal arm with the *Ring of Calling* that you need to open the Seal of Mythanthor and exit the Dwarven Dungeons. Climb the tower and take it from them. The top of the tower contains some worthwhile treasure.

The House of Gems Grounds

The grounds are very straightforward. Clear the undead from the area before entering the house. After you find your way to the roof, restore the ancient pumping system, destroying another spawn pool in the process.

The House of Gems

The first floor of the House of Gems features several deadly traps and mechanical defenses. Defeat them and climb the stairs to the 2nd floor, where you find Harldain. You have to cleanse the pump system of corruption before he'll talk to you, but it's worth the effort; Harldain has numerous pieces of useful information, the Starstone to complete the Wizard's Torc, and some extremely powerful magic items for sale.

After you have spoken to Harldain, return to the Dwarven Dungeons and finish the last remaining quest: Plinshree's waterbells. To find the first one, enter the Halls of Light through the Round Tower and walk west to the Rhonglyn Room. Go to the Halls of Stone through the Rhonglyn Room and go north to the last door sealed by the Glyph of Water at location 45. Then go to locations 76 and 79 of the Deep Halls. When you have collected all three waterbells, go back to Plinshree's fountain at location 3 in the Glim-Gardens to collect your reward.

When you have spoken to Plinshree, go across the overland south and west. Speak to Anorrweyn at the Shrine of Mystra and turn in any idolons for Fading Rings at the stone idol. Finally, return to Ualair's Circle in the Speculum Grounds and use the completed Wizard's Torc to open a passage to the Elven Catacombs.

169

POOL OF RADIANCE
RUINS OF MYTH DRANNOR
Prima's Official Strategy Guide

Dungeon Master's Notes

The House of Gems
Round Tower

> ### Note
>
> This adventure starts from the Halls of Light (Dwarven Dungeon level 1). Locations 1–5 are in the House of Gems Tower, which is accessible from underground. The party starts in location 6 of the aboveground map shown on the next page.

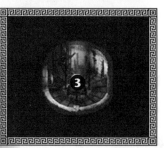

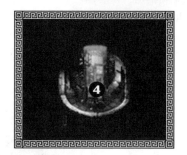

Inside the Round Tower of the House of Gems

1 Upon entering the ground floor of the House of Gems Round Tower, the party is attacked by four skeleton lords. The door to the east leads to location 37 in the Halls of Light. The stairway leads up to location 3 on the tower's 2nd floor.

Return to this room after escaping the Dwarven Dungeons to meet four orogs. They speak about the wickedness of the Cult and ask you to join them in their fight against it. The also speak about the *Helm Cleaver*, which you can help them retrieve from the Cult. If you agree to help them, they will join your fight. Proceed to the Halls of Light and find them at location 29 (or an unnumbered location southeast of location 33) prepared to begin their raid.

2 This door is locked from the other side. When it is unlocked, it leads to location 18 in the House of Gems.

3 Three soulless orogs attack the party here on level 2. Stairs lead up to location 4 on the 3rd floor and stairs lead down to location 1 on the 1st floor.

4 This is the Room of Words. The three cult mages here are speaking all the words in the room in an attempt to remove the *Ring of Calling* from the skeletal arm, but to no avail. They carry the *Eye of Ranman* and the skeletal arm with the *Ring of Calling*. If the party knows the Word of Oblivion, taught by Caalenfaire in the Hall of Wizards, the word speaks itself and the party receives the *Ring of Calling*.

5 This is the roof of the Round Tower. Here the party faces two gargoyles. They are hiding some gold and the *Gauntlets of Light Burden*.

Tip

These three mages are a tough fight. Spread your characters out as soon as you enter this level to keep the mages from blasting you with area effect spells such as *fireball*. Have a warrior close to melee range with each mage right away to minimize their ability to cast spells, then weaken them all gradually until they fall.

Note

This treasure appears after you have escaped the Dwarven Dungeons.

The House of Gems Grounds

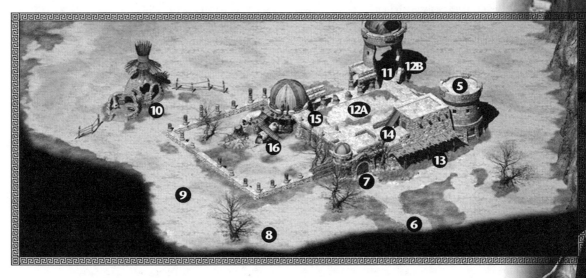

The grounds area surrounding the House of Gems

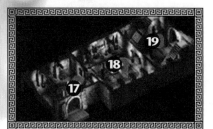

The interior of the House of Gems

6 This is the entrance to the House of Gems grounds from location 17 of the Glim-Gardens.

7 This door leads to location 17 in the House of Gems interior, Safekeep Halls.

8 Two ghasts and two shambling ghasts attack the party here.

9 Two ancient zombies, two skeleton lords, and two ghasts loiter on this plain. They carry a small amount of gold.

10 This structure has been taken over by undead, who have killed the previous occupants and are now eating them. Two shambling ghasts are eating a gargoyle, and to the east, three more shambling ghasts and two ancient zombies are eating a dead ormyrr. All attack the party when disturbed. They have a *Stalwart Shield* among their treasures. Rest in the two hollowed-out huts.

11 Three skeleton lords guard a chest holding the *Talisman Staff*. This ruin is one of the only safe places in which to rest in the overlands.

12A Five ghasts and two ancient zombies infest this courtyard. The statue here requires a hinged device to open it, so the party must return after finding it. See Chapter 20 for details.

12B The party encounters four ghasts and three ancient zombies.

13 Four skeleton lords and a shambling ghast dwell in the shade of this awning.

14 This door leads from the roof of the House of Gems to location 20 in the interior. Make your way here after exploring the interior, Hearthhame Halls.

15 Two margoyles attack as the party follows this parapet.

16 The party comes across another spawn pool here. Someone pinned the corpse of a woman to the side of the pump house with a *Flame Blade*. The spawn pool was drawn to the symbol of corruption. Four arraccats and a black arraccat were drawn to the twisted totem by the pool and have made their nest around it. To destroy the pool, defeat the arraccats and destroy their nests. Remove the *Flame Blade* from the corpse, freeing the woman's spirit and destroying the pool. With the pool gone, the pump house returns to working order.

172

The House of Gems

17 A dwarven statue guards the entry to the Safekeep Halls. Like the Lifespring Guardian, it is a powerful golem, capable of taking and dealing tremendous physical damage, and immune to all magic. It is the primary reason the House of Gems hasn't been overrun by scavengers in the centuries since the fall of the city. When defeated, the golem drops the *Axe of the Phoenix* and a Copper Key, which will unlock the door to the next room.

18 This room is a giant lightning trap. When the party steps into the room, massive arcs of lightning shoot continuously from the walls. The floor is littered with the bones of former victims. A device on the opposite side of the room will disable the trap if the party has the Pass Key.

19 This room is free of traps. The chest in the middle of the room contains the Pass Key the party needs to disable the lightning trap in the previous room. The door to the east is barred on this side and lets the party move freely into and out of the tower. The staircases lead up to location 20.

20 When you enter this room, the Hearthhame Hall, you see the ghost of Harldain. Because he is frozen, he can only stutter. The stairs on the east side of the room lead down to location 19, and the door to the west leads to the roof of the House of Gems, location 14.

Tip

Mob the dwarven statue with your warriors. Equip the *Mountain Fist* if you have it. Have the rest of your characters focus on healing. Use *bull's strength* to pump up your fighters.

Tip

To deal with this room, have one character with lots of hit points and a good Reflex saving throw bonus (such as a monk, paladin, or rogue) run across the lightning bolts and disable the trap before the rest of the party crosses.

When the pump house is freed from corruption, Harldain returns to normal. The pool slowed the pump house, thus slowing Harldain, whose spirit is tied to the ancient dwarven machinery. He tells the party about the Elven Orrery, a great machine that, when operational, allows people to teleport across the city in moments. He explains that the colored stones the party has found are pieces of the Orrery, and he frees the blue Orrery stone the party has been carrying since the beginning of the adventure. He also has suggestions about where to find the remaining stones. Harldain tells the party how to use the completed Wizard's Torc to enter the Elven Catacombs at Ualair's Circle in the Speculum Grounds, and he gives them the Starstone to complete the Wizard's Torc the party found in location 119 of the Dwarven Dungeons' Main Hall. Finally, Harldain has numerous powerful magic items for sale, including the *Shield of House Starym*, the *Lancer's Guard*, a suit of *Full Plate +4*, *Olortynnal's Heartmail*, a *Longbow +3*, *Ildacer's Satin Gloves*, and *Ranman's Meditations* (this needs to be added to a monk's inventory to be effective).

Chapter Sixteen

First Cellar
(The Elven Catacombs, Level 1)

You enter the catacombs through the amphitheatre in the Speculum Grounds, and are immediately in another world. The Elven Catacombs were created to provide space in which to do the Castle Cormanthor's work: hide prisoners, furnish work space for reclusive mages, and bury elven heroes who couldn't be buried under the sun. Level 1 is home to a large family of drow elves, a contingent of cult members, and various undead who have encroached on this area over the years.

Quick Overview

Orog Rebels

South of where you enter the dungeon is the hideout of a group of orog rebels making trouble for the cult on this level of the dungeon. You see signs of the group's work as you explore. It is not hostile to you, and there are several useful treasures and keys in and around the group's hideout.

The Cult Torture Chamber

In this region, the cult is creating soulless orogs from the orogs that it's captured. This makes it the primary target for the roaming bands of orog rebels to the south. When you enter this area, you walk in on a heated battle between orog marauders and cult members.

The Cult Stronghold

The Cult Stronghold is a linear, straightforward area. The cult members are weakened by their battles with the orogs, so strike them a blow. Tear through their camp, defeat any cult members you find, and take their treasure. It will come in handy in your future explorations.

The White Orrery Planet

At last you have the opportunity to complete the Orrery machine that Harldain told you about. When it is finished, you can warp between spinning spires anywhere in the city. Don't get too excited, however, as the white planet is in a treasure trove protected by a large horde of powerful monsters. Ready your weapons, because this fight is going to be tough!

The Undead Prison

Due to its secure location in the center of the level, this area of the Catacombs was once used by the elves to hold various prisoners. Since the fall of the city, it has been overrun with undead.

Ghosts of the Past

As you explore the far west of the dungeon, you notice that this area is free of undead or monsters, but the once-stately walls have been destroyed in a cataclysm. The spirits of Myth Drannor confront you here, then give you their blessing as your exploration continues to the lower levels.

The Freth Drow Stronghold

This incredibly difficult stronghold is full of powerful drow, including guards, commanders, assassins, inquisitors, and more. Defeating these enemies is very difficult without *The Sacred Staff of Sunlight* and other weapons you will find on levels 2, 3, and 4, so leave most of this stronghold for later. You have to conquer it eventually, it's just a question of when.

Dungeon Master's Notes

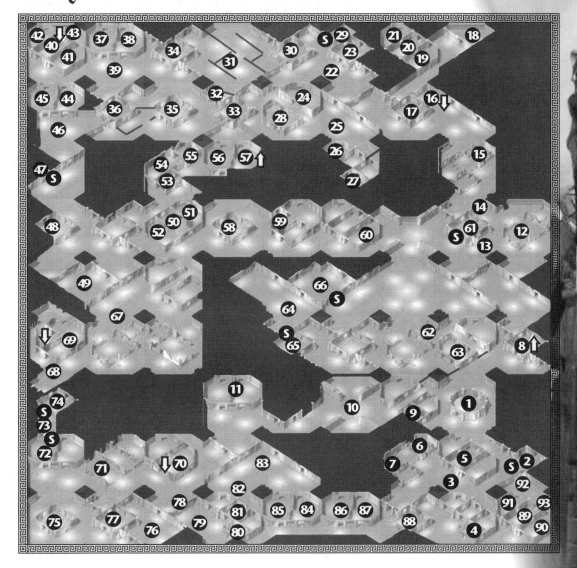

⬆ ⬇ Staircases leading up or down   **S** Secret door

177

Orog Rebels

1 This round room is where you appear after warping into the Elven Catacombs from Ualair's Circle in the Speculum Grounds, location 14 (see Chapter 10).

2 A lich lives here and protects its treasures fiercely. There is a *Large Shield +4* and a *Greataxe +2* on the ground. The chest is trapped and contains a large sum of gold and a *potion of full healing*.

3 Entering this hallway, the party finds a pile of Cult of the Dragon soldiers burning on a pyre. They are recently dead, so whoever killed them must still be nearby.

4 In this room, one of a series of suites once used to temporarily house important dwarven visitors, the party encounters a single mohrg. His coffin holds gold, gems, and a *Staff of Flame*.

5 Two margoyles attack the party in this room. They possess gems and a *potion of moderate healing*. The door in the northwest of this room requires the Greenish Copper Key. The Greenish Copper Key is held by the orogs at location 6, but you have to kill them to get it.

6 These rooms are the hideout for orog rebels, who are currently resting between cult harassment outings. After the orog rebels realize that you are not cult members, they are very tolerant, even allowing the party to take supplies from their hideout. However, if the party becomes hostile, the rebels will fight back viciously. The first two rooms house four orog marauders, an orog marauder boss, an orog marauder big boss, an orog marauder hoodoo, and an orog marauder brute. The chest in the barracks holds healing potions, a *Ring of Strength*, and the Old Elven Key. The orogs have the Greenish Copper Key; you'll have to kill them to get it.

7 The remaining two rooms of the orog hideout house two orog marauders, an orog marauder boss, and an orog marauder brute. They are part of the same party in location 6, so don't attack them if they haven't attacked first. The table holds a *Greataxe +2* and an orog dungeon map that gives general locations of the cult and drow elves on level 1. The two chests contain a *Large Shield +2* and a *Battleaxe +1*.

8 The two master wraiths that attack the party in this room are the spirits of long-dead elven warriors whose final task was to guard the stairway to the surface to the very end. They continue their duty even in death. The stairs here lead to the formerly barred door at location 15 in the Speculum Grounds (see Chapter 10).

9 The well here contains a *Wand of Stinking Cloud* and a *Ring of Stamina*.

10 This is the forward vanguard of the drow fortress on this level. A drow elf steps out of an unnatural cloud of darkness and threatens the party. If the party tells her that she is the one who will die, she brings a couple of her warriors out of the darkness. If the party continues to taunt her, she drops her darkness, giving the party an advantage. Bergos (the drow elf) is joined by eight Freth drow commandos, two guard arraccats, and a Freth drow high priest. They carry the Silver Spider Key, a suit of *Drow Chainmail* +1, a *Drow Shortsword* +1, and some healing salves.

11 There are some corpses on the ground, but both of these rooms are safe places to rest.

The Cult Torture Chamber

12 Fifteen zombies and a zombie lord pray to a dark god at this ruined temple. The zombie lord carries a *Wand of Slay Living*, and there is gold in the back room.

13 To open this door, you must have the Rusty Elven Key, which is found in location 17.

14 This door requires the Old Elven Key, which can be found in the orog rebels' hideout at location 6.

15 Six wights and four zombies attack the party here.

16 This stairway leads down to location 1 on level 2 of the Elven Catacombs.

17 This room contains a freshly dead cult soldier and some mundane weapons scattered about. There is also a note to Lieutenant Garesh. The chest in the middle of the room contains the Rusty Elven Key.

18 The fountains in this room impart a number of magical benefits on characters who drink from them. The fountains grant boons of *restoration* (front left, one charge), *shield of faith* (front right, one charge), *cure critical wounds* (back left, three charges), and *protection from evil* (back right, three charges).

> ### Note
>
> There is a dark naga lair with a powerful weapon near the staircase on level 2. It is well worth your time to make the quick diversion. See Chapter 17 for details.

19 Two orog marauder brutes and an orog marauder boss fight a cult archmage in this room. Terrible experiments are being performed on orogs here, and these marauders have come to free their brothers. After the fight, you'll find a *scroll of fireball* and the *Staff of Firestorms*.

20 Two soulless orogs defend their cult masters against two orog marauder brutes and an orog marauder big boss. The furnace in this room contains a *Ring of Teeth*. A thorough search of the room will unveil a *scroll of invisibility sphere*, a *Great Warhammer +4*, and a note.

21 An orog marauder fights against a soulless orog here. Five chests are in this room. The leftmost two do not contain anything. Of the remaining three, the rightmost chest is locked and contains gems and healing potions. The middle remaining chest is trapped with *cone of cold* and locked; it contains a *Ring of Dodging* and various mundane gear. The final chest is trapped with *fireball* and locked; it contains *Boots of Stalking*, a *battleaxe*, and a couple of *daggers*. A shelf contains a *scroll of bull's strength*.

The Cult Stronghold

22 A cult mage and four soulless orogs patrol this area. You may or may not encounter them. To the southeast, the party meets Tudo and Nottle, arguing (as usual) over the treasure from some cult mages they have dispatched. At this point, add Tudo to your party. He is a high-level rogue who can help disarm traps and find secret doors.

23 The door to this room is locked; the lock can be picked or the door smashed.

On the table is a *Dagger +1* and a note to Lieutenant Garesh threatening him unless he can deal with the orog rebels. There are also two chests. The chest on the northwest wall is locked and contains a *Small Shield +1*. The chest on the northeast wall is trapped with *lightning bolt* and locked; it contains a *Dagger +3*.

Tip

Picking locks gives your rogue experience. When you have a choice between picking a lock and breaking it open, pick it!

24 The door to this room is locked; pick the lock or smash the door. The Jail Cell Key is inside. Six cult soldiers, a cult archmage, and a cult lieutenant lurk outside the cell.

25 Four ghouls, four wights, and a ghast attack the party as they try to exit the area.

26 The chest in this room is empty, except for a note saying that things are being stolen.

27 Five ghouls and two ghasts feed on dead cult members in this room.

28 The door to this room is locked; pick the lock or smash the door. The kegs in this room, from left to right, can restore, strengthen, and heal the characters who drink from them, for one charge each keg.

29 This secret room has a number of useful treasures. There are scrolls on the bookshelves, and the three chests contain gems, healing potions, and the *Crypt Cleanser* mace. All the chests are locked, however, so bring a rogue or a weapon to break them open!

30 A cult mage and his two soulless orog minions attack the party here.

31 A cult mage, two cult soldiers, and two soulless orogs are working in this disheveled storage room when the party finds them. The keg in this room heals a character who drinks from it.

32 This out-of-the-way corner houses two coffins, which contain a *Longbow +2* and a little gold.

33 Both doors into this room are locked. A cult mage and his two soulless orog minions live here.

34 The chest in this room holds a *Ring of Defense*, a Rusty Key, and a Bronze Key. The door to the south is locked; pick the lock or smash the door.

35 A cult mage and his two soulless orog minions dwell here.

36 This elven tomb is protected by an ancient warning that has kept the cult out of it so far. Inside are six sarcophagi, each with a valuable treasure that once belonged to their occupants. The various tombs contain the *Ring of the Protected*, *Bloodbow*, the *Armor of Shadows*, a *Shield of Purity*, the *Hammer of Justice*, and a *Scimitar of Slaying*. As you exit the tomb, you are attacked by wraiths, one for each sarcophagus you looted. Loot a single sarcophagus and then leave, unleashing a single wraith at a time.

37 A cult mage and two soulless orogs guard this room. They have a *Ring of Defense*, a Rusty Key, and a Bronze Key. A Bronze Key is required to open the door to the east.

38 Some gems lie on this table, and the fountain casts *bull's strength* on one who drinks from it. You need a Bronze Key, which is in location 37, to open the trapped chest. After all that trouble, the only thing it contains is a *potion of neutralize poison*.

39 As you exit this room, you may surprise a cult war party consisting of a cult archmage, two cult lieutenants, six cult soldier elites, and three soulless orogs. They are likely on their way to confront the rebel orogs, and as such, carry no treasure. This encounter doesn't always occur, as these cult members are on patrol, moving about this area.

40 Five cult soldiers and a cult quartermaster reside in the three rooms of this barracks.

41 The chest to the south in this room holds a cult map of the 1st level of the Catacombs. The middle chest holds a *Dagger +2*. The north chest is trapped with *poison*, and holds just a few gold pieces.

42 The southernmost chest in this room is locked and contains gold. The middle chest contains an Elven Royal Necklace (a nonmagical trinket). The third chest holds some gems and a threatening note to the local cult leader.

43 The stairway here connects to location 5 of the Elven Catacombs's 2nd level (see Chapter 17).

44 The door to this room is locked. Pick the lock or smash the door. The chest inside is locked and requires the Old Iron Key, which is in the next room. There are gemstones inside the chest. The fountain here can heal a character.

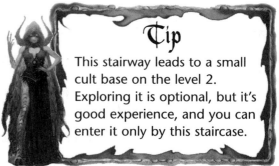

Tip

This stairway leads to a small cult base on the level 2. Exploring it is optional, but it's good experience, and you can enter it only by this staircase.

45 A cult mage is in this room, and a couple of soulless orogs hover outside the door to the south. The chest here is trapped with *lightning bolt* and locked; it contains two *potions of remove fear* and an idolon. The cult mage carries a *salve of remove paralysis*, a *Staff of Halt Undead*, and a *Shield of Purity*. The Old Iron Key is on the table.

46 The two soulless orogs carry the Brass Key. It opens the door on the south side of this room.

The White Orrery Planet

47 This secret room is the final resting place of a mysterious archer, whose corpse carries a suit of *Leather Armor +3*, a nonmagical shortbow, and an *Arrow of Dire Flatulence*. Beware of the mohrg and three wights waiting outside this door.

48 Five mohrgs attack. Rest safely in this room when the monsters are defeated.

49 Six orog marauders patrol outside of this ancient elven prison cell. A master spectre attacks when you enter the cell. The corpse that rots here has a *Necklace of Prayer Beads*.

50 Upon entering this room, you receive an invitation to rest and heal inside, but a warning about taking anything from within! A variety of healing potions are on the table in this room, making good on the first part of the message. If the characters take any of the treasure from locations 51 or 52 and try to leave, they will find a closed door trapped with *lightning bolt*. Leave the door open to avoid activating the trap.

51 Ten skeleton lords line the wall of this room. They do not attack until someone opens the chest, which contains a *Ring of Electra*.

52 Ten skeleton lords line the wall of this room also. They likewise do not attack the party until someone opens the chest, which contains a *Wand of Electra*.

53 This empty chest is trapped with *fireball*. If the trap is sprung, the orogs from location 54 hear and attack.

54 Four orog marauders, an orog marauder boss, and an orog marauder big boss lurk in this room. They carry a *Halberd* +2. One chest holds a *Large Shield* +2, the other some healing potions.

55 The room contains two orog marauders, four orog marauder brutes, an orog marauder hoodoo, two soulless orogs, and a dark naga. One monster has a *Ring of Equilibrium*, and there are several scrolls and potions on the shelves. Other shelves contain a *Clerics' Tome of Truths* and a *Sorcerers' Cyclopedia Illuminati* on other shelves. The fountain in the middle of the room contains a treasure, but fish bite your hand when you reach in. First poison the fish with the vial of poison found in the room immediately to the northeast (location 56). At the bottom of the fountain is *Nightshade*, a small star-patterned shield.

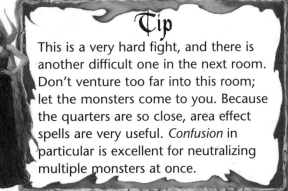

Tip

This is a very hard fight, and there is another difficult one in the next room. Don't venture too far into this room; let the monsters come to you. Because the quarters are so close, area effect spells are very useful. *Confusion* in particular is excellent for neutralizing multiple monsters at once.

56 Exhausted by the fight in the previous room, you find another huge group of monsters in this room! To survive, you must defeat four soulless orogs, two orog marauder brutes, an orog marauder hoodoo, and a dark naga. The monsters have a *Ring of Mothers*, and there are several potions on the shelves and on the round barrel, including the vial of poison needed in location 55.

57 This room holds the monsters' main treasure trove. In the center of the room is the white Orrery Planet. When you release it, it flies back to the Orrery in the Speculum Grounds. Three chests are here as well. The northwest chest holds a suit of *Full Plate +3*, the south chest has *Terrilan's Crimson Wand* and an idolon, and the east chest contains *Kluusar's Chain of Warding*. The door in the back of the room leads up to the cave at location 5 in the Stillwater Ruins.

The Undead Prison

58 When you walk into this room, you are surrounded and attacked by four mohrgs and eight wights. The Fountain of Despair in the center of the room heals any character (six charges of *cure light wounds*) who drinks from it.

59 Four wights and two master wights are eating cult member corpses here, but they immediately attack in the hopes of winning fresher flesh.

60 Three mohrgs, a master wight, and three wights attack you here.

61 The door to this secret room is trapped with *lightning bolt*. Inside is the secret chamber of a powerful mage (who has long since departed). A *potion of restoration* and *Draude's Illustrated Codex Maleficus* are on the table in the center of the room, and numerous unfinished or flawed scrolls and potions line the walls.

> ### Tip
>
> Cadaverous dead such as wights, zombies, and mohrgs have many hit points, but relatively low armor classes. Take advantage of this by using the Power Attack feat to maximize your attacks. Power Attack is especially useful with weapons that double or triple the amount of damage dealt. Try to inflict 100 points of damage with a single hit!

62 A master wight and two wights lurk in this rubble, ready to attack.

63 These two rooms contain a total of five wights. Proceed southwest from here to location 64, as moving north again sometimes results in a confrontation with three roaming Freth drow scouts.

64 This guard room has been converted into a storage area of sorts. A Prison Key Ring lies on the table here, but the rest of the clutter in the room is not magical nor useful.

65 This secret crypt is protected by two mohrgs and a spectre. The sarcophagi contain healing potions, scrolls, and a *Shortbow +4*.

66 This large cell has a single corpse in it. On the floor is a *Ring of Freedom* and a note that tells of a secret door "to the right." The secret door is on the southeast side of the room, but you have to kill a revenant that attacks from the corner first. To enter the revenant's cell, use the Prison Key Ring found at location 64.

Ghosts of the Past

67 A large area of the dungeon here is completely clear of monsters. The silence is a welcome change of pace, but a little unsettling. If you loiter long enough, you'll encounter some patrolling undead: three mohrgs and five skeleton knights.

68 Don't be misled by this wall. The hole on the west side lets you walk through to the rooms behind.

69 As you walk through the corpses in these rooms, the ghosts of dead elven spirits rise to speak to you. They tell of the final days of Myth Drannor, how they held the stair to the last and were finally brought low by treachery. It is their presence that keeps this area free of scavengers, but having finally told their story, they depart to their final rest. The stairs here lead down to level 2 of the Elven Catacombs, location 12. If you choose not to proceed to the second level, three wraiths lie in wait for you south of location 68.

The Freth Drow Stronghold

70 You likely entered this room from location 87 on level 3 of the Catacombs. The door to the southeast is locked, requiring the Adamantine Key, which is lying on the floor of this room.

71 One master wight and four wights linger around this well. A *Necklace of Confidence* is hidden inside the well.

72 Three skeleton knights call this room home. It is safe to rest here when they are defeated. There's a secret door to the north.

73 Walking through the secret door in location 71, you surprise a lich and a wraith in their lair. Another secret door lies to the north.

74 This is a lich's inner sanctum (along with his wraith buddy). *Aasirak's Book of Dancing Dead* is on the table, along with a *potion of restoration*. There are numerous incomplete or failed magical items scattered about. The ornate box in the corner is the lich's phylactery, and smashing it scatters the lich's spirit.

75 Three margoyles surround you and attack when they enter this room. Two arraccats and a single drow priest lie dead, victims of some unknown attacker.

76 Five margoyles attack in this maze-like room.

77 Two margoyles and a margoyle queen guard their treasure in this lair. Their treasure consists of some gems, healing potions, and a *Sling +4*. Don't be intimidated by these opponents' taunts.

78 This door requires the Silver Spider Key, which can be won from Bergos in location 10.

79 Four drow commanders and two drow assassins appear from behind columns in this room when you enter, winning the advantage of surprise.

80 You come across two Freth drow warriors and a Freth drow priest. The priest carries a *Staff of Darkness*, and the bookcase holds healing potions. A cult map of level 1 lies on the table. A *Drow Dagger +3* is in the room to the northeast.

81 A Freth drow commander and four Freth drow warriors are in this room. There are potions on the bookcase, a *scroll of healing*, and a drow map of level 1 on the table. In the next room, the chests hold a suit of *Drow Chainmail +3* and a *Drow Shortsword +2*.

82 Four Freth drow warriors surround a fountain here. Two guard arraccats, a Freth drow high priest, and a Freth drow inquisitor also attack. The Fountain of Drow Elixir here inflicts severe poison damage and drains Constitution temporarily from anyone who drinks from it.

Tip

Be sure to spread out before entering this room so that *flame strike* and *firestorm* can't hit so many of your party members, and close to melee range with the drow priests immediately.

83 This is the Temple of Lolth, the drow fortress. The priests carry *scrolls of destruction* and *firestorm*, and *potions of mage armor* and healing are on the tables. Touch the spider idol to open the altar, revealing a *Drow Ceremonial Dagger* and a *Drow Spinnan Trisagion*.

186

84 This is a drow barracks. The enemies here and from location 85 attack as soon as you enter either room. Two Freth drow commanders and six Freth drow warriors jump to attack when they see you. The victors can claim a *Drow Assassin's Dagger* and a *Wand of Cure Serious Wounds*. It is safe to rest here after the enemies have been defeated.

85 Another drow barracks, this one is home to two Freth drow commanders and two Freth drow warriors. Find some more maps of the Catacombs in this room as well. This room is also safe to rest in.

86 These arraccat pens are home to two Freth drow warriors, four arraccats, and a guard arraccat. These arraccats don't like being confined, and they turn on their trainers at the first opportunity.

87 This room is home to a Freth drow commander, four Freth drow priests, and a Freth drow high priest. The chest on the left side contains *Drow Boots of Displacement*, while the right chest only holds gold. A city records book lies on a shelf nearby.

88 This room is blocked by four Freth drow guards, a Freth drow guard master, a Freth drow high priest, and two guard arraccats. The Freth guards are some of the most powerful type of drow, so this battle is significantly tougher than the ones before.

89 This is the home of Greyanna, leader of the Freth drow elves. She tells you that you seek the Bodach Swan in vain.

She summons her guards. Greyanna, her mate Foluben, and a specially trained arraccat, Kalannar, are in the main room. Depending upon how long you allow Greyanna to talk to you, the ensuing combat will be with six, seven, or eight additional enemies, a mixture of Freth drow guards and guard arraccats, attacking from adjacent rooms via secret doors. When they are all defeated, you find Anorrweyn's skull, a suit of *Drow Chainmail +5*, and a *Drow Shortsword +5* on the elves. The shelves hold a *scroll of raise dead* and a *scroll of domination*. The three chests (none locked or trapped) contain a *Necklace of Magic Resistance*, a *Ring of Precision*, and a *Drow Lamp of Darkness*.

> ## Note
> She is talking about the Bodach Swan to stall for time so her warriors can sneak closer. The trick is to not be distracted by her discourse, and attack right away. If you do, you'll surprise the warriors. If you don't, there will be more enemies or even worse, they will get the surprise attack.

> ## Tip
> This fight is very difficult. Sorcerers should be casting *confusion* and *mass suggestion* in all directions, warriors should try to close with the archers to help take the pressure off the sorcerers, and clerics should assist with *heal* if a companion needs it, and *firestorm* otherwise. Rummage through all the magic items you have been collecting and saving up to this point. Some of them may be useful in this combat. Good luck.

90 A *potion of neutralize poison* is on the shelf in this room, and the chest here contains a *Drow Shortsword +4*.

91 The chest in this room contains a *Drow Dagger +2*.

92 This is the first part of Greyanna's treasure trove. The shelves contain a *scroll of healing* and some healing potions. The three chests (none locked or trapped) contain a *Drow Shortbow +3*, a suit of *Drow Chainmail +2*, an idolon, and the *Great Knife of Shyde*.

93 The two chests in this corner are not trapped or locked and contain three *potions of sleep* and a *Wand of Command*.

Chapter Seventeen

Second Cellar (The Elven Catacombs, Level 2)

Quick Overview

The Dark Naga's Lair

This very small area takes only a little time and has a huge payoff, making it well worth climbing the stairs a couple times. The dark naga has set a trap for unwary adventurers such as your party. However, when he springs the trap on your party, he will probably find he bit off more than he can chew! Search his home for a powerful weapon against the undead.

Northwest Cult Stronghold

This area is optional. There are only a couple minor treasures in this area, so the reward for clearing it doesn't really measure up to the effort required. However, there is some background info about the Cult here, so tear through it if you're being thorough.

Western Catacombs

This is where most players begin their assault on the Second Cellar in earnest. A well-defended orog base is in this region, a wraith guards an ancient treasure, and a pair of beleaguered Sisters of the Silver Fire can become potent allies. The section of the dungeon just south of the Cult Stronghold (locations 19–23) is mostly just weaker undead, so skip it, unless your party needs the experience.

189

Southwest Catacombs

This region is populated by minor monsters that guard relatively minor treasures. It is, however, a good place to earn experience.

Margoyle Fortress

In the southeast is a canyon that marks the entrance to an extensive margoyle complex. If your party holds the Stone Mouth (found in the Ancient Tomb in the Glim-Gardens), talk the guards into lowering the drawbridge so you can ransack the complex, earning some very nice weapons and other treasures.

Eastern Catacombs

This area is not controlled by any one faction, but there's a large platoon of orog marauders and they have a necessary key. A lich's lair lies to the north.

Cult Fortress

A large contingent of Cult of the Dragon members have set up a camp over the only stairway deeper into the dungeon, and the best way to get past cult members is to go right through them. The party faces a couple of really tough battles here, especially the final fight for access to the stairs. Save your game often and be thorough in your search for treasure.

Northern Cult Fortress

You tackle this area of the Cult Fortress later in the game, after you have finished exploring the Elven Dungeons. You find the local cult overseer here as well as his personal treasures.

Dungeon Master's Notes

The Dark Naga's Lair

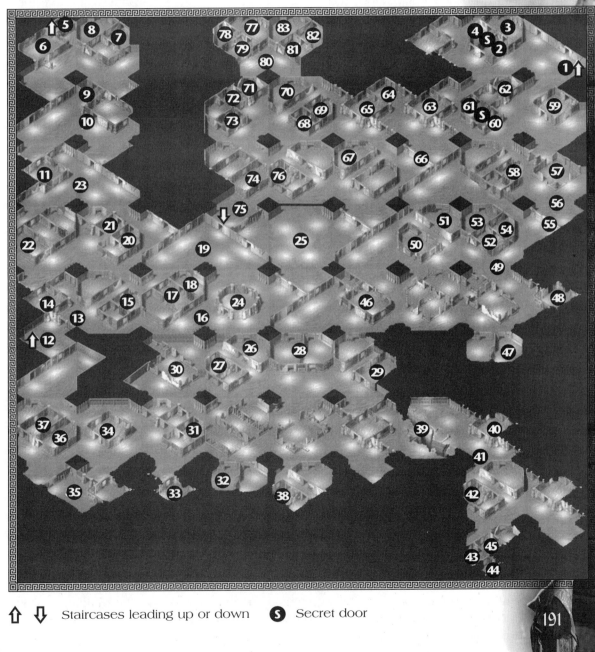

⇧ ⇩ Staircases leading up or down   **S** Secret door

1 These stairs lead up to location 16 on level 1 of the Elven Dungeons (see Chapter 16). A cult mage and six soulless orogs patrol this area; sometimes they're nearby when you come down the stairs.

2 A magical battle happened in this room recently. As your party walks into the room to the northeast, a dark naga opens a secret door to the northwest and attacks you from behind. It carries a *Quiver of Arrows* +5 and the Oily Iron Key. Prevent the naga from sneaking up on you by finding and opening the secret door yourself. This gives you surprise when attacking the naga.

3 A dead cult member lies by this fountain. Not surprisingly, the fountain is poison. The Slender Silver Key is required to open the door to location 3.

4 This is the dark naga's lair. There's a healing potion on the shelf. The metal chest is trapped and contains the Slender Silver Key, which opens the door to location 3. The wooden chest is trapped and contains some gems, some healing potions, and *Dawnpike*, a powerful weapon against undead.

Northwest Cult Stronghold

5 These stairs lead up to location 43 in the First Cellar (see Chapter 16).

6 A huge contingent of cult warriors attacks you here, including a dangerous lieutenant. They come in from the hallway to the southeast. They total eight cult soldiers elite, two cult mages, a cult quartermaster, and a cult lieutenant. In the room itself are three cult soldiers, who are fairly easy opponents, provided you don't have to fight the larger contingent at the same time.

7 A single cult mage and his soulless orog servant are using this room as a study. They have a scroll of *fire shield* and a New Iron Key, which is used at location 11. The metal chest in this room is trapped with fire and locked. It contains gold and a potion of displacement. A map of the Catacombs sits on a table nearby.

> ### Tip
> Due to their large numbers, these cult soldiers can quickly overwhelm even the most skilled party. Incapacitate as many of them as possible with spells such as *confusion* and *hold person*.

8 This room is a barracks. Inside are six cult soldiers, a soulless orog, and three chests. The chest on the left contains a suit of *Full Plate* +1. The middle chest is locked and contains a *potion of bull's strength*. The right chest is trapped and contains a *Light Hammer* +2.

9 The southeast door to this small room is locked, but the lock can be picked. The two cult soldiers within carry a Dull Metal Key. This is used to exit the chamber to the southeast.

10 A cult mage and five soulless orogs patrol this section of the stronghold. They may happen upon you, they might not.

11 This room is occupied by a cult archmage, four cult soldiers, and two soulless orogs. They have an amusing note. The New Iron Key from location 7 is required to exit this room to the northeast.

Western Catacombs

12 This stairway leads up to location 69 in the First Cellar (see Chapter 16).

13 Three Freth drow scouts patrol this hallway. If you happen upon them, they are likely to run.

14 This room is full of sarcophagi. The tombs are home to two mohrgs and a master wraith, but otherwise empty.

15 Two wights and a master wight lurk in this room. Again, the sarcophagi are empty.

16 Three more Freth drow scouts patrol here. As with all the scouts, sometimes they see you, and sometimes they are patrolling elsewhere.

17 This is the first room of a massive orog marauder base. This room contains two orog marauders, and when your characters enter, they are also attacked by an orog marauder hoodoo and four orog marauders from the south. It's very likely that the fighting will attract the marauders in location 18 as well.

18 This is the second room of the orog marauder base. An orog marauder hoodoo, two orog marauders, and an orog marauder boss occupy it. When the fighting begins, six orog marauder brutes and an orog marauder big boss join the fight from the north. After the fight, the party can find some gems, some healing salve, and a Worn Elven Key.

> ### Tip
> This fight is huge. Be sure to save first, and use the same tactics you've been using before. Use fighters to block doors, close to melee range against spellcasters, and use debilitating magic such as *hold person* to remove attackers from combat.

19 Three mohrgs, two spectres, two wraiths, two master wights, and three wights block the party's access to the Orrery Spire here. After the monsters are defeated, use the spire to transport to any other spire in Myth Drannor.

20 This Fountain of Sanctus casts *protection from evil* on the first party member who drinks from it.

21 Three shadows haunt this well. The well contains a *Pike +3*.

22 Six wights and two master wights guard this tomb. The chest here is locked and contains gold and a healing potion. The sarcophagus contains a *Shortsword +2*.

23 You need the New Iron Key to enter here. Eight wights, a master wight, and three mohrgs haunt this area, just outside the entrance to the Northwest Cult Stronghold. Sometimes they attack you when you move through, sometimes they don't.

24 This circular chamber is home to a master spectre. His treasure is the remarkable *Aasirak's Ebony Twin Ring of Power*.

25 This is the Shrine of the Silver Fire. Its regular protectors are missing, and it's currently guarded by two Sisters of the Silver Fire, whose war party met with a disastrous fate. The sisters, Bronwyn and Kellan, have a great deal of useful information about the baelnorn in the Catacombs and about the Cult presence in the area. After you have found the guardians of the

Note

Aasirak created two rings, each of which grants great bonuses and horrible debilitations and allows the wearer to cast a powerful spell. When both rings are worn, bonuses and debilitations cancel out, leaving the wearer with the ability to cast powerful spells from both rings. The *Ebony Ring* weighs 250 pounds, making it very hard to carry. The *Ivory Ring* (found in location 44) reduces a character's load by 249 pounds, making it easy to carry the *Ebony Ring*. On the other hand, you may wish to just leave the *Ebony Ring* behind and take advantage of the unencumbrance bonus the *Ivory Ring* grants all on its own.

shrine (Lower Keep, location 20, Chapter 18), add one or both of them to your party. Sometimes when exiting this room the party is attacked by two orog marauders, one orog hoodoo, and six mohrgs on a patrol.

Southwest Catacombs

26 The southwest door in this room requires the Worn Elven Key, found in location 18.

27 Four cult soldiers fight a mohrg here. The soldiers have a Blackened Elven Key, some gems, a *Shortbow* +3, and a *Small Shield* +3.

28 Five margoyles and a margoyle queen block this entrance to the Southwest Catacombs. They hoard some gems and healing potions.

29 Four wights and a master wight lie in wait in this room. They have no treasure.

30 Three shadows attack the party here.

31 A skeleton lord, a zombie lord, and a master wight team up against the party here.

32 Two arraccats, a guard arraccat, and a black arraccat hoard gems and healing potions here. As you leave this location for location 33, you may encounter three drow robbers who have stolen gems and a healing salve. If you aren't careful, they'll snag some of your gold as well.

33 Three mohrgs, four wights, a master wight, a skeleton lord, a skeleton knight, and two skeletons are holed up in this room. After clearing out the undead, the party can rest here safely.

34 Four Freth drow warriors, a Freth drow commander, and a Freth drow priest have established a small outpost here. They won't make it home to report to their superiors.

35 Three arraccats and three black arraccats live in this room. Their lair holds some gems and healing potions.

36 A wraith and four shadows attack the party here.

37 This room is safe to rest in.

38 This room holds three margoyles. Numerous gems and potions are scattered about their lair.

Margoyle Fortress

39 There is a large chasm here with a drawbridge across it that is raised. The controls for the drawbridge are on the other side, under the control of four margoyles. If the party has the Stone Mouth (found in the Ancient Tomb, location 19, Chapter 13), they can talk to the margoyles by activating the signpost

195

marker. The margoyles have been ordered not to lower the bridge, but if your characters say they're wounded, then elaborate by saying they're badly wounded, the margoyles will lower the drawbridge to attack the weakened party. If you don't convince the margoyles to lower the bridge, go away and come back later, as the margoyles get tired of waiting and lower the bridge.

40 Four margoyles and a margoyle queen guard this treasure room. The chest is trapped with a *firestorm* spell, and contains an idolon, a healing salve, a *Shortsword* +5, a *Light Hammer* +5, a *Battleaxe* +5, a *Quarterstaff* +5, and a ton of gold. Defeat these enemies quickly; otherwise, the five margoyles from location 41 will join the combat.

41 Freth drow scouts sometimes patrol this hallway.

42 This room houses three black arraccats. Their treasure consists of some gems and a healing potion.

43 Four mohrgs block this room.

44 This room is the lair of an archlich. The sarcophagus here holds *Aasirak's Ivory*

> ## Tip
>
> This is a very significant treasure hoard! Distribute the +5 weapons so that your characters can all switch to one when they have trouble hitting enemies with high armor classes.

Ring of Power, a remarkable ring that weighs negative 249 pounds. The chest on the east side of the room is trapped with a *fireball* and holds *Elhrain's Lanthorn*. The chest to the west is locked and holds healing potions. Be sure to search around this room and the room to the northeast across the hall for the small ornate box that holds the lich's spirit. Destroy it.

45 As you leave the lich's lair, three spectres, four wights, a master wight, and four mohrgs attack.

Eastern Catacombs

46 This ancient wine cellar is a good place to rest.

47 Encounter a black arraccat and three guard arraccats here.

48 This room is infested with undead. You face two wights, two mohrgs, a zombie lord, two skeletons, and a zombie.

49 Six orog marauder brutes, an orog marauder hoodoo, and an orog marauder boss patrol in this area. You may meet them when you pass this way, you may not.

50 A revenant haunts this room. It is safe to rest here after he has been put down.

51 The well on the left in this room contains some gold.

52 Four orog marauder brutes are inside this room.

53 This is the home of numerous angry orog marauders. Between the two remaining rooms here, the party is attacked by five orog marauder brutes, an orog elite, four orog marauders, and an orog marauder big boss. The chest in this room contains healing potions, and the orogs carry a healing salve, a *Great Warhammer* +4, a suit of *Chainmail* +4, and a Scarred Elven Key.

54 The metal chest in this room is trapped and locked. It contains a suit of *Chainmail* +5 and a rough map of the Second Cellar. The wooden chest is also trapped and locked. It contains a *Battleaxe* +4.

55 This door is locked and requires a Scarred Elven Key to open, which is in location 53.

56 Six cult soldiers and a cult quartermaster are exploring the Eastern Catacombs here. If you show up when they do, they attack. If not, you might not see them.

57 Six Freth drow warriors, a Freth drow priest, and a Freth drow commander were just preparing to defend themselves against the cult members at location 56 when your party interfered. They carry a *Wand of Cure Serious Wounds* and a *Shortsword* +3.

58 A black arraccat, three arraccats, and two guard arraccats make their lair here. They hoard gems and a healing potion.

59 A cult archmage and four enthralled drow hold this room. The mage carries a *Ring of Restoration*. A scroll of *searing light* and a note lie on the table. The note describes an unfortunate encounter for the Cult in this area of the dungeon.

60 The secret door on the northwest wall of this room leads to a lich's lair.

61 A lich and a spectre attack in this room. Some failed magical experiments are scattered about and a *Dagger of Warding* lies on the table. The lich's phylactery, a small ornate box, is hidden in a cage in the back of the room. It is trapped in and emits lightning on the first strike. Destroy it to scatter his spirit and gain experience.

62 This minor margoyle lair is occupied by a margoyle queen and five margoyles. They have some gems and healing potions.

Cult Fortress

63 This room marks the beginning of Cult territory on this level. Four cult soldiers guard the room. They carry a Dull Brass Key, which is needed to open the door in the southwest of the room. There is a nonmagical Elven Royal Dagger on the table.

64 This area is full of barrels. The keg of elven mead heals one character.

65 The door to this room requires a Fragile Iron Key, which is in location 81 in the Northern Cult Stronghold. Inside, nonmagical weapons are on all the tables, a *Large Shield +2* and several nonmagical shields lie on the shelves, and nonmagical halberds and pikes are hidden in the barrels. One chest is empty, and the other contains a *Warhammer +3*.

Tip

Your party will likely be equipped with better gear than this by the time you find the Fragile Elven Key, so returning here isn't necessary.

66 The Oily Iron Key found in location 2 is required to open this door.

67 There's a *Ring of Souls* on the body in this jail cell.

68 A cult mage and two enthralled drow are in this room. There's a *potion of protection from poison* on the table and a scroll of *invisibility sphere* on the shelf. The trapped chest contains healing potions.

69 Two enthralled drow guard this room. You might find yourself battling the forces from locations 68 and 69 together if you are not careful. There is a poison potion on the table and scrolls of *inflict wounds* and *fear* on the shelves. The locked chest contains only gold.

70 Four cult soldiers, a cult quartermaster, and a cult lieutenant face the party here. The door to the north requires a Large Metal Key, which is found in location 80 of the Northern Cult Stronghold.

71 Five cult soldiers guard this room. The locked wooden chest contains a suit of *Chainmail* +2.

72 The chest in this room contains a *Longsword* +3.

73 Six cult soldiers are holed up in this barracks room. The chest to the east contains a *Longspear* +1, and the chest to the west contains a *Sling* +2.

74 Bloody tracks run from the north into this room. The zombie lord inside has apparently been preying on the Cult, unbeknownst to them.

75 This room contains the staircase leading down to location 1 of the Lower Keep (see Chapter 18), but getting to it won't be easy. The Cult has built its base around the stairs, and many cult members guard them. In this room, the party faces two cult mages, a cult archmage, two enthralled drow, and three cult soldiers elite. If the party does not defeat them quickly, reinforcements appear from the rear.

76 This area houses a cult brigadier, a cult lieutenant, and two cult soldiers elite. A note here instructs these cultists to find the remaining Sisters of the Silver Fire, Kellan and Bronwyn. The metal chest on the left is locked and contains gold. The metal chest on the right is trapped and locked and contains a *Longspear* +4.

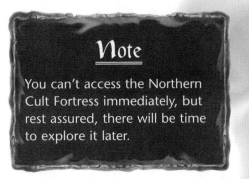

Note

You can't access the Northern Cult Fortress immediately, but rest assured, there will be time to explore it later.

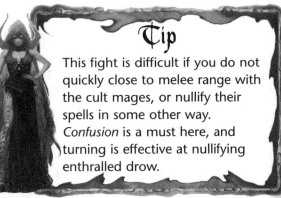

Tip

This fight is difficult if you do not quickly close to melee range with the cult mages, or nullify their spells in some other way. *Confusion* is a must here, and turning is effective at nullifying enthralled drow.

Northern Cult Stronghold

This section covers the areas you visit when you return to this level later in the game.

77 A cult mage, two cult soldiers, and three enthralled drow attack immediately when the party warps through the portal. They carry a Flat Brass Key, which is required in the door to the south.

78 This is where Beriand (and Faeril, if she's not in your party) are being held. They've already freed themselves by the time you enter the room, and they quickly return to their sanctuary after healing everyone. The two chests here are empty.

79 A cult archmage, four cult soldiers, and two enthralled drow guard this room. They carry a *Wand of Cloudkill*.

80 Four cult soldiers and a cult lieutenant block this hallway. They carry a Large Metal Key, a suit of *Chainmail +3*, and a *Greatsword +4*.

81 The left chest in this room is trapped and contains a Fragile Iron Key and a *Light Mace +4*. The middle chest is locked and holds a *Longbow +3*. The right chest is locked and holds a *Small Shield +2*.

82 A *Greataxe +2* is on the table and a scroll of *domination* is on a bookshelf. The metal chest is trapped and locked and contains a *potion of protection from poison* and a *potion of spell resistance*.

83 This room is the living quarters of the local cult overseer. He has two enthralled drow servants with him, and they all attack the party. The overseer carries *Druul's Kiss*, the *Sceptre of Leogans*, and a note from the leader of the Cult. Another note is on the table, a scroll of *fear* is on the bookshelf, and some healing potions are on another shelf. The chest is trapped and locked and contains an idolon, the *Boots of Grace*, and a *Sling +4*.

Chapter Eighteen

Lower Keep
(The Elven Catacombs, Level 3)

Quick Overview

The Mad Mage

The 3rd floor of the Elven Catacombs begins with a conversation with a mysterious drow elf named Nathlilik. Her goal, destroying the Freth drow, happens to match yours, so agree to help her and she'll drop a bridge across a chasm for you.

If you choose not to help her, fight your way through the lair of Thyaast Ammath, a long-dead mad wizard. Thyaast's final days were filled with experimentation with immortality and the nature of death, but it is unknown if she ever discovered anything. Even if you don't have to, explore her lair; it is filled with useful history and gear, including *Wroth's Executioner*, a very powerful axe.

Guardians of the Flame

In this short sequence of rooms, you right a great wrong and free a pair of innocent prisoners, defeat Gulrithi in a thrilling, mortal battle, pick up a key you'll need later, and gather treasure!

Dwarven Tombs of Myth Drannor

These tombs are where the greatest dwarven heroes of Myth Drannor were buried. Numerous dwarven statues guard the tombs and punish lawless intruders. The dwarves of yesteryear were not blind to the heroes of today, however, and if you are clever, you can find a great deal of assistance in the tombs. Exploring them is optional, but it's worth the effort.

The Northern Catacombs

Your party must fight through these catacombs to reach the bottom level. A couple of encounters are of interest, including a fortified orog marauder base and a squadron of cult members escorted by a new type of monster. To exit to the Southeast Catacombs, your characters must find a key from the Guardians on this level.

Southeast Catacombs

In this region, your party encounters a dark naga necromancer and a powerful cult exploration party. The treasures of the necromancer will prove useful in defeating the Cult of the Dragon.

Southwest Catacombs–Arraccat Infestation

This region of the dungeon is overrun with arraccats. Unfortunately, they hoard little of value, carrying only gems and the occasional healing potion. Still, their presence here is significant, so there is likely a nest around. Also, you finally find the staircase down to the final level in this region, as well as the mage with *The Sacred Staff of Sunlight* that Nathlilik spoke of. Be sure to look out for traprunes (marked with an X on the map).

Dungeon Master's Notes

The 3rd level of the Elven Catacombs is primarily a burial place for the dwarves and elves of old Myth Drannor. The prevalent threat here is undead, but there are strong infestations of arraccats and other menaces as well. This level is very linear compared to the other areas in the game, and it's essentially a gauntlet with some interesting lairs and tombs to explore.

This is also the first area in which you encounter traprunes. Marked with an X on the map, these runes often escape your party's notice until you're right on top of them. They explode when you walk on them, causing a small amount of damage.

Tip

The best way to avoid the traprunes is to find the *Necklace of Safe Footfalls* in the Ancient Tomb (location 24 in the Glim-Gardens, Chapter 13). Wearing it while navigating this area deactivates each traprune as you step on it.

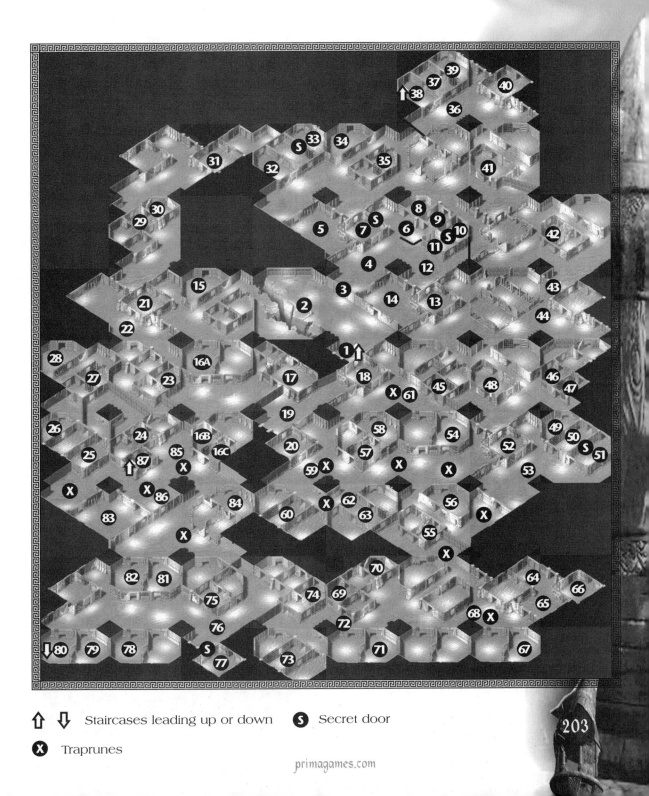

⬆ ⬇ Staircases leading up or down   **S** Secret door

X Traprunes

The Mad Mage

1 This stairway leads up to location 75 in the Cult Fortress on the 2nd level of the Elven Catacombs.

2 On the other side of this bridge, Nathlilik of the House Kilsek, a drow elf, parleys with you. If you listen to her, she tells you of a cult mage blocking her way southwest of the dungeon (location 80). If you ask why she wants to pass him, she tells how the Kilsek drow were betrayed by the Cult of the Dragon and how now they are used to feed the dracolich. Agree to help and she lowers the drawbridge. A corpse near the bridge has the Gem Studded Key.

3 This door requires the Gem Studded Key (from location 2) to open. Behind it is the lair of Thyaast Ammath, the mad mage.

4 Immediately after entering the mage's lair, you are attacked by a dark naga, two master spectres, two master wights, two mohrgs, two master shadows, and a zombie lord. One among this veritable smorgasbord of undead carries a *Wand of Heal*, and a *scroll of mass suggestion* is on a shelf.

5 A wraith, a mohrg, and two skeleton knights lurk in this room. Unfinished potions and rings are scattered about the room and a Delicate Gold Key lies on the table. The metal chest here is trapped and locked, but it contains a valuable suit of *Vulcan Mail*. The Delicate Gold Key opens the door to the northwest.

6 A *potion of haste* is on one shelf here and a *potion of spell resistance* is on another. A shelf holds a *scroll of lightning bolt*. A secret door is to the southwest, and the door to the northeast is trapped with *silence*. Also, be sure to check out Thyaast's Journal; it's on the table in the northwest corner.

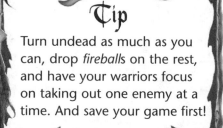

Tip

Turn undead as much as you can, drop *fireballs* on the rest, and have your warriors focus on taking out one enemy at a time. And save your game first!

Note

Rather than leaving the mage's lair now, leave to the west the way you came in if you agreed to help the drow. If you didn't agree to help the drow, you need to use this door to reach the rest of the dungeon.

7 This room is the secret resting place of Thyaast Ammath. The bookcase contains an idolon, a *scroll of undead control*, and a note from Thyaast. Surprisingly, you also find a small, trapped, ornate box that holds the undying soul of a lich! Perhaps Thyaast is not so dead as was believed...

8 The door to this room is trapped. Find a *scroll of find traps* on a bookcase.

9 A *scroll of finger of death* lies on a bookshelf here.

10 This room is Thyaast's final resting place. Her corpse is on the ground, and *Thyaast's Staff* and a *Dagger +5* lie next to her. There is a *Ring of Harvest* on the shelf and a secret door to the southwest.

11 This is Thyaast's treasure room, and it's guarded by Thyaast herself! Thyaast is fast and powerful, and she can paralyze with a touch. After you defeat her, you find a *scroll of dispel magic* on a table along with a *Dagger of Magus*. All three chests in this room are trapped and locked. The chest on the left holds a large sum of gold and a healing potion. The chest in the middle holds an *Amulet of Invulnerability* and two *potions of spell resistance*. The last chest holds a *scroll of neutralize poison* and a *Wand of Flame Strike*.

12 There is a mysterious note and a *scroll of cone of cold* on a shelf here.

13 This room is full of coffins.

14 A master wight and 11 mohrgs attack you in this room. They carry *Woundwulf* and *Wroth's Executioner*—powerful weapons indeed.

Guardians of the Flame

15 The door to this room is locked, but the lock can be picked. It is safe to rest here.

16A Four wights and a mohrg are in this room.

16B Three mohrgs and three wights are holed up in this room.

16C The *Meat Cleaver* is on the table in the center of this room. The trapped chest contains the *Wand of Entanglement*.

Tip

This fight is difficult. The mohrg in this room can overwhelm your party quickly, especially if it paralyzes some of your characters. Act quickly to neutralize it with spells such as *halt undead*. The *scroll of undead control* from location 7 can come in very handy here.

17 The door to this room is locked, but it can be picked. The room is dark and full of shadows, both mundane and monstrous. There are two master shadows and four shadows here.

18 The door to this chamber is trapped and locked. A metal chest inside is also trapped and locked. It contains *Theodore's Gloves of Kinship*, an Iron Cell Key, a Bent Elven Key, and a Flat Brass Key. The shelves and table hold healing potions and a *scroll of slow*.

19 Gulrithi the Naga awaits you, supported by a master wight and two mohrgs. They carry a Serpent Key, an *Amulet of Perfect Health*, and *Delvendoor's Chisel*.

20 The door into this room is trapped and locked with the Serpent Key (from location 19). Two guardian nagas are held by magic on the edges of this room. Destroying the skull totem releases the nagas, who are the guardians of the Shrine of the Silver Fire on level 2 of the Catacombs (location 25).

Dwarven Tombs of Myth Drannor

21 Sleethur, a dark naga, parleys with your characters here, promising them Nezras' chainmail if they will only spare him. If you pause, he attacks with surprise. He carries *Nezras' Mysterious Chainmail*.

22 Two dwarven statues guard the entrance to the Dwarven Tombs here, but they do not attack when you first arrive. Two wights attack you as they explore. Writing on the walls identifies the tombs and warns you against stealing without giving.

23 Three mohrgs, four wights, and a master wight have taken up residence in this tomb. A mundane shortsword lies on the floor in the room to the southwest. The *Moonsplinter* dagger is in the sarcophagus. Place a mundane dagger in the receptacle here before taking it, or the nearby dwarven statues will attack. Find a mundane dagger in location 24.

24 Two dwarven statues guard this room. Two mohrgs and three wights attack you in this tomb. A mundane dagger lies on the ground. The sarcophagus contains *Shadowhisper*, but place a shortsword in the receptacle before taking it, or the guardians will attack. A shortsword is in location 23. It's safe to rest in this room after clearing it of enemies.

25 This crypt contains *Asterfellon—Mace of Power*. Appease the guardians by placing the light mace from the next room in the receptacle here before taking *Asterfellon*.

26 Three wraiths attack you in this tomb. Place a longsword in the receptacle before taking *Valamir's Slayer* from the sarcophagus. A longsword is in location 27.

206

27 A warhammer and a longsword lie on the floor of this tomb. Two spectres live here, and they attack when they see you. The tomb contains *Sunderstone*. Place a warhammer in the receptacle before taking it to avoid being attacked by the tomb's defenders.

28 There is a master spectre in this tomb, and a battleaxe on the ground. Place it in the receptacle to take *Atroth's Bane* from the sarcophagus without fear of reprisal.

The Northern Catacombs

29 This orog marauder base is occupied by two orog marauders, two orog marauder bosses, an orog marauder big boss, an orog marauder hoodoo, and five orog marauder brutes. They carry a *Ring of Blessing*, a Crude Metal Key, a *Handaxe* +4, a suit of *Chainmail* +3, and a Bent Key. The chest in the western room is locked and contains a healing potion. The left hand chest in the southern room is locked and contains a *potion of neutralize poison*. The right hand chest in the southern room opens with the Crude Metal Key and contains *Mortissa's Beads of Rigor*.

30 The door to this room requires the Bent Key from location 29. This is an orog brewery. The barrel to the north here is trapped, but it will fully heal a character who drinks from it. Watch out for the wraith that attacks when anyone approaches the barrel.

31 Two orog marauder bosses are squatting in this room. They have a healing potion, a *Light Mace* +4, and the journal of a doomed elven war party led by an elf named Victoria.

> ## Tip
> Use the doorways to your advantage in this fight, minimizing the number of orogs that can attack you at any time and trapping them in the main room. Rain down spells on them from a distance to prevail.

32 A trail of gold leads out of (or into) this room. Place the ancient skull found at location 34 in the sarcophagus, and a voice tells you to avenge her. This is the corpse of Victoria. Her adventuring gear is in the room to the north.

33 The secret door to this room opens when you restore the corpse in location 32. This room holds five chests. From left to right, the first chest contains *Victoria's Gloves of Electric Touch* and a *scroll of repulsion*. The second chest contains a *Dagger of Angels*. The third chest contains a *potion of bull's strength* and *Victoria's Leather Corset*, a decent suit of armor for a sorcerer who does not mind a small (5 percent) chance of spell failure. The fourth chest holds *Victoria's Boots of Beguiling Gait*, and the fifth chest holds a *potion of true seeing*, a *scroll of shield of faith*, and the bow *Arrowflight of Angels*.

34 The gate to this room is locked and must be picked.

35 Four wights, two mohrgs, a skeleton lord, and a master wight haunt this room. After they are destroyed, it is safe to rest here.

36 You may find three Freth drow scouts here. They roam around this area, and may or may not be here when you arrive on the scene.

37 In this room, you hear voices coming from the south, one speaking and one translating. The translating voice says they must take some mysterious item "up to the castle..."

38 Inside this room are the speakers from location 37: a dragon-kin, four enthralled drow, two cult soldiers elite, a cult lieutenant, and a cult archmage. They carry a Heavy Key, a *Wand of Magic Missiles*, and a crude map of the 3rd level of the Catacombs. They were discussing a *Ring of Health*, which lies on the ground. A door here leads to the Stillwater Ruins, behind Faeril and Beriand's tree, making this a good time to sell gear and hear tales.

39 The door to this room is locked, but the lock can be picked. The room is empty.

40 Two mohrgs hold this room. It is safe to rest when they are gone.

41 Two shadows and a master shadow lurk in this room.

42 Two master wights and five wights hold court in this room.

43 This door is locked with the Bent Elven Key, which is in the lair of Gulrithi the Naga, in location 18.

Southeast Catacombs

44 Nine wights and three mohrgs are directly on the other side of the door here, waiting for you.

45 A revenant lurks in this room, far from the main thoroughfare. Some Freth drow scouts patrol a nearby passageway and may attack after you've finished off the revenant.

46 The doors leading into this complex from the north are locked, but the locks can be picked. Alternately, use the open door to the south at location 47. Inside are three margoyles and a margoyle queen. They have a *potion of full healing*, some gems, and a *Ring of Silence*.

47 Eight margoyles make their lair here. They have some minor gems and a healing potion. They will assist the margoyle queen if you don't destroy her quickly enough.

48 Three mohrgs and two wights lurk in this room. Rest here safely when they are gone.

49 Three margoyles and a margoyle queen guard some gems and healing potions. The door to location 50 is locked and trapped with *lightning*.

50 Scattered around this room are a necromancer's tools. The area is guarded by two mohrgs and four wights. You find a *scroll of fear*, a healing potion, and *Gauntlets of Necromancy*. There is a secret door to the southeast, and you can hear a voice behind the wall, but whoever is there hears you too.

51 In this room is a dark naga and an orog marauder hoodoo, plus their servants: a master wight, two mohrgs, and a zombie lord. Find a *Quiver of Arrows of Second Death*, a *Wand of Undead Control*, a *Great Warhammer +5*, *salve of undead repair*, and a *scroll of slay living*.

52 You can hear some cult members talking behind the door to the south. They sound wary of something called "traprunes."

53 You come across a huge cult war party, consisting of four enthralled drow, six cult soldiers elite, 10 soulless orogs, a cult quartermaster, a cult lieutenant, a cult mage, and a cult archmage. They carry healing potions, a *Halberd +4*, a *Longsword +5*, and a *Staff of Deadly Splinters*.

Tip

This fight really tough! If you have the *Wand of Undead Control* from location 51, use it to bring some of the enthralled drow over to your side, and use halt undead against the soulless orogs. As always, *confusion* works wonders, and be sure to take those mages out early through whatever means possible. Good luck!

209

54 The three doors in this pair of rooms are locked, but the locks can be picked. The rooms are empty, and it is safe to rest in them. After exiting, the party may encounter a patrol of varioius arraccats.

55 A spectre haunts this room.

56 Two guard arraccats, a arraccat, and a black arraccat use this room as their lair. They carry gems.

57 Five Freth drow commandos and a Freth drow commander are exploring this area. They carry a *drow quiver of arrows* and a *scroll of darkness*.

58 Five Freth drow commandos and a Freth drow priest hold this room. They have a *potion of remove blindness*, a *Dagger +4*, and an Old Elven Prison Key. They will assist in the battle at location 57 if you don't prevail quickly.

59 A guard arraccat, a black arraccat, and an arraccat patrol.

60 This is the lair of two guard arraccats. They have some gems and a healing potion.

61 Two black arraccats, three guard arraccats, and an arraccat call this region home.

62 This door is locked and requires the Old Elven Prison Key to open. Some drow elves have it in location 58.

63 Five wraiths haunt this prison.

64 Two mohrgs and two spectres lurk in this dark chamber.

65 Outside this room, you may be attacked by a single drow assassin. As you move into this area, three drow assassins attack from behind.

66 This is the lair of an archlich. His phylactery, a small ornate box, is in the room outside his chamber. Disable its trap, then destroy it to scatter his spirit forever.

67 The door here is locked, but the lock can be picked. It is safe to rest inside.

68 A black arraccat, an arraccat, and two guard arraccats block this passageway.

69 Two wraiths and a mohrg wait in this room.

70 Three mohrgs and four wights attack you in this dark room.

71 Eight wights and two mohrgs lurk here.

72 Two Freth drow robbers may ambush you here, if you show up when they are in the area. They carry some gems and a healing salve they've taken from the local arraccats. Take care: they may lift some of your gold if you aren't careful.

Southwest Catacombs

73 This is the lair of a guard arraccat and a black arraccat. They have some gems and a healing potion.

74 This room is infested with two mohrgs, a master wight, and five wights.

75 Two black arraccats and three guard arraccats attack the party here. They have gems, a healing potion, and a *potion of invisibility*.

76 Three guard arraccats, a black arraccat, and an arraccat lurk here.

77 The secret door to this room conceals a lich's lair. Destroy his phylactery to defeat him permanently.

78 The two guard arraccats here have some gems.

79 A black arraccat and a guard arraccat block the sealed door in this room. They have a healing potion and some gems. The door is sealed with the Glyph of Safekeeping, and can be opened only with the Word of Necessity, which you learn from Anorrweyn Evensong at Mystra's temple in Nightingale Court, after they bring her the token of Mystra from Faeril and Beriand. This door is the only access point to the next level of the dungeons, so it is important to have learned the Word of Necessity before coming here.

80 These stairs lead down to location 1 of the 4th level of the Elven Catacombs. This is where the mage with *The Sacred Staff of Sunlight* Nathlilik spoke of should be, but he and his staff are missing. However, there are signs of a struggle and arraccat claw marks.

81 There are some gems on the floor here, and it is safe to rest.

82 Three guard arraccats live in this room. They have some gems.

Tip

Rest now. There is a tough fight coming up.

83 This is the nexus of the arraccat infestation in this corner of the dungeon: a massive arraccat nest! When the party enters this room, huge groups of arraccats appear at both entrances, scissoring the party between them. In total, there are two arraccats, nine guard arraccats, two black arraccats, and an arraccat mother. Inside the nest, find the corpse of a cult mage and his *Sacred Staff of Sunlight*, a massively powerful weapon against drow elves. Pick through the nest to find a *scroll of firestorm*, a *potion of full healing*, two *potions of restoration*, a suit of *Leather Armor +5*, a Corroded Metal Key, *Prince Antonae's Stormbow*, and the final entry from the cult mage's journal, describing the traprunes he set.

84 Three mohrgs attack you here.

85 Three guard arraccats and two arraccats roam this area.

86 Two guard arraccats and an arraccat are all that remain of the once massive infestation on this level.

87 The stairs here lead up to location 70 on the 1st level of the Elven Catacombs. Taking these stairs allows you to get the Adamantine Key and sneak past the border guards of the drow complex.

Tip

In small groups, arraccats aren't much trouble, but they can be dangerous in large groups. Come at the nest from the south. Drop some *fireballs* into the center of the nest to clear out the debris and make it easier to move, then make your stand inside the nest and let the arraccats come to you. Arraccats are vulnerable to all types of magic, but *fireball*, *flame strike*, and *confusion* work particularly well. When they are dead you are free to either take the stairs at location 80, or clear out the rest of the level.

Note

Return here after you have finished exploring the bottom level of the Catacombs. The drow on the 1st level are firmly entrenched, and items you find on the bottom level can help you defeat them.

Chapter Nineteen

The Prisons
(The Elven Catacombs, Level 4)

The final level of the Elven Catacombs was once used as a burial ground for the greatest heroes of the city. Those tombs are still there, but they have been pushed aside by the Cult of the Dragon and Freth drow, who have turned this level into a massive living and training ground. In the farthest corner of the level, the Cult holds the baelnorn, *Miroden Silverblade*, your only hope for restoring the Mythal and destroying the Pool of Radiance.

Quick Overview

Tombs of Heroes

There is a line of spacious tombs along the south wall of the 4th level of the Elven Catacombs, known as the Prisons. Inside are buried elven and dwarven heroes, who for some reason couldn't be buried outdoors like most. Many of the tombs are empty, but one heavily guarded, magically protected tomb contains the single most dangerous treasure of Myth Drannor, a blade of such immense diabolical power that in the wrong hands, it could bring all of Faerûn to its knees: the *Dreadsword Daemonic*! In your hands, it is a noble tool indeed.

Freth Drow Treasure Chamber

The drow have collected and stockpiled treasures from all over Myth Drannor, and they're currently boxing them up for transport into the Underdark, never to be seen by the goodly races again. By braving the tombs, you can sneak into the treasure chamber without fighting through the stronghold. The treasures inside are particularly powerful against drow, making the Freth Drow Stronghold that much easier to conquer, should you choose to conquer it.

213

Freth Drow Stronghold

The Freth Drow Stronghold on this level is even more strongly fortified than the stronghold on the 1st level, though you should be more prepared to face it now. Numerous drow guards and high priests viciously protect their base in Myth Drannor. Weapons such as *The Sacred Staff of Sunlight* and the *Baneblade Faervian*, which have extreme bonuses against drow, are particularly useful. Because the drow are so strong, it is possible to rise a level in this region alone. Whether that's worth the struggle is up to you.

Freth Drow Command Post

In this corner, the Freth elite commanders plan the infiltration of Myth Drannor and their triumphant return to the Underdark. Sadly, they are in your way, so it's unlikely they will ever make it home. Be sure to stop in and say "hi" to Dreydre, their leader on this level.

Cult Facility Outskirts

This section of the dungeon is largely unclaimed territory. It is patrolled by members of the Cult of the Dragon, but they haven't established a true base here because of the local undead, and because they want a buffer between their base and the Freth drow to the south.

Cult Facility

Outside of Castle Cormanthor, this is the most fortified Cult facility in Myth Drannor. It includes living spaces, a training area, storage space, and a holding cell for one baelnorn: Miroden Silverblade. It will not be easy to fight through all the cult members, but the safety of the realms demands it. Once Miroden is free, he can finally help you restore the Mythal.

Dungeon Master's Notes

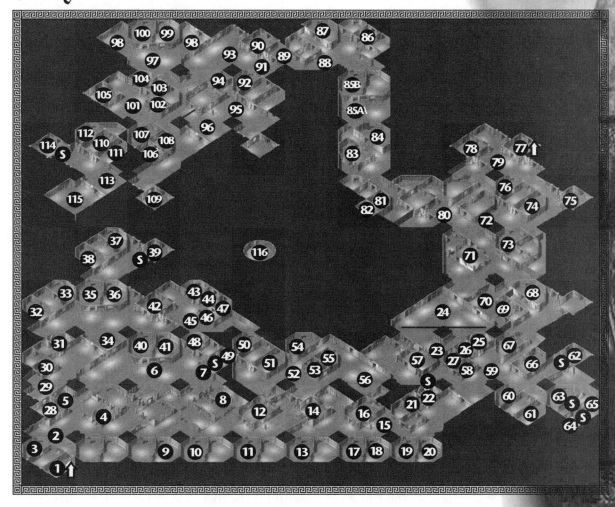

⇑ ⇓ Staircases leading up or down   **S** Secret door

Tombs of Heroes

❶ The stairs here lead up to location 80 on level 3 of the Elven Catacombs (see Chapter 18).

❷ Three Freth drow scouts explore this hallway. They may be there when you arrive, and they may not.

215

3 This room is the lair of three black arraccats. They have hoarded a small amount of gold.

4 Several dead drow are scattered about this ruined room and some gems lie on the ground. You may also encounter a patrol of eight Freth drow commandos and their commander.

5 This door is locked with the Iron Spider Key, which is on the drow in location 12.

6 Three margoyles attack the party here. To the west, another patrol group made up of five Freth drow commandos, a Freth drow priest, and two guard arraccats may happen by.

7 This small chamber is home to a zombie lord. A secret door in the back of the room leads into the Drow Stronghold.

8 Two black arraccats and a guard arraccat jealously hoard gems in their lair.

9 This is the tomb of Kerym, of Clan Ildacer. Two spectres live here now.

10 This tomb belongs to Alea, of Clan Aunglor. Two wraiths and a master wraith attack the party.

11 This is the resting place of Finolas, of Clan Ulondarr. It is haunted by two spectres and a master spectre. It's safe to rest here when they are vanquished.

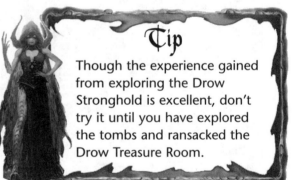

Tip

Though the experience gained from exploring the Drow Stronghold is excellent, don't try it until you have explored the tombs and ransacked the Drow Treasure Room.

12 In this room, a revenant assaults a drow robber who was attempting to steal from the tombs. The robber carries an Iron Spider Key, gems, and a healing potion.

13 This tomb, the final resting place of Aolis Ammath of Clan Alastrarra, is now home to two mohrgs, two wights, and a revenant.

14 The trapped ornate box here holds the spirit of the lich in location 15. If it is smashed, killing the archlich ends his existence permanently.

15 This hallway is blocked by an archlich and three master shadows. Find this lich's phylactery in location 14.

16 Five margoyles attack the party here.

17 This is the tomb of Penaal Thrist of Clan Aulamyr. His tomb houses two mohrgs, two wights, and a master spectre.

18 In the tomb of Fieryat of Clan Nierdre, the party is attacked by four mohrgs, two wights, a master wight, and two master wraiths.

19 Four mohrgs and two master spectres have desecrated this tomb, the final resting place of Laele of Clan Ainesilver.

20 The name on this tomb has been blotted out with a magical rune of everlasting blood, and powerful protections have been placed over it. The sarcophagus inside perpetually radiates a *circle of death*, and the two gates into the tomb are both locked and trapped with *cloudkill* and *firestorm*, respectively. If the party approaches the sarcophagus, a revenant attacks, and simultaneously, two liches, an archlich, and nine mohrgs attack the party from behind. Inside the tomb is the *Dreadsword Daemonic*.

Tip

The *Dreadsword Daemonic* is one of the most powerful weapons in the game, and its powerful guardians aim to keep it out of unworthy hands. Your characters should all be higher than 9th level, so you won't have to concern yourself with the *circle of death*. The bulk of the enemies appear from behind, so keep your strongest fighters at the rear of your party. Cast *freedom of movement* on them before the fight begins to protect them from the mohrgs, then use *halt undead* or *control undead* to thin the ranks of the opposition.

Freth Drow Treasure Chamber

21 Two spectres and a mohrg haunt this room.

22 A secret door in the north wall leads into the back door of the Drow Treasure Chamber. Just north of the secret door, a patrol of two Freth drow commanders and two guard arraccats may attack when you come through.

23 This is the outer part of the Drow Treasure Chamber, where many of the Freth drow's minor treasures are kept. Two Freth drow robbers carry gems and gold, and they may add some of your gold to their own, if you don't finish them off in a timely fashion. A *scroll of firestorm* and a *scroll of incendiary cloud* are on a shelf, a *potion of spell resistance* and a *potion of invisibility* are on a bookcase, and a metal chest contains a *scroll of resurrection* and a *Drow Quiver of Assassin's Arrows*. To the north, the party can hear a large number of drow moving treasure about, preparing it for transport to the Underdark. To the west, a single Freth drow assassin stalks the hallways. If he's there when you are, he'll attack.

24 The valuable treasures here are guarded by four Freth drow guards, five Freth drow warriors, a Freth drow guard master, a Freth drow priest, a Freth drow high priest, and a Freth drow assassin. All the chests in this room are trapped with powerful magic and locked. Four chests line the south section. From west to east, the first contains gold, a healing potion, and a *Ring of Azular*. The second contains the *Daemonclaws of Gr'Zak*. The third contains gold, the *Morolith* hammer, and *Ravenskin* armor. The fourth chest, the easternmost, contains gold, the *Eye of the Witch*, and *potion of insect plague*. The chest in the far north of the room contains the greatest treasure of all: the *Baneblade Faervian*, the legendary weapon of Hachaam Selorn, and a vital tool in the war against the drow.

25 The door to this room is locked, but the lock can be picked. The *Beacon of Grigori* is on a table inside.

> ## Tip
>
> You can enter the main Drow Treasure Chamber (location 24) from two directions: from the west and from the east. Either way, the drow may surprise you. Given their proficiency with bows and magic, keep your spellcasters out of sight of the archers.

> ## Note
>
> The *Baneblade Faervian* is part of a quest to attain another powerful weapon, the *Baneblade Morvian*. To continue that quest, take the *Baneblade Faervian* to Hachaam's tomb at location 57 in the Halls of Light (see Chapter 9) after you have finished the Elven Catacombs. This is a long trek, but well worth it, as the *Baneblade Morvian* is one of the game's most powerful weapons.

26 The door to this armory is locked, but the lock can be picked. The *Drakulwyng* shortsword is on a table inside, *Seethre's Tongue* is on a bookshelf, and *The Ilrazor of Sholg'Gliath* is inside a trapped and locked metal chest.

27 The door to this library is locked, but the lock can be picked. Inside are numerous scrolls on shelves, but you'll have to defeat a single Freth drow high priest before collecting the treasure. With a thorough search, the party can find a *scroll of destruction*, a *scroll of slay living*, a *scroll of control undead*, and a *scroll of finger of death*. On the way to location 28, the party may encounter a patrol of two spectres.

Freth Drow Stronghold

28 This "greeting room" for the stronghold is manned by four inhospitable Freth drow guards. Getting in requires the Iron Spider Key, which is in location 12.

29 This hall is guarded by eight Freth drow warriors, a Freth drow priest, and a Freth drow commander. The enemies here are well dispersed, so the drow priest is hard to reach.

Tip

Don't forget to use *confusion*! Drow have magic resistance, but it still works well enough.

30 Three Freth drow warriors, a Freth drow priest, and a Freth drow commander watch this room. The bookcase holds healing potions, and the drow carry a *Ring of Confusion*.

31 Four Freth drow guards attack the party in this room.

32 Two Freth drow commanders and six Freth drow warriors occupy this barracks. The chest on the left is locked, trapped, and contains a *Drow Shortbow +5*, an excellent ranged weapon for rogues. The right side chest is locked but empty.

33 The left chest in this room is trapped, locked, and contains gold and a *Drow Longsword +3*. The right chest is locked and contains gold and a *Drow Shortsword +4*.

34 This is the Well of Wishes. Despite its promising name, all it does is *daze* any character who drinks from it. Keep your eyes open! A Freth drow assassin may be lurking near the well. Also, in the open area north of the well, a squad of 10 Freth drow commandos and their commander sometimes appear when you enter.

35 This room and location 36 are arraccat pens. The drow train the vicious arraccats as guards and pets. There are three black arraccats, two guard arraccats, and two Freth drow warriors in this pen.

36 This arraccat pen is watched by two Freth drow warriors and houses three black arraccats and two guard arraccats.

37 A Freth drow commander and seven Freth drow warriors are packed into this room. Both chests are trapped and locked. The chest on the left contains gold and a *Drow Shortsword +4*, and the chest on the right contains gold and a *Drow Mace +4*. A healing potion is on the shelf. The party may encounter three Freth drow scout when they exit this room.

38 Two Freth drow commanders and five Freth drow warriors attack the party here. The chest on the left is locked and trapped and contains gold and a *drow quiver of arrows*. The right side chest is locked and contains more gold and another *drow quiver of arrows*. A healing potion is on the shelf.

39 After finding this room through the secret door, the party is struck with the feeling that the drow are watching them. This trapped and locked chest contains one of their greatest treasures: the *Wraithmael of Drenofiend*.

40 This arraccat pen holds two guard arraccats and three black arraccats, and is watched by two Freth drow guards.

41 This arraccat pen holds two guard arraccats and three black arraccats, and is watched by two Freth drow guards.

42 Four tough Freth drow guards protect this room. A *potion of invisibility* sits on the shelf.

43 The party finds a potion of displacement, a *scroll of lightning bolt*, and a *scroll of repulsion* on the shelves in this library.

44 The party encounters two Freth drow priests in this sector of the library. There is a *scroll of dispel magic*, a *scroll of bestow curse*, and a *potion of shield of faith* on the shelves.

> ## Note
> As 14–hit die fighters, Freth drow guards are the most powerful standard Freth units. They are especially mean with arrows, and they like to target your sorcerers. Have your fighters close to melee range with them quickly.

45 Several squads of drow protectors attack when the party steps into the vulnerable space of this open hallway. A Freth drow assassin is in the center; the group to the west is composed of three Freth drow guards, a Freth drow priest, a Freth drow assassin, and a Freth drow guard master; and the group to the east consists of a Freth drow high priest, a Freth drow assassin, and four Freth drow guards.

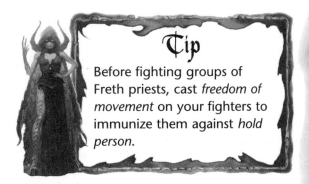

Tip

This is quite a fight! As always, *confusion* is your savior. Use it liberally. Their clustered position makes the two groups of drow great targets for area effect spells as well. Take one group out completely with your warriors, and then focus on the other. To take pressure off your spellcasters while you are killing the first group, send the character equipped with T*he Sacred Staff of Sunlight* (who has a +7 AC bonus and is thus nearly impossible to hit) into combat against the second group.

46 A Freth drow high priest and a Freth drow priest guard this room. After the encounter in location 45, they're pushovers. A shelf holds a full healing potion.

47 A Freth drow commander, four Freth drow priests, and a Freth drow high priest attack the party here. There is a *Dagger of Magus* in a cupboard, a *Wand of Melf's Acid Arrow* in a locked and trapped metal chest, and a *Necklace of Spiritual Weapon* in a locked and trapped wooden chest.

48 A *potion of delay poison* sits on a shelf in this room, and a *potion of fireshield* is in a cupboard in the next room to the southeast. Also in the room to the southeast are a *scroll of cone of cold* and a *scroll of remove paralysis* on various shelves.

Tip

Before fighting groups of Freth priests, cast *freedom of movement* on your fighters to immunize them against *hold person*.

49 In the southwest wall of this room is a secret door leading out of the drow stronghold. This entry room is guarded by three Freth drow priests, a Freth drow high priest, a Freth drow inquisitor, and a Freth drow commander. The shelves hold healing potions. The metal chest here is trapped and contains *Bernard's Unforgivable Boots*. The wooden chest is also trapped, and contains *Gauntlets of Destruction*. The party may run into a drow assassin while heading for location 50.

221

50 This room is the gateway to the eastern portion of the stronghold. It is blocked by two guard arraccats, four Freth drow warriors, a Freth drow commander, and a Freth drow priest. A healing potion is on a shelf. In the hallway to the south, three Freth drow scouts may attack when you enter.

51 This drow barracks is home to two Freth drow commanders and seven Freth drow warriors. It also contains a healing potion on a shelf and two locked chests. The left chest is trapped as well and contains the *Pigsticker* spear. The right chest contains the *Headsplitter* axe.

52 Four Freth drow priests mill about in this open hallway; they may or may not be there when you enter.

53 This room houses a small library. On the shelves are a *scroll of circle of death*, a *scroll of raise dead*, and a *potion of globe of invulnerability*.

54 The door to this armory is locked, but the lock can be picked or the door broken down. Two *drow quivers of arrows* are on the shelves. On the tables, the party finds two *Drow Shortbows +5* and three *Drow Shortswords +3*. In the barrels are five *Drow Longspears +4* and a *Drow Longsword +5*. Both chests are locked. The left chest contains healing potions and a *Drow Mace +5*, and the right chest holds four *Drow Daggers +4* and some damaging potions.

55 This small room is home to a Freth drow commander, four Freth drow priests, and a Freth drow high priest. It also contains a *scroll of heal* on a shelf, and two trapped and locked chests. The wood chest contains a *Staff of Harm*, and the metal chest contains a *Wand of Firestorm*.

56 Three Freth drow commandos, two Freth drow commanders, a Freth drow priest, and a Freth drow high priest fight among themselves here. From what the party can tell, they appear to be fighting over leadership, with some drow claiming loyalty to "Greyanna" and others following "Dreydre."

57 Here the party finds two black arraccats, four Freth drow guards, a Freth drow guard master, and a Freth drow priest. The Heavy Spider Key found on a shelf unlocks the door to the northeast.

Freth Drow Command Post

58 Three Freth drow guards and a Freth drow priest occupy this room.

59 Four Freth drow assassins ambush the party in this hallway, one from each direction.

60 The metal chest in this room is trapped and locked; it contains gold.

61 Two Freth drow commanders and six Freth drow commandos, a portion of Dreydre's personal guard, live in this room. The chest here is locked and contains some of the Freth drow's ill-gotten gold.

62 This command room is hidden behind a secret door and guarded by several high-level drow. The party faces a black arraccat, two Freth drow guards, and a Freth drow guard master. There are healing potions on the shelf, and the locked and trapped metal chest contains gold and the *Spellfoil* shield.

63 This is Dreydre's living room. It is well guarded, but the party can use a secret door to the south to ambush her and her guards. Dreydre is a 16–hit die drow priestess. Her personal guard consists of two Freth drow guards and a Kalannar, a powerful breed of arraccat. They carry the *Venom* dagger and a map of level 4. The locked wooden chest contains gold and a *Medallion of Lolth*. The locked metal chest contains gold and a suit of *Drow Spidersilk Armor*. There is also a *scroll of fear* in the bookcase and a *potion of freedom movement* on the shelf.

64 Two Freth drow guards, part of Dreydre's elite retinue, hide in this room. They carry a *potion of invisibility*. They come only if you don't defeat Dreydre quickly.

65 Behind a secret door, find this room. A shelf holds a *scroll of dispel magic*. The trapped and locked metal chest contains gold and a *Ring of Cursing*.

66 This drow barracks is abandoned. A *potion of hold poison* is on a shelf, and a *Small Shield +4* is in a locked chest.

67 A Freth drow commander and five Freth drow warriors attack the party in this room. They guard a healing potion and a locked and trapped chest full of gold.

68 This abandoned room contains drow treasure. A healing potion is on a shelf. The chest to the left is trapped and locked and contains *Samigel's Dead Slayer*. The right chest is locked and contains only gold.

69 Three Freth drow commandos and a Freth drow high priest inhabit this room. They carry potions of healing.

70 These drow guard the northern entrance to drow territory. Although they do not expect the party to be coming from the south, they react quickly. There are four Freth drow guards, a Freth drow guard master, a Freth drow high priest, and two guard arraccats here. A nearby shelf holds a *potion of blink*.

223

Cult Facility Outskirts

71 Margoyles lurk in the shadows of these ruins. Seven margoyles have killed a group of cult wizards and undead.

72 A cult archmage, a cult brigadier, four enthralled drow, and six soulless orogs patrol the right side of this hallway. A cult brigadier and eight soulless orog are in charge of the left side. It's possible to avoid both groups.

73 Two mohrgs, two master wraiths, and a wraith haunt this crypt. The coffins here are empty.

74 Three enthralled drow, two soulless orogs, and a cult mage guard this open room.

75 Four zombie lords inhabit this room. It's a safe place to rest once they are gone.

76 Four margoyles make this room their home.

77 A mohrg and two wraiths inhabit this room. The door in the back of the room leads to the cave (location 5) in Stillwater.

78 Two shadows and a master shadow thrive in the darkness of this forgotten room.

79 Seven enthralled drow and a cult archmage patrol here. As with most of the patrols, they are not always in this location.

80 A cult brigadier sometimes leads a group of eight enthralled drow here. They attack the party as they explore the ruins.

81 A cult archmage and six enthralled drow are locked in combat with five margoyles. This leaves them vulnerable to vicious attack from the party.

82 A margoyle queen hides in this room from the fight in location 81.

83 Seven margoyles fortify this room.

84 Two spectres haunt this room, protecting it from margoyle infestation.

85A This area is inhabited by two parties that are split between rooms. First, a cult archmage, a cult lieutenant, four soulless orogs, and four enthralled drow patrol the area. They are backed up by the rest of their team, who wait in 85B. They occasionally patrol this area, which means it's possible to avoid them.

85B The passage north through these rooms is blocked by a cult archmage, a cult lieutenant, four enthralled drow, and four soulless orogs.

86 The door to this room is locked, but the lock can be picked. The chest inside is empty, but it is safe to rest here. Behind a door to the southeast wait three mohrgs.

87 Four master wraiths haunt their final resting place. The sarcophagi here are empty.

88 The party encounters Nottle and Tudo here. They are arguing, but Tudo quickly asks to join the party. If the party chooses not to take him, he goes to Nottle's pavilion to wait for them. You may encounter Nottle and Tudo at other locations in the game. As soon as you do, they return to the aboveground world.

89 This door to the Cult of the Dragon facility is locked tight. But when the characters approach and look through the keyhole, they see a dramatic appearance by Kya Mordrayn. In the end, the Cult forces are fortified and the door is unlocked.

90 The stairs here lead up to location 14 in Nightingale Court (see Chapter 11).

Cult Facility

91 Immediately upon opening the door to the Cult Facility, the party is attacked by cultists. The cult forces consist of a cult lieutenant, a cult archmage, six cult soldier elites, and four soulless orogs. After you defeat that group, a cult lieutenant, a cult brigadier, a cult archmage, two cult soldiers elite, four enthralled drow, two dragon-kin, and a dragon-kin captain attack from the west, and you won't have time to rest in between.

Tip

This is a good time to return Anorrweyn's skull to the shrine of Mystra. It grounds her spirit in the present, but she can't help you further until you find Miroden Silverblade, the baelnorn. This is also a good time to rest up, as the Cult Facility is securely fortified, and there's no way to conquer it other than through the front door.

Tip

Despite their preparation, this is not the most powerful cult force. Kill the archmage quickly with ranged weapons or magic (try *destruction*), and finish off the rest with standard tactics, such as *confusion* and *flame strike*. Finish this battle quickly or the cultists will call for reinforcements from the surrounding rooms. The enemies listed in areas 92 and 93 below can easily join this fight, stacking the odds a bit more in their favor.

92 A cult lieutenant, a cult brigadier, a cult archmage, and two cult soldiers elite await the party in this room. This group is called only as reinforcements to defend the attack in 91.

93 Two dragon-kin, a dragon-kin caption, and four enthralled drow come late to fortify the front door against the party. These reinforcements may be called to battle when you start combat at location 91.

94 Two cult soldiers elite loiter in this small storage area. In the middle of the corridor to the west of this room is a patrol area frequented by a cult archmage, a dragon-kin, and eight enthralled drow. If they're here when you are, they will attack.

95 This storage area and the cell within it are completely devoid of enemies or treasure.

96 A cult lieutenant and three cult soldiers elite attack the party here.

97 Two dragon-kin watch the entrance to the cult training area.

98 In both of these locations, a cult lieutenant trains cult soldier recruits (four recruits on the left, six on the right). Training tools, such as blunt arrows and wooden longswords, are scattered about.

99 A cult archmage and four cult mage recruits have lost control of a soulless orog, and they frantically use their best spells to incapacitate it, leaving them vulnerable to the party. There is a healing potion on a shelf and a scroll of *undead control* on a table.

100 A cult archmage and four cult mage recruits practice their lightning magic. A healing potion is on a shelf and a *scroll of lightning bolt* is on a table.

101 Walking into this area, the party comes across a strong cult contingent. There are eight cult brigadiers, two cult archmages, a cult field marshal, and a cult overseer.

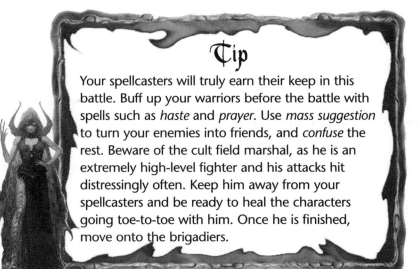

Tip

Your spellcasters will truly earn their keep in this battle. Buff up your warriors before the battle with spells such as *haste* and *prayer*. Use *mass suggestion* to turn your enemies into friends, and *confuse* the rest. Beware of the cult field marshal, as he is an extremely high-level fighter and his attacks hit distressingly often. Keep him away from your spellcasters and be ready to heal the characters going toe-to-toe with him. Once he is finished, move onto the brigadiers.

102 A cult brigadier and two cult soldiers elite occupy this room. They carry a Blackened Key, which opens the door in location 108.

103 The two chests in this room are locked. The chest on the right contains a *Quiver of Arrows* +5, and the chest on the left contains a potion of healing.

104 Three cult soldiers elite and a soulless orog guard the chests in this room. The chest on the left contains only gold, but the chest on the right is locked and contains a *Small Shield* +4.

105 This room is an officer's quarters. Sadly, the cult lieutenant here is completely alone. The table holds a *Drow Dagger* +5 and healing potions are on the shelf. The chest on the left is locked and contains a *potion of bull's strength*. The chest on the left is locked and trapped and contains a suit of *Full Plate* +4.

106 The door to this room requires the Blackened Key, found in location 102. A cult archmage and four enthralled drow reside here. A healing potion is on a table. The chest here is locked and trapped and contains *Thoggua's Tooth*.

107 The cult overseer and two enthralled drow who guard this room protect a note and a map on the table. When the fight is over, you find *The Guulstau of M'Raelhorrid*. The shelves hold potions of healing, a *scroll of restoration*, and a *scroll of raise dead*. The chest is locked and trapped and holds gold, a *Ring of Searing Light*, a *Wand of Mass Suggestion*, and an idolon.

108 A cult brigadier watches this room. A note and a Simple Iron Key lie on the table. The northern chest is trapped and locked and contains gold and the *Ravensong* longsword. The middle chest is locked and contains a potion of healing. The southern chest is locked and contains a *potion of remove fear*.

109 A cult mage and two enthralled drow hide out in this secluded room. The mage carries a *Wand of Stinking Cloud*. The chest is trapped and locked and contains a *scrolls of destruction*, *incendiary cloud*, *firestorm*, and *disintegrate*. Outside the door to this room, a dragon-kin, cult archmage, and six enthralled drow sometime patrol. Be ready in case they're around when you are.

110 Two cult soldiers elite attempt to block the party's progress through this room.

111 Five cult soldiers elite and a soulless orog guard one chest that contains a little gold. They join in the fight at location 110 after one round of combat.

112 Both chests in this room are locked and contain gold.

113 The party stumbles across a massive cult force. A cult lieutenant, four cult brigadiers, a cult field marshal, and four cult soldiers elite stand ready in parade formation. Their leaders carry a note and a Black Steel Key.

114 This room, hidden behind a secret door, confines two shadows and six master shadows, which can quickly drain even the hardiest barbarian of Strength. The well in the center of the room is trapped and contains the *Wraithmael Shield*.

Tip

This fight is notably easier than the one in location 101. The cult soldiers elite are in a tight formation, and tend to stay in and fire arrows, making area effect spells amazingly effective. Have your clerics drop *firestorms* on them and your sorcerers use their most damaging spells, such as *cone of cold*, while your warriors face the leaders.

115 This is the cell where the Cult of the Dragon is holding Miroden Silverblade. The door of the cell requires the Black Steel Key carried by the soldiers in location 113. A cult overseer, two cult archmages, a cult brigadier, and eight cult soldiers elite guard Miroden. When Miroden is free, he warps the party to his lair at location 116.

116 This is Miroden the Baelnorn's home. He has tended the Mythal for centuries, but he was deceived by Kya Mordrayn, who convinced him to betray his sacred duty with tales of the revival of Myth Drannor. He tells the party that he destroyed the sapphire that controls the weave rather than let it fall into her hands. To restore the Mythal, the party must help Anorrweyn attune a new gem to the Mythal and take control. He suggests the party talk to Harldain to obtain a suitable gem. To drive the party on their quest, he opens his treasure trove to them. The chests arranged about the room contain healing potions, *potions of restoration*, a suit of *Chainmail* +5, a *Light Mace* +5, a *Shortsword* +5, a *Pike* +5, a *Club* +5, a suit of *Leather Armor* +5, a suit of *Full Plate* +5, a *Greatsword* +5, and a *Greataxe* +5. Miroden also opens a portal that transports the party to location 19 in Nightingale Court.

Chapter Twenty

Overland Revisited

After you free Miroden Silverblade in the bottom of the Elven Catacombs, the Cult of the Dragon finally realizes that your party is a dangerous threat, and it sends out patrols in force to weaken and hopefully destroy the party. As you visit your allies throughout the overlands, cult patrols, mercenaries, and other enemies constantly attack you. You have never been so close to success—only a few steps stand between you and victory.

　　The numbers in the Dungeon Master's Notes in this chapter refer to numbers on the maps from each of the overland chapter maps (Chapters 5, 10, 11, 13, 14 and 15). Therefore, in this chapter, the numbers appear out of order. To follow the walkthrough, simply visit the locations in this chapter in the order they are listed and as marked on the maps in the chapters noted above.

Quick Overview

Nightingale Court (Chapter 11)

The first thing to do after speaking to Miroden Silverblade is to speak to Anorrweyn at the Shrine of Mystra. Now that you have her skull, she can manifest herself completely in the present, and upon Miroden's advice, she agrees to help you restore the Mythal. She suggests you speak to Harldain in the House of Gems. First, use the spinning spire to visit Faeril and Beriand in Stillwater.

Stillwater (Chapter 5)

Upon visiting Faeril and Beriand's sanctuary, you find that they've been kidnapped by the Cult of the Dragon in retaliation for your interfering with their plans. Follow the cultists to the prison where they're holding Faeril and Beriand to rescue them, and gain access to another area of the Cult's fortresses. Once Faeril and Beriand are rescued, either walk south to the Windrider Glade to speak with Odelinde, or travel to the Glim-Gardens using the spires.

Windrider Glade (Chapter 14)

Odelinde has tales of Castle Cormanthor, one of your next destinations. In particular, she has an idea of how you can actually get inside, as the Cult has sealed almost all entrances.

Glim-Gardens (Chapter 13)

Your party must pass through the Glim-Gardens to reach the House of Gems, and the Cult has posted several patrols to try to prevent you from doing that. They want to prevent you from creating a new gem of the weave.

House of Gems (Chapter 15)

Speak to Harldain. He tells you where to find a gem of the weave, but once you have obtained the gem, you face a tough fight against a special squad of cult soldiers, the doomkin, and their leader Azmark Duathel. They do their utmost to prevent you from returning the gem to Anorrweyn. When you escape to the Glim-Gardens, use the spire to travel to Speculum Grounds, or simply walk through the Windrider Glade.

Speculum Grounds (Chapter 10)

Your goal here is to take the emerald of the weave to the top of the Speculum. Use the gateway at location 3, then walk up the steep path to the top of the Speculum, fighting the dragon-kin who ambush you on the way. Once this is complete, you are transported to the Castle Passage to continue your quest.

Dungeon Master's Notes

Nightingale Court (Chapter 11)

8 When you have returned her skull and spoken to Miroden Silverblade, Anorrweyn agrees to assume Miroden's responsibility as defender of the city, but first she needs your help to find a new gem of the weave. Anorrweyn also marks you so that you may pass through Antarn's Gate at location 3 in Speculum Grounds (see Chapter 10). Next, visit Harldain.

11 After you complete the Elven Catacombs, this statue dispenses more powerful rings in return for idolons than it did before. The five new rings it can dispense are *Garras' Keen Sight*, *Misery's Embrace*, *Fist of Saint Cuthbert*, *Arknor's Vile Voice*, and *Stillness of Dawn*.

21 Use the spinning spire here to transport yourself to Stillwater to visit Faeril and Beriand.

Stillwater (Chapter 5)

6 Faeril and Beriand have been kidnapped by the Cult of the Dragon! Their home is overrun with two cult soldiers, two cult archmages, a cult brigadier, and a cult lieutenant; they carry a *Longsword* +2 and a healing salve. Faeril and Beriand must have been taken through the portal in the back of the room. Follow it through to location 77 in the second level of the Elven Catacombs (Chapter 17).

7 Use this bridge to travel to the Windrider Glade if you'd like to speak to Odelinde.

1 Use this spire to travel to the Glim-Gardens if you don't wish to speak to Odelinde.

Windrider Glade (Chapter 14)

3 Odelinde can tell you tales of Castle Cormanthor, including a possible entrance. The Cult of the Dragon has sealed most entrances to the castle, but she suggests that you can enter through the aerie on the roof.

2 Use this staircase to enter the Glim-Gardens after you've spoken to Odelinde.

Glim-Gardens (Chapter 13)

3 Two dragon-kin, two cult quartermasters, and a cult overseer ambush the party here. If you haven't returned the waterbells to Plinshree, do so now.

8 Two cult quartermasters, two cult archmages, and a cult brigadier patrol this area, looking for the party. They carry a *scroll of bull's strength* and a healing salve.

16 The staircase up to the House of Gems is blocked by three dragon-kin and two dragon-kin captains.

House of Gems (Chapter 15)

20 This is where you visit Harldain. He gives the party the Tumblebar Key to open the statue in the back of the House of Gems. Under the statue is a dwarven treasure hoard containing an emerald of the weave, the last remaining weave stone in Myth Drannor.

12 The Tumblebar Key opens this statue. Under it is a treasure trove containing an emerald of the weave. As you exit, you're attacked by four doomkin cult fighters. They are servants of Azmark Duathel, the mage of whom Faeril and Beriand spoke.

13 Five doomkin cult fighters attack as the party rounds the eastern tower.

6 Azmark Duathel himself and five doomkin cult fighters guard the pathway down to the Glim-Gardens. They demand the party turn over the emerald of the weave, then fight to their deaths to obtain it. When the fight is over, you find gems, a *Longbow +5*, and the *Doomkin Scarab* necklace.

Tip

Doomkin fighters are more potent than normal cult soldiers, but they're not especially challenging. Use the same tactics you use against cult soldiers and you will be victorious.

Speculum Grounds (Chapter 10)

3 After speaking to Anorrweyn, after freeing Miroden Silverblade and returning her skull, the party can open this gate and walk up the path behind it to the dragon's spine atop the Speculum. Four dragon-kin captains guard the path.

18 When your characters place the emerald of the weave here, they are joined by Anorrweyn, who attunes the gem to the Mythal. However, she encounters some problems, and she takes the party with her to question Miroden Silverblade. After a quick discussion, she and Miroden transport your characters to location 1 of the Castle Passage (Chapter 21) so that they may strike at the heart of the Cult of the Dragon: Castle Cormanthor.

Chapter Twenty-One

Castle Passage

You arrived in Myth Drannor as novices. You took up Athan's quest, though it overwhelmed even him. Now, your bravery and adventures in Myth Drannor have honed you into one of the most powerful fighting forces in the Realms. You have conquered the drow House of Freth single-handedly. You have freed Myth Drannor's Baelnorn and uncovered some of the greatest treasures of the ancient city.

Now it's time to strike at the heart of the Cult of the Dragon infestation of Myth Drannor: Castle Cormanthor. You have sent cult members running back to the castle every time you have met. They know you oppose them, and they fear your coming.

And rightly so.

Quick Overview

The Demon's Lair

The most notable feature of the eastern Castle Passage is the chamber where ancient gold dragons sealed the Demon Rivener. He stole one of the elven Baneblades years ago and was sealed in because he couldn't be defeated. Hachaam Selorn, the great elven hero that Eadred freed, helps the party release him and recover the treasure.

Cult Prison

Cult members have taken some enemies hostage here to learn about their opponents throughout Myth Drannor. Several prisoners are very important, including one warrior, long thought dead, whose valor and strength could prove valuable to your party in this final stretch.

Ghosts of the Past

In a last-ditch effort, the Cult of the Dragon has assembled a massive force to block your entry to Castle Cormanthor through the Castle Passage. Defeating them is no easy task, but the halls below Castle Cormanthor are haunted. The spirits of long ago recognize righteousness when they see it, and if you are open minded and observant, they will assist you in your fight against the Cult of the Dragon's taint.

Dungeon Master's Notes

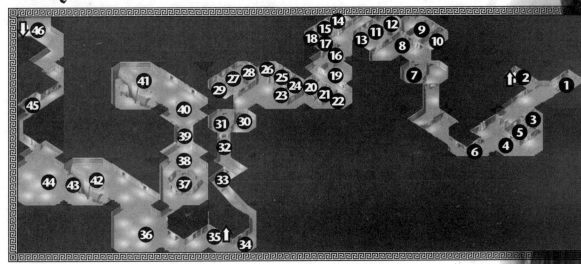

⬆ ⬇   Staircases leading up or down

The Demon's Lair

❶ This is where Miroden warps your party after you and Anorrweyn confront him about the gems of the weave.

❷ A master spectre, two spectres, and two mohrgs guard this room. These stairs lead up to location 14 in Nightingale Court (see Chapter 11).

❸ A fallen skeleton knight here bemoans a great failure, and mentions a "stone of fate" and a dwarven defense system. This is the ancient elven Armanthor, charged with protecting Castle Cormanthor from the forces of darkness in the siege of Myth Drannor.

235

4 This door is sealed with the Glyph of the Moon, the mark of the elven god Corellan Larethian. To open this door, the party must return the Baneblade Faervian to the tomb of Hachaam Selorn in location 57 (Halls of Light, Chapter 9).

5 This room is the holding chamber of the Demon Rivener, a beast so powerful that the gold dragons of the past could not defeat him, only entomb him. By opening the seal on the door, your characters release him, and now only they stand between him and total freedom. He also hoards the great elven sword: the Baneblade Morvian.

Tip

The Demon Rivener has been weakened over his centuries of confinement, but he is still a potent opponent. He has waited ages for a chance to be free, so when you open the door to his cage, he fights hard to get past you and wreak havoc on an unsuspecting Faerûn.

When you approach him, he summons eight clones of himself, each with one hit point. Don't get cocky, however. The Rivener and his clones are all highly resistant to magic, get six attacks per round, cause paralysis with a successful hit, and can be damaged only by +3 weapons or better.

Cast *freedom of movement* and *haste* on your warriors before the battle begins and kill him with melee weapons as quickly as possible. Use your spellcasters to inflict *magic missile* on his clones even though they get to make a magic resistance roll against each missile. The clones get a full complement of attacks, so destroying them is almost as important as the Rivener himself. Your reward, the *Baneblade Morvian*, is especially potent against dragons and dragon-kin.

6 Three mohrgs and two master wraiths block this passageway.

Cult Prison

7 These are the entry rooms to the Cult Prison. All the doors into and out of these rooms are locked, but you can pick the locks. A single cult soldier elite guards this room. You find a suit of *Chainmail +4* on a shelf, a *Longsword +4* on a table, a *Quiver of Arrows +3* in a barrel, and a *Shortbow +4* in a chest.

8 A cult lieutenant and four cult soldier elites guard this area.

9 Four dragon-kin guard these cells. One of them carries a Large Iron Key.

10 A voice calls the party to this cell. Inside, after unlocking the door with the Large Iron Key from location 9, you find a weakened, dying man. This is Athan, the leader of the party of heroes Elminster sent into Myth Drannor. He has listened carefully to the cult members who have tortured him since his capture, so he has useful information. The fires of vengeance still burn in him, and he will join the party if they will have him.

11 Two dragon-kin guard these cells.

12 The ormyrr in this cell nearly tramples the party in his haste to escape when his cage is opened.

13 The orog marauder hoodoo in this cell was actually friends with his guards, and he's angry that the party has killed them! He attacks viciously.

14 A Freth drow high priest occupies this room. A note on the door says that he is bound for the Pool of Radiance.

15 The zombie lord in this cell is absent-minded but well read. He is harmless, but the party can choose to kill him.

16 A large force consisting of a cult lieutenant, a cult archmage, two dragon-kin, two dragon-kin captains, and four cult lieutenants attempts to halt the party's progress in this hallway.

17 Two cult quartermasters and a cult lieutenant guard this room. They protect the cult leaders in the next room, who will reinforce these cult members if you don't finish them off quickly.

18 This is the office of the prison's wardens: two cult archmages, a cult brigadier, and a dragon-kin captain. Gems lie on the table, and the chest contains a roster of the 10 prisoners, stating that Athan is one prisoner, and Nathlilik is another. Athan is locked in location 10, and Nathlilik is in a cell in location 28.

19 Four cult soldier elites and a cult brigadier are re-equipping themselves in this armory when the party enters. The metal chest contains a healing potion. The wooden chest on the left is locked and contains a *Dagger +3*. The right side wooden chest is locked and contains a *Quiver of Arrows +4*.

20 This room is home to a cult archmage and his four enthralled drow servants. There is a *potion of cat's grace* on the shelf and a *scroll of repulsion* on the table. The chest is trapped and locked and contains a *Ring of Hushing*.

21 A scroll of *prayer* lies on the table in this room and a healing potion and scroll of *raise dead* are on the shelves.

22 Three cult soldier elites, a cult lieutenant, and a cult archmage gather around a fire here to keep warm.

23 Four cult soldier elites guard this room. The two from location 24 join their comrades in combat after the first round.

Tip

They want to be warm?! Drop a couple fireballs on them! *That* should warm them up!

24 Two cult soldier elites occupy this room. An old map of the Elven Catacombs lies on the table.

25 The lizardfolk taskmaster locked in this cell is loyal to Malgi Hi, but peaceful. He will leave without confrontation if the party is not hostile.

26 This cell appears to be empty, but a Kilsek drow attacks from the shadows if the party unlocks the door and enters.

27 Two dragon-kin guard this cell block. They have a Heavy Prison Key.

28 Nathlilik is in this cell. She promises the party information if they agree to help her. She tells how the Cult of the Dragon enslaved the Kilsek and what she plans to do about it. If the party agreed to help her on level 3 of the Elven Catacombs, she leaves without confrontation. Otherwise, she casts *darkness* and attacks.

29 The orog berserker in this cell attacks when he is freed.

30 The first of two rooms leading out of the Cult Prison, the room is guarded by a cult lieutenant and four cult soldier elites. All three chests in this room are locked but are not trapped. The metal chest contains a *potion of bull's strength*. The western wooden chest contains gold. The eastern wooden chest contains a *Greatsword +4*.

31 A dragon-kin, two cult soldier elites, and four enthralled drow, the last remaining prison guards, futilely attack the party here. They carry gems and reinforce the combat at location 30 after one round.

Ghosts of the Past

32 A black arraccat blocks this narrow hallway.

33 A zombie is trapped by a rock. If the party breaks the rock, he wanders off happily, leaving behind Aasirak's Brain.

34 Two black arraccats and one guard arraccat block this corner.

35 Behind this doorway, a long, winding path leads to the cave next to Faeril and Beriand's hideout in Stillwater (location 5, Chapter 5).

36 The Castle Passage opens into a massive cavern here. Two black arraccats fight against three mohrgs and two wights over control of this territory. The party can feel the presence of ghosts. They seem to be walking north.

37 Eight mohrgs guard a lich's phylactery in this room. They carry a scroll of *hold monster*, and there are healing potions on a shelf. Both chests are trapped and locked. The right chest contains the *Hammer Veneficus*, which has a very favorable critical hit range of 18–20. The left chest contains an idolon and *Sylmorrir—Shield of Power*.

38 Just north of the lich's quarters, the party encounters the archlich whose phylactery they just destroyed. He's not happy about it.

39 These nine barrels are all trapped with fireballs. Setting off one will set off a painful chain reaction. The presence of ghosts grows very strong here.

> ## Tip
> As always, *control undead* and *halt undead* are much more useful against mohrgs than turning undead, due to their high number of hit dice.

40 Three black arraccats and an arraccat mother block the party here.

41 The ghosts of the past crossed the bridge that once led into the castle, seeking safety. However, they were betrayed, and all of them were killed. Their grief at the failure of the guardians of the passage is palpable. On the ground is the *Stone of Fates*, which seems to have some connection to the defenses of the passage and the failure of the Armanthor at location 3. There is also a *scroll of fireball*.

42 The spirit of an elf appears before the party here. She says "The stone. The defenses. All is not lost."

43 This is the Well of Fates. If the party drops in the Stone of Fates, four dwarven statues will join the fight as allies in location 44.

44 A large cult contingent has set up camp here to stop the party's progress. You face a cult field marshal, four cult lieutenants, two cult quartermasters, two cult archmages, a cult overseer, two enthralled drow, and three dragon-kin captains. Four dwarven statues assist against these enemies if the party dropped the Stone of Fates in the well at location 43.

45 Two black arraccats block this pathway.

46 These stairs lead up to location 1 in the Castle Cormanthor exterior (see Chapter 22).

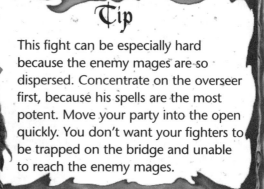

Note

You have to be fast to put the stone in the well before the fight begins. If you examine the well but don't put in the stone, a dragon-kin to the west spots your party, and then you won't have the chance.

Tip

This fight can be especially hard because the enemy mages are so dispersed. Concentrate on the overseer first, because his spells are the most potent. Move your party into the open quickly. You don't want your fighters to be trapped on the bridge and unable to reach the enemy mages.

Chapter Twenty-Two

Castle Exterior

Castle Cormanthor was, and still is, the most prominent structure in Myth Drannor. Though it was central to the fall of the city, its solid construction and protective magic kept it mostly intact throughout the battle. Many elves fled to the castle for protection, and they died by the thousands when their magical defenses failed them against the intruders. Since then, no group or creature has been able to hold the castle for long.

Something about it undermines the plans of squatters. They are always overthrown, and the castle becomes deserted once again.

Quick Overview

Castle Cormanthor is a very linear area. There is only one path to take, and the only people you meet are cultists who are trying to stop the party in its tracks. Rest whenever you have an opportunity, as the fights are very difficult; you can't afford to take on these fights at half strength.

241

Dungeon Master's Notes

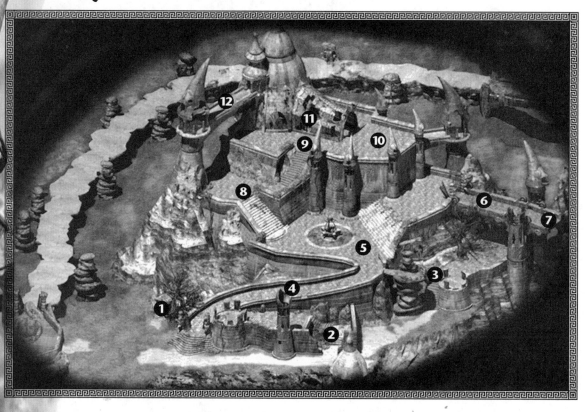

1 This is the staircase where the party emerges from location 46 in the Castle Passage. Four dragon-kin and a dragon-kin captain await you here.

2 A cult archmage, a cult overseer, eight cult soldier elites, a cult brigadier, and a cult lieutenant, determined to defend the castle, attack the party here. They carry some gems and a *scroll of finger of death*.

3 Three black arraccats and an arraccat mother nest here. A black arraccat and an arraccat mother also attack from the south if the party invades the nest. A dead cult soldier in the nest has some healing potions. It is safe to rest here.

4 Two dragon-kin, two cult archmages, a cult lieutenant, and seven cult soldier elites guard this narrow corridor.

5 Gathered around the fire here are six dragon-kin, a dragon-kin captain, a cult overseer, and three cult archmages. They carry a *Quiver of Arrows +5*, a *Battleaxe +4*, and a suit of *Chainmail +5*.

6 Four gargoyles and a gargoyle leader have snuck into Castle Cormanthor from the Windrider Glade.

7 When the drawbridge here is raised, it allows the party to travel back and forth between this location and location 15 in the Windrider Glade (see Chapter 14). When the party first finds it, it is raised.

8 Four dragon-kin, a dragon-kin captain, three cult soldier elites, and a cult lieutenant guard this landing. They leave a note explaining the presense of the gargoyles to the east.

9 At the top of these steps, the party is attacked by a dragon-kin, a dragon-kin captain, two cult archmages, and four cult quartermasters. After two rounds, the combat attracts the attention of the force at location 10.

10 This is the Cult of the Dragon's last chance to keep the party out of the interior of Castle Cormanthor. They have posted a contingent of three dragon-kin, a dragon-kin captain, two cult lieutenants, a cult brigadier, a cult archmage, and a cult overseer to meet your party. They carry a *Wand of Flame Strike* and a *scroll of circle of death*.

11 This is the entrance to location 1 of the top floor of Castle Cormanthor (see Chapter 23).

12 This elevated walkway is guarded by a cult archmage, four cult soldier elites, a cult lieutenant, and a cult brigadier. They carry a *Greatsword +4*. It is safe to rest here once they are defeated.

Note

You cannot reach this walkway from the castle's exterior; you must go inside and find the staircase that climbs up to it.

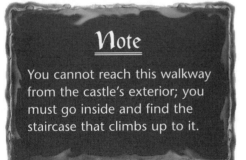

Chapter Twenty-Three

Castle Cormanthor

Castle Cormanthor is occupied by the Cult of the Dragon. It has turned the highest floors into a lair for its dragon-kin allies, created a massive vessel to hold the souls of drow elves and other minions, and summoned a Pool of Radiance in the deepest cavern. The most powerful enemies in the game appear here in large numbers.

In the deepest caverns below Castle Cormanthor await your greatest enemies: Kya Mordrayn and the dracolich, Pelendralaar. The time to conquer the Cult of the Dragon is now, and all of Faerûn is counting on you.

Quick Overview

Top Floor

The top floor is a massive lair for the Cult of the Dragon's dragon-kin allies. Dragon-kin are notoriously selfish and greedy creatures, and they like to collect shiny, magical treasures. As a result, a number of unique magical items are scattered throughout the dragon-kin lair.

Middle Floor

This is where the Cult of the Dragon holds its soul vessel, which cultists use to hold the souls of the drow and orog they enslave to their cause. Every enthralled drow and soulless orog the party has faced has a soul trapped in the vessel, and destroying it allows those souls to go to their final rest.

Bottom Floor

This is the cultists' main "thoroughfare." From here, their mages create portals to places all over Myth Drannor. Using these portals, cultists could send strike forces behind the defenses of the inhabitants of Myth Drannor. The creatures inhabiting the Dwarven Dungeons and Elven Catacombs were powerless against a rampaging dracolich that suddenly warped into their back yard.

Pool Cavern

At last, you make your way to the cavern below the castle where Kya Mordrayn summoned a Pool of Radiance. Here she communes with the sapphire of the weave that controls the Mythal. Armed with the Word of Redemption, you can break her hold on the city and force her to face you in combat. But beware, she is a dangerous foe, and when she falls, you have to face her greatest ally: the dracolich Pelendralaar.

Dungeon Master's Notes

Dragon-kin Aerie (Top Floor)

Tip

Castle Cormanthor is the most difficult area in the game. A battle can turn against you very quickly. Stack the odds in your favor by using as many expendable magic items as possible. Drink your potions, use your wands, and equip your +5 arrows. There's nothing to save them for after this.

❶ This is where the party enters from location 11 in the Castle Exterior (see Chapter 22). You are met with the stench of dragon-kin.

❷ Two dragon-kin meet the party here.

3 This elven hall has been converted into a treasure chamber and breeding room for the dragon-kin. A single dragon-kin guards the stairway up to location 12 of the Castle Exterior (see Chapter 22). When the party comes down the ramp into this chamber, the dragon-kin attacks. After you have defeated him, the other seven dragon-kin attack. The party may also trigger combat with the group of seven by clicking on them or moving too close. Scattered about the main room are several healing potions, a number of magic scrolls, valuable gems, a *Dagger* +5, a *Dagger* +4, a *Jeweled Dagger* +2, *Farland's Fabulous Footwear*, *Ethanniel's Sling*, an idolon, a *Quiver of Arrows* +3, a *Large Shield* +1, a *Staff of Harm*, a *Shortbow* +1, a *Handaxe* +1, a *Battleaxe* +3, a suit of *Studded Leather* +2, and plenty of gold.

4 These stairs lead out to location 12 in the Castle Exterior (see Chapter 22).

5 Four dragon-kin feed on the corpse of an arraccat. They attack the party on sight.

6 Two dragon-kin captains, two dragon-kin, a cult lieutenant, a cult brigadier, and a cult archmage watch over the dragon-kin from here. They drop a healing potion and a *Dagger* +5.

> ## Note
> It's easy for the enemies in location 5 and 6 to get involved in this battle. Do not advance your characters—let the dragon-kin come to you. If the other enemies become involved, quickly eliminate their magic users.

7 Two dragon-kin guard the stairs down to location 8 on the middle floor of Castle Cormanthor.

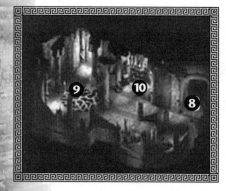

Silverspear Armory (Middle Floor)

8 These stairs lead up to location 7 on the castle's top floor. When your characters stand here, they can feel the torment of the thousands of ghosts still haunting the castle.

9 This is the Cult of the Dragon's soul vessel. The souls of all their undead minions are stored here for some later nefarious purpose. If the party didn't kill Nathlilik, and did release her from her prison in the Castle Passage, she appears to assist the party against the vessel's guards: a cult archmage, a dragon-kin captain, and eight enthralled drow. If you are victorious, Nathlilik destroys the vessel, then kills herself in order to be with her beloved. She leaves behind a *Drow Longbow +4*, a *Drow Shortsword +4*, a *Drow Shield +2*, and a suit of *Drow Chainmail +4*. Find *Dydimm's Ring of False Hope* to the west, beyond the vessel. Stairs under the vessel lead down to location 11 in the bottom floor.

10 There are two locked and trapped chests in this small study. The chest on the right contains *potions of displacement*, *slow*, and *prayer*, and *scrolls of disintegrate* and *raise dead*. The left chest contains a *Wand of Magus*, a *Death's Head Ring*, healing potions, a *potion of bull's strength*, and a note.

Hall of Armanthors (Bottom Floor)

11 The stairs down to this level are built on the remains of thousands of bodies. This is where the citizens who fled to the castle were killed, and their presence still haunts this chamber. The stairs lead up to location 10 on the middle floor.

12 A cult lieutenant and two cult soldier elites patrol back here.

13 Another cult lieutenant and two cult soldier elites attack the party here.

14 Entering the main chamber, the party comes across a number of cult mages maintaining portals. As soon as you approach, the mages and their guards attack. There are three dragon-kin, two dragon-kin captains, three cult overseers, a cult grand overseer, a cult lieutenant, five cult brigadiers, and two cult field marshals. After four rounds, four enthralled drow, two cult mages, two dragon-kin, and a cult archmage show up from behind. When they are all defeated, the party finds a *Wand of Fireballs*, a *Dagger +5*, some potions and gems, a *Ring of Slowing*, a *Ring of Disbelief*, and a *Ring of Hold Person*. The grand overseer has *Dragonbone Talisman*, which summons a portal to location 15 in the Pool Cavern.

Tip

This fight is hard because each opponent is very powerful, and because they are so spread out. Try to disable groups of cultists with *confusion* magic, and keep your cleric out of the thick of battle so that he or she can cast healing spells with impunity. These soldiers are smart enough to run behind your party and attack your magic users; encircle your mages with warriors to keep them safe.

Pool Cavern

15 When they warp in, your characters are met by a cult grand overseer, a cult overseer, a cult archmage, four enthralled drow, four dragon-kin, and a dragon-kin captain. They carry some potions and a *Ring of Protection +4*.

16 This is the Pool of Radiance itself. As the party observes it, the Pool weaves an insidious spell that leads them to consider how they could use it to accomplish good. However, it is only a ploy to distract them for an ambush. If the characters consider the Pool too long, an overwhelmingly large troop of cultists attacks.

After Kya and Pelendralaar have been defeated, a portal appears here. It transports the party to location 7 of the Castle Exterior (see Chapter 22).

17 Kya Mordrayn stands here, lost in the weave and the Mythal. The party cannot harm her, but she does not notice their presence. Walk behind her to the sapphire of the weave, then use the Word of Redemption to summon Miroden, who smashes it. When the sapphire is destroyed, Kya breaks out of her reverie, creates two simulacra, and attacks.

When Kya falls, the demons she made pacts with pull her down to her final fate, leaving behind only the Gauntlets of Moander that she wore. She calls out to Pelendralaar to avenge her, and he immediately breaks through a nearby wall and attacks! In the moment of Kya's defeat, Anorrweyn breaks through the Cult's protections and heals and rejuvenates the party. They'll need it, for Pelendralaar is incredibly deadly.

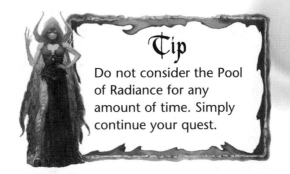

Tip

Do not consider the Pool of Radiance for any amount of time. Simply continue your quest.

Tip

Kya begins the fight by casting *fireball*, *chain lightning*, *cone of cold*, and other damaging magic. This can quickly decimate your party. To prepare for the fight, cast *freedom of movement* (which is actually a preparation to fight Pelendralaar) and *haste* on your warriors, and have only one character approach the sapphire of the weave, leaving the rest in position to attack Kya. She relies on magic, and when she is overwhelmed with fighters, she will fall.

Tip

Pelendralaar is mostly about preparation and diligence. He has very high magic resistance, so the best way to damage him is with weapons, such as the *Baneblade Morvian*. He has a deadly breath weapon that can do more than 100 hit points of damage to your characters, so have your fighters attack him from different sides and spread your characters out so he cannot affect more than one or two characters at a time. *Freedom of movement* helps against his dragon fear, but be prepared to *remove paralysis* and *heal* injured characters. Pelendralaar has more than 800 hit points, so this won't be a quick fight, but if you keep your fighters and cleric alive, you will eventually emerge victorious.

After Pelendralaar and Kya are defeated, the party uses the *Gauntlets of Moander* to destroy the Pool of Radiance and save the Realms. You find *Fau'Bluhdg'Ne*, *Praung*, and *Plaeg* on Pelendralaar, and you are now free to explore the rest of Myth Drannor and complete any quests you missed.

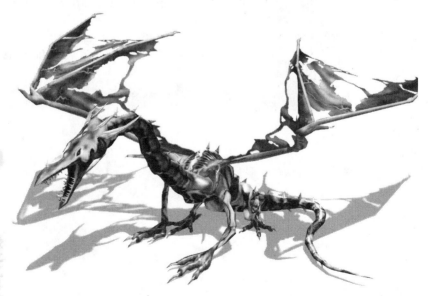

Chapter Twenty-four
Multiplayer

Getting Started

One of the best parts of *Pool of Radiance™: Ruins of Myth Drannor* is the Multiplayer feature. Fight with your friends against hordes of enemies in terrain that is dynamically generated, which means it's rare that you'll play through anything close to the same adventure twice. However, all multiplayer games begin at the same place, so that's where we'll start.

Configuration Menu

The first step is to select Single Player on the game menu to create a new character(s). You can use your characters from the single-player game, but remember that if your characters are of a significantly higher level than those of

your multiplayer allies, it will throw off the game balance.

If one player has high-level characters and another has low-level, the encounters are too easy for the high-level characters, and too hard for the low-level ones. That means the high-level characters will beat all the monsters and help the low-level characters earn experience.

Note

You can take characters from a single-player game into a multiplayer game, but not the other way around. Taking a character into a multiplayer game does not remove him or her from the single-player experience; you can still resume play there any time you want, but experience earned and items gained in multiplayer are not accumulated for use in that single-player game.

The level of the characters in a multiplayer adventure party dynamically determines the game's difficulty. Your characters can be anywhere from 1st level to 32nd level to play on the multiplayer arena. You can control more than one character, but six is the maximum number of characters who can join a multiplayer adventure party.

Joining a Party

Once you create your character, or if you know which character you are going to use, go back to the main menu and select Multiplayer Game. Then select your character's name. Then select Server. If you are playing on a Local Area Network (LAN), then the party leader is the host. Select his or her computer as the server and the party leader will be prompted to

> ### Note
>
> It is possible to play a "multiplayer" game with only one player. Using the multiplayer menu, start the game normally, and keep all the characters assigned to yourself. This is a lot of fun, as you'll quickly beat up random monsters, collect treasure, and advance in levels. Because no story unfolds, the pace is quicker than in the single-player game, and you'll accumulate experience more quickly.

let you join the party. Select the character you want to play from your list of characters and then wait for the host to add your character to the party.

If you are the host of the game, select Player Character to add to the slot. The Character Arbitration menu pops up, allowing the host to see the stats of the characters. Once you approve of the characters, select Locked and then add them to your party. This prevents other players in your party from changing characters or character stats. To start a multiplayer game, human players must occupy all six character slots in the host's party (less than six people can play, but they'll have to control more than one character) Computer controlled characters cannot be substituted.

Playing a Multiplayer Game

All Multiplayer games begin on the same maps: Nightingale Court (easiest), Windrider Glade (more difficult), Speculum Grounds (medium), and Castle Cormanthor (very hard). Each of these maps has entrances to dungeons of varying difficultly levels. Each door to a dungeon is color coded: red is the hardest, yellow is difficult, and green is easy.

Each dungeon is 2–5 levels deep and contains a major boss encounter near the end of it. You find more valuable treasure after defeating the boss. A portal also opens up, allowing your party to return to the surface.

Multiplayer Strategies and Tactics

Tip

Remember that you can transfer treasure, weapons, armor, and magic (assuming that there aren't any class restrictions on the magic) between party members just as in the single-player version.

Pay attention to when it is your turn! Nothing will annoy your other party members faster than having to prompt you to take your turn.

✤ Explore the aboveground areas first. Each aboveground area contains a chest or two with some minor treasure in it to help you get started. See the maps at the end of this chapter for where each chest is located and where the entrances to each dungeon are found.

✤ Use the chat bar at the bottom by moving your mouse over it and then typing. Coordinate your strategy with your party members if you can't talk to them directly.

✤ Remember that XP is divided evenly once a battle is completed, so don't jump into battle prematurely, without properly configuring the party for battle.

Tip

There are two Nottles on each map, allowing the party to trade as they please. Keep in mind that a Nottle carries more than 96 unique magic items that haven't been previously seen in all your adventures through the single-player game. Thus, it pays to trade!

253

Multiplayer Maps

⇩ Location of each dungeon entrance　Ⓧ Location of each treasure chest

Multiplayer Nightingale Court

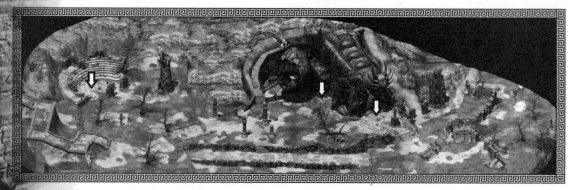

Multiplayer Speculum Grounds

Multiplayer Windrider Glade

Multiplayer Castle Cormanthor, where the great challenges exist

255

PART THREE
The Appendices

Appendix A: Magic Items

Under the "Where Found" column in the following tables, the first number represents the chapter number, and the second number represents the location number. For example, 18-24 is Chapter 18, location 24.

Key for "Usable By" Column

Ba: Barbarian	**Mo:** Monk	**Ro:** Rogue
Cl: Cleric	**Pa:** Paladin	**So:** Sorcerer
Fi: Fighter	**Ra:** Ranger	

Melee Weapons
Axes

Name	Enchantment	Base Damage	Crit Range	Crit Multiplier	Usable By	Where Found
Artoth's Bane	+5, Double Damage, Cast *Hold Person* Level 20	1d8	18–20	3	Fi, Ba, Ra, Pa	18-24
Axe of the Phoenix	+4 to Hit, +2 Damage, Very Light	1d12	20	3	Fi, Ba, Ra, Pa	15-17
Battleaxe	up to +5	1d8	20	3	Fi, Ba, Ra, Pa	Common
Greataxe	up to +5	1d12	20	3	Fi, Ba, Ra, Pa	Common
Handaxe	up to +4	1d6	20	3	Fi, Ba, Ra, Pa	Common
Headsplitter	+5, STR +2	1d6	18–20	3	Fi, Ba, Ra, Pa	19-51
Helm Cleaver	+4, STR +3	1d12	20	3	Fi, Ba, Ra, Pa	9-32
Hextor's Vengeance	+2, Reflex Saving Throws +6	1d8	20	3	Fi, Ba, Ra, Pa	7-11
Meat Cleaver	+2, +4 vs. Orc and Orog, STR +1	1d6	20	3	Fi, Ba, Ra, Pa	18-17
Ritual Battleaxe of Blessing	+1, Cast *Bless* Level 15	1d8	20	3	Fi, Ba, Ra, Pa	6-94
Silverleaf Hatchet	+2, +3 vs. Orcs and Orogs, Protection vs. Orcs and Orogs +1	1d6	20	3	Fi, Ba, Ra, Pa	11-25

257

Name	Enchantment	Base Damage	Crit Range	Crit Multiplier	Usable By	Where Found
Wroth's Executioner	+5, +7 vs. Humanoids, STR +2, INT -6, Fortitude Saving Throws +4, Reflex Saving Throws +1, Cast *Bestow Curse* Level 10	1d8	18–20	3	Fi, Ba, Ra, Pa	18-24

Clubs

Name	Enchantment	Base Damage	Crit Range	Crit Multiplier	Usable By	Where Found
Brewmaster's Cudgel	Triple Damage Vs. Undead	1d6	20	2	All	9-23
Club	Up to +5	1d6	20	2	All	Common
Fau'Bluhdg'Ne	+6, DEX +4, CHA -4, Fortitude Saving Throws +1, Willpower Saving Throws -1, Cast *Cloudkill* Level 15	1d6	18–20	3	All	23-17
Hextor's Cruelty	+2, Will Saving Throws +6	1d6	20	2	All	6-11
Massive Club +3	+3, Double Damage	1d6	20	2	All	6-33
Mountain Fist	+2, +5 vs. Constructs, STR +1	1d6	20	2	All	8-55
Samigel's Dead Slayer	+4, +7 vs. Undead, Reflex Saving Throws +1, Cast *Protection from Evil* Level 5	1d6	18–20	3	All	19-68

Daggers

Name	Enchantment	Base Damage	Crit Range	Crit Multiplier	Usable By	Where Found
Ancient Dwarven Ceremonial Dagger	+1, +2 vs. Orcs and Orogs	1d4	19–20	2	All	6-14
Blunted Dagger of Armor	-2, AC +5	1d4	19–20	2	All	6-99
Boghurst's Putrefication	Cast *Bestow Curse* Level 10	1d4	19–20	2	All	7-28
Borea's Blood	+2, Protection +4, Cast *Cone of Cold* Level 15	1d4	19–20	2	All	8-17

NAME	ENCHANTMENT	BASE DAMAGE	CRIT RANGE	CRIT MULTIPLIER	USABLE BY	WHERE FOUND
DAGGER	Up to +5	1d4	19–20	3	All	Common
DAGGER OF ANGELS	+5, CON +1, Cast *Raise Dead* Level 10	1d4	19–20	2	All	18-33
DAGGER OF DEFENSE	Cast *Mage Armor* Level 5	1d4	19–20	2	All	7-2A
DAGGER OF MAGUS	+3, CON -1, INT +3, Cast *Searing Light* Level 10	1d4	19–20	2	All	18-11, 19-47
DAGGER OF RITUAL	+3, +5 vs. Undead	1d4	19–20	2	All	13-3
DAGGER OF WARDING	Cast *Protection from Evil* Level 5	1d4	19–20	2	All	17-61
DELVENDOOR'S CHISEL	+4, +5 vs. Constructs, STR +1	1d4	18–20	3	All	18-19
DEXTROUS DAGGER	+5, DEX +2, Reflex Saving Throws +2	1d4	19–20	2	All	In Nottle's equipment for sale to 14th
DROW ASSASSIN'S DAGGER	Increased Base Damage	2d4+3	15–20	3	All	16-84
DROW CEREMONIAL DAGGER	Cast *Hold Person* Level 20	1d4+6	17–20	2	All	16-83
DROW DAGGER	Up to +5	1d4	18–20	2	All	16-80, 16-91, 19-105
DRUUL'S KISS	+5, CHA -4, Cast *Poison* Level 10	1d5+2	18—20	3	All	17-83
INFERNO KNIFE	+3, Cast *Burning Hands* Level 5	1d4	19–20	2	All	9-47
JEWELED DAGGER	+2 or +3	1d4	19–20	2	All	6-24, 14-7
JEWELED DWARVEN DAGGER—ORCKILLER	+1, Double Damage vs. Orcs and Orogs	1d4	19–20	2	All	6-121
MARSHBANE DAGGER	+2, Triple Damage vs. Reptiles	1d4	19–20	2	All	9-1
MOONSPLINTER	+5, AC +1, All Saving Throws +1, Init +1, Spell Resistance +13, Cast *Globe of Invulnerability* Level 15	1d4	18–20	3	All	18-23
OBSIDIAN EDGE	+3, Spell Resistance +7	1d4	19–20	2	All	11-12
THOGGUA'S TOOTH	+4, STR +2, DEX -1, Cast *Cloudkill* Level 15	1d4	19–20	2	All	19-106
VENOM	+5, Double Damage, Cast *Web* Level 5	1d4	18–20	3	All	19-63

259

Hammers

Name	Enchantment	Base Damage	Crit Range	Crit Multiplier	Usable By	Where Found
Dwarven Great Warhammer of Death	+2, +5 vs. Undead	1d10	19–20	2	Fi, Ba, Ra, Pa	6-14
Great Warhammer	up to +5	1d10	19–20	2	Fi, Ba, Ra, Pa	17-53
Hammer Veneficus	+5, All Saving Throws +2, Cast *Dispel Magic* Level 10	1d8	18–20	3	Fi, Ba, Ra, Pa, Cl	21-37
Hammer of Justice	+1, +3 vs. Undead, Double Damage vs. Undead	1d8	20	3	Fi, Ba, Ra, Pa, Cl	16-36
Hammer of Martel	1	1d10	17–20	2	Fi, Ba, Ra, Pa	7-59
Hammer of Splintering	+1, +3 to Hit vs. Humanoid, Double Damage vs. Humanoid	1d8	20	3	Fi, Ba, Ra, Pa, Cl	9-92
Hextor's Might	+2, Fortitude Saving Throws +6	1d10	19–20	2	Fi, Ba, Ra, Pa	7-11
Light Hammer	up to +5	1d6	20	3	Fi, Ba, Ra, Pa, Cl	Common
Miners' Great Warhammer	Double Damage	1d10	19–20	2	Fi, Ba, Ra, Pa	6-108
Morolith	+6, STR +2, Cast *Cloudkill* Level 15	1d10	19–20	2	Fi, Ba, Ra, Pa	19-24
Sunderstone	+4, +7 vs. Constructs, STR +2, INT -2, Cast *Remove Paralysis* Level 5	1d10	18–20	3	Fi, Ba, Ra, Pa	18-27
Warhammer	up to +4	1d8	20	3	Fi, Ba, Ra, Pa, Cl	Common
Warhammer of Death	+2, Cast *Poison* Level 10	1d8	20	3	Fi, Ba, Ra, Pa, Cl	6-33, on Mol's shaman, can't retrieve
Wings of Diabolicus	+2, Cast *Slay Living* Level 15	1d10	19–20	2	Cl	7-14

Maces

Name	Enchantment	Base Damage	Crit Range	Crit Multiplier	Usable By	Where Found
ASTERFELLON– MACE OF POWER	+6, DEX -2, WIS +3, Willpower Saving Throws +1, Cast *Divine Power* Level 10	1d6	20	2	All	18-25
CRYPT CLEANSER	+4 vs. Undead, Protection from Undead +4, Cast *Control Undead* Level 20	1d6	18–20	2	All	16-29
DROW MACE	up to +5	1d6	18–20	2	All	19-37
LIGHT MACE	up to +5	1d6	20	2	All	Common
ORCISH LEAD MACE	-2 to Hit, +6 Damage	1d8	20	2	All	6-34
SILVERLEAF ROD	+2, +3 vs. Orcs and Orogs, Protection vs. Orcs and Orogs +1	1d6	20	3	All	11-25
WINGS OF DOMINION	+2, Cast *Raise Dead* Level 15	1d8	20	2	All	7-65

Polearms

Name	Enchantment	Base Damage	Crit Range	Crit Multiplier	Usable By	Where Found
HALBERD	up to +5	1d10	20	3	Fi, Ba, Ra, Pa	Common
HALBERD OF VIGILANCE	+2, AC +2, Init +2	1d10	20	3	Fi, Ba, Ra, Pa	9-58
THE ILRAZOR OF SHOLG'GLIATH	+6, STR +2, DEX -2, Fortitude Saving Throws +1, Cast *Harm* Level 15	1d10	18–20	3	Fi, Ba, Ra, Pa	19-26

Spears

Name	Enchantment	Base Damage	Crit Range	Crit Multiplier	Usable By	Where Found
DAWNPIKE	+4, +6 vs. Light Sensitive and Undead, Reflex Saving Throws +3, Willpower Saving Throws +2, Fortitude Saving Throws -4, Cast *Searing Light* Level 5	1d10	18–20	3	Fi, Ba, Ra, Pa	17-4
DEATHSPIKE, SPEAR OF SKEWERING	+2 to Hit, Triple Damage	1d8	17–20	5	All	5-14
LERAJA'S SPEAR	+2, +5 vs. Gargoyles	1d8	20	3	All	9-81
LIBERTAS	+2, Willpower Saving Throws +3, Cast *Freedom of Movement* Level 10	1d10	20	3	Fi, Ba, Ra, Pa	7-51
LONGSPEAR	up to +5	1d8	20	3	Fi, Ba, Ra, Pa	Common
PIGSTICKER	+3, +5 vs. Orc and Orog, STR +1	1d10	20	3	Fi, Ba, Ra, Pa	19-51
PIKE	up to +5	1d10	20	3	Fi, Ba, Ra, Pa	Common
SPEAR OF STABBING	+3	1d8	20	3	Fi, Ba, Ra, Pa	6-126

Staffs

Name	Enchantment	Base Damage	Crit Range	Crit Multiplier	Usable By	Where Found
DEATHBANE	Cast *Heal* Level 20	1d6	20	2	All	6-17
DWARVEN CEREMONIAL STAFF	+1 vs. Orcs and Orogs, Protection from Magic +2	1d6	20	2	All	6-95
LUTHER'S PROTECTOR	+3, Init +3	1d6	20	2	Mo	8-67
QUARTERSTAFF	up to +5	1d6	20	2	All	Common
RODERICK'S WALKING STICK	Fires Poisonous Missiles	1d6	20	2	All	11-16

Name	Enchantment	Base Damage	Crit Range	Crit Multiplier	Usable By	Where Found
STAFF OF DARKNESS	+1, Cast *Darkness* Level 5	1d6	20	2	So	16-80
STAFF OF DEADLY SPLINTERS	+5, Cast *Harm* Level 15	1d6	18–20	3	Ra, Cl, Pa	18-53
STAFF OF FIRESTORMS	+3, Cast *Firestorm* Level 20	1d6	20	2	Ra, Cl, Pa	16-19
STAFF OF FLAME	+4, Cast *Flame Strike* Level 15	1d6	20	2	Ra, Cl, Pa	16-4
STAFF OF FLAME STRIKE	Cast *Flame Strike* Level 20	1d6	20	2	Ra, Cl, Pa	6-126
STAFF OF HALT UNDEAD	Cast *Halt Undead* Level 20	1d6	20	2	So	6-81, 16-45
STAFF OF HARM	+3, Cast *Harm* Level 15	1d6	20	2	Ra, Cl, Pa	19-55, 23-3
TALISMAN STAFF	INT +1	1d6	20	2	All	15-11
THE GUULSTAV OF M'RAELHORRID	+5, STR -3, INT +3, Willpower Saving Throws +3, Cast *Circle of Death* Level 15	2d6	18–20	3	So	19-107
THE SACRED STAFF OF SUNLIGHT	+7 vs. Drow, Triple Damage vs. Drow, AC +7 vs. Drow, All Saving Throws +7 vs. Drow, Init +7 vs. Drow, Spell Resistance +7 vs. Drow, Cast *Searing Light* Level 20	3d6	19–20	2	Ra, Cl, Pa	18-83
THYAAST'S STAFF	+5, STR -2, CON +2, All Saving Throws +1, Cast *Resurrection* Level 15	1d6	20	2	Ra, Cl, Pa	18-10

Longswords

Name	Enchantment	Base Damage	Crit Range	Crit Multiplier	Usable By	Where Found
DROW LONGSWORD	up to +5 +3, Cast	1d8	18–20	2	Fi, Ba, Ra, Pa	19-33
FLAME BLADE	*Flame Strike* Level 15	1d8	19–20	2	Fi, Ba, Ra, Pa, Cl	15-16

263

NAME	ENCHANTMENT	BASE DAMAGE	CRIT RANGE	CRIT MULTIPLIER	USABLE BY	WHERE FOUND
LONGSWORD	up to +5	1d8	19–20	2	Fi, Ba, Ra, Pa	Common
PUREBLADE	+1, +3 vs. Undead	1d8	19–20	2	Fi, Ba, Ra, Pa	7-4
RAVENSONG	+5, DEX +2, Reflex Saving Throws +2, Willpower Saving Throws -3, Cast *Feeblemind* Level 10	1d8	19–20	2	Fi, Ba, Ra, Pa	19-108
SWORD OF FIREBRAND	+3, Cast *Burning Hands* Level 5	1d8	19–20	2	Fi, Ba, Ra, Pa	9-26
SWORD OF VENGEANCES	+3, +5 vs. Evil, CON +2, WIS -5	1d8	19–20	2	Fi, Ba, Ra, Pa	In Bronwyn's equipment at 16th level
BANEBLADE FAERVIAN	+3, +6 vs. Drow, AC +3, Cast *Flame Strike* Level 15	1d8	19–20	2	Fi, Ba, Ra, Pa	19-24
VALAMIR'S SLAYER	+5, CON +2, Spell Resistance +5, Cast *Slay Living* Level 15	1d8	18–20	3	Fi, Ba, Ra, Pa	18-26
WOUNDWULF	+5, STR +2, Fortitude Saving Throws +1, Cast *Vampiric Touch* Level 10	1d8	18–20	3	Fi, Ba, Ra, Pa	18-14

Shortswords

NAME	ENCHANTMENT	BASE DAMAGE	CRIT RANGE	CRIT MULTIPLIER	USABLE BY	WHERE FOUND
BACKSTABBER	+4 to Hit, +2 Damage, DEX +2	1d6	19–20	2	Fi, Ba, Ra, Ro, Pa	Carried by Tudo
BLADE OF LARCENY	+2, DEX +2	1d6	18–20	2	Ro	8-5
BLADE OF VENOM	Increased Base Damage	1d6+3	19–20	2	Fi, Ba, Ra, Ro, Pa	8-64

Name	Enchantment	Base Damage	Crit Range	Crit Multiplier	Usable By	Where Found
DRAKULWYNG	+4, STR +1, CON -2, CHA +2, Fortitude Saving Throws +1, Cast *Vampiric Touch* Level 10	1d6	18–20	2	Fi, Ba, Ra, Ro, Pa	19-26
DROW SHORTSWORD	up to +5	1d6	18–20	2	Fi, Ba, Ra, Ro, Pa	16-10, 16-81, 19-33
PRAUNG	+7, STR +3, DEX +3, CON -5, Fortitude Saving Throw +1, Reflex Saving Throws +1, Willpower Saving Throws -3, Cast *Resurrection* Level 5	1d6	18–20	3	Fi, Ba, Ra, Ro, Pa	23-17
SCIMITAR	up to +5	1d6	18–20	2	Fi, Ba, Ra, Ro, Pa	Common
SCIMITAR OF SLAYING	+3, STR +2	1d6	18–20	2	Fi, Ba, Ra, Ro, Pa	16-36
SHADOWHISPER	+5, All Saving Throws +3, Cast *Improved Invisibility* Level 10	1d6	18–20	3	Fi, Ba, Ra, Ro, Pa	18-24
SHORTSWORD	up to +5	1d6	19–20	2	Fi, Ba, Ra, Ro, Pa	Common
SOUL BITER	+2, Strength Stealing Touch	1d6	19–20	2	Fi, Ba, Ra, Ro, Pa	9-19
THE GREAT KNIFE OF SHYDE	+4, STR +2, DEX -2, Willpower Saving Throws +1, Cast *Searing Light* Level 5	2d6	18–20	2	Fi, Ba, Ra, Ro, Pa	16-92
THE WINTER BLADE	+2, Protection +2, Cast *Cone of Cold* Level 10	1d6	19–20	2	Fi, Ba, Ra, Ro, Pa	8-1

Two-Handed Swords

Name	Enchantment	Base Damage	Crit Range	Crit Multiplier	Usable By	Where Found
BLADE OF DESTRUCTION	+2, Critical Hits Cause Triple Damage	2d6	19–20	3	Fi, Ba, Ra, Pa	13-21
GREATSWORD	up to +5	2d6	19–20	2	Fi, Ba, Ra, Pa	Common

Name	Enchantment	Base Damage	Crit Range	Crit Multiplier	Usable By	Where Found
GREATSWORD OF FIRE	+1, Cast *Burning Hands* Level 5	2d6	19–20	2	Fi, Ba, Ra, Pa	6-81
SWORD OF MARSHBANE	+1, +4 vs. Reptiles	2d6	19–20	2	Fi, Ba, Ra, Pa	9-18
THE BANEBLADE MORVIAN	+5, +7 vs. Dragonkind, Spell Resistance +20, Cast *Firestorm* Level 20	2d6	19–20	2	Fi, Ba, Ra, Pa	21-5
THE DRAEDSWORD DAEMONIAC	+6, STR +4, DEX +2, Reflex Saving Throws +2, Willpower Saving Throws -3, Cast *Destruction* Level 20	4d6+6	17–20	3	Fi, Ba, Ra, Pa	19-20
TWILIGHT GUARDIAN	+2, +14 Magic Resistance vs. Orcs and Orogs	2d6	19–20	2	Fi, Ba, Ra, Pa	7-34
THE DAEMONCLAWS OF GR'ZAK	+5, Double Damage, AC +3, STR +3, WIS -3, Cast *Inflict Critical Wounds* Level 10	2d6+2	18–20	3	All	19-24

Ranged Weapons
Longbows

Name	Enchantment	Base Damage	Crit Range	Crit Multiplier	Usable By	Where Found
ARROWFLIGHT OF ANGELS	+5, CON +2, Cast *Resurrection* Level 15	1d8	18–20	3	Fi, Ba, Ra, Pa	18-33
BLOODBOW	+4, Cast *Slay Living* Level 10	1d8	18–20	3	Fi, Ba, Ra, Pa	16-36
LONGBOW	up to +5	1d8	20	3	Fi, Ba, Ra, Pa	Common
PRINCE ANTONAE'S STORMBOW	+5, Double Damage, STR -3, DEX +3, Reflex Saving Throws +1, Cast *Lightning Bolt* Level 10	1d8	18–20	3	Fi, Ba, Ra, Pa	18-83
SEETHRE'S TONGUE	+5, DEX +1, CHA -3, Cast *Melf's Acid Arrow* Level 10	1d8	19–20	3	Fi, Ba, Ra, Pa	19-26

Shortbows

Name	Enchantment	Base Damage	Crit Range	Crit Multiplier	Usable By	Where Found
Bow of Accuracy	+3 to Hit	1d6	20	3	Fi, Ba, Ra, Ro, Pa	10-10
Drow Shortbow	up to +5	1d6	19–20	3	Fi, Ba, Ra, Ro, Pa	19-32
Jaws of Malice	-1 to Hit, Damage +3	1d6	17–0	3	Fi, Ba, Ra, Ro, Pa	8-24
Plaeg	+6, STR -3, DEX +4, Reflex Saving Throws +2, Cast *Flame Strike* Level 15	2d6	18–20	3	Fi, Ba, Ra, Ro, Pa	23-17
Shortbow	up to +4	1d6	20	3	Fi, Ba, Ra, Ro, Pa	Common

Slings

Name	Enchantment	Base Damage	Crit Range	Crit Multiplier	Usable By	Where Found
Ethanniel's Sling	+5, DEX +2, Reflex Saving Throws +2, Cast *Magic Missile* Level 5	1d4	18–20	3	All	23-3
Sling	up to +4	1d4	20	2	All	Common
Sling of Striking	+6, STR +4	2d4	20	2	All	In Kellan's equipment

Armor
Armor

Name	Enchantment	Base AC Bonus	Max Dex Bonus	Dex Check Penalty	Spell Failure	Location	Usable By	Where Found
Arcane Mail	AC +2, Movement -20	8	1	-6	0	Torso	All	13-21
Armor of Shadows	AC +3, Init +2, Spell Resistance +12	2	6	0	10	Torso	All	16-36

Name	Enchantment	Base AC Bonus	Max Dex Bonus	Dex Check Penalty	Spell Failure	Location	Usable By	Where Found
Burnished Dwarven Plate Mail +1	AC +1, Movement -20	7	+0	-7	40	Torso	All	6-88
Chainmail	up to AC +5, Movement -20	5	2	-5	30	Torso	All	Common
Drow Chainmail	up to AC +5, Movement -15	5	3	-3	15	Torso	All	16-10, 16-80
Drow Spidersilk Armor	DEX +2, Reflex Saving Throws +2, Movement -5, Cast *Web* Level 5	11	5	-1	5	Torso	All	19-63
Full Plate	up to AC +5, Movement -20	8	1	-6	35	Torso	All	Common
Girdle of Serenity	AC +2, Protection +6	2	6	0	10	Torso	All	9-50
Half-Plate	up to +2, Movement -20	7	0	-7	40	Torso	All	Common
Holy Armor	AC +3, All Saving Throws +3, Movement -20, Cast *Prayer* Level 15	5	2	-5	40	Torso	All	In Eadred's equipment at 12th &15th level
Leather Armor	up to AC +5	2	6	0	10	Torso	All	Common
Miners' Burnished Light Plate of Protection	All Saving Throws +3, Init +3, Movement -10	8	1	-6	35	Torso	All	6-108
Nezras' Mysterious Chainmail	AC +5, DEX +3, WIS -3, Reflex Saving Throw +2, Willpower Saving Throw -2, Movement -10, Cast *Blink* Level 15	5	3	-4	20	Torso	All	18-21
Olortynnal's Heartmail	AC +4, +5 Damage vs. Dragonkind, Movement -20	7, 7	+0	-7	40	Torso	All	15-20
Quimbee's Armor of Many Pockets	AC +4, +100 Weight Limit	2	6	0	10	Torso	All	16-92
Ravenskin	AC +6, STR -1, DEX +2, CHA +1, Fortitude Saving Throws -1, Reflex Saving Throws +1, Movement -10, Cast *Improved Invisibility* Level 10	5	3	-3	20	Torso	All	19-24

Name	Enchantment	Base AC Bonus	Max Dex Bonus	Dex Check Penalty	Spell Failure	Location	Usable By	Where Found
Reptilian Scale Mail +3	AC +3, Movement -20	4	3	-4	25	Torso	All	6-46
Ring Mail	up to AC +2	4	3	-2	20	Torso	All	Common
Sacred Vestments	AC +2, WIS +1, Spell Resistance +7	2	6	0	10	Torso	All	7-48
Studded Leather	up to AC +2	3	5	-1	15	Torso	All	6-73
The Wraithmael of Drenofiend	AC +6, STR +3, INT -2, Fortitude Saving Throws +2, Reflex Saving Throws -3, Willpower Saving Throws +1, Movement -20, Cast Fear Level 20	8	1	-6	35	Torso	All	19-39
Victoria's Leather Corset*	AC +5, CHA +6, Fortitude Saving Throws -2, Cast Domination Level 15	2	7	0	5	Torso	All	18-33
Vulcan Mail	AC +4, Protection +6, Movement -20, Cast Burning Hands Level 5	8	1	-6	35	Torso	All	18-5
Windswept Armor	AC +2, Protection from Gargoyles +4, Movement -20	7	+0	-7	40	Torso	All	9-75

* There is a 5% chance of spell failure.

Gauntlets

Name	Enchantment	Location	Usable By	Where Found
Dymon's Dutiful Gloves	Reflex Saving Throws +4, Cast Haste Level 10	Forearms	All	8-6
Fists of Ranman	+4 Damage	Forearms	Mo	6-25
Gauntlets of Destruction	Cast Destruction Level 20	Forearms	All	19-49
Gauntlets of Dexterity	DEX +1	Forearms	All	6-17

269

Name	Enchantment	Location	Usable By	Where Found
Gauntlets of Light Burden	AC +1, +10 Weight Limit	Forearms	All	15-5
Gauntlets of Necromancy	WIS +3, Willpower Saving Throws +1, Protection from Undead +4, Cast *Halt Undead* Level 15	Forearms	All	18-50
Gauntlets of Ogre Power	STR +2	Forearms	All	8-30
Gauntlets of Ogre Size	AC +2, -5 to Hit Throws +4, Cast *Bull's Strength* Level 10	Forearms	All	13-20
Gloves of Courage	CON +1, Fortitude Saving	Forearms	All	9-66
Gloves of Steadiness	+2 to Hit	Forearms	All	9-89
Gloves of the Archmage	AC +4, INT +1	Forearms	All	9-32
Ildacer's Satin Gloves	CHA +4, Cast *Improved Invisibility* Level 20	Forearms	All	15-20
Theodore's Gloves of Kinship	CHA +2, Init +2, Cast *Charm Monster* Level 10	Forearms	All	18-18
Thundergrip	+2 Damage, Cast *Shocking Grasp* Level 20	Forearms	All	8-24
Victoria's Gloves of Electric Touch	STR +2, Willpower Saving Throws +1, Cast *Shocking Grasp* Level 10	Forearms	All	18-33

Boots

Name	Enchantment	Location	Usable By	Where Found
Bernard's Unforgivable Boots	CHA -2, Movement +10, Cast *Stinking Cloud* Level 10	Feet	All	19-49
Boots of Grace	DEX +1, Reflex Saving Throws +1, Movement +5, Cast *Cat's Grace* Level 5	Feet	All	17-83
Boots of Health	AC +2, CON +1, Movement +10	Feet	All	6-73
Boots of High Wisdom	WIS +3	Feet	All	6-100
Boots of Mobility	Movement +10	Feet	All	7-32
Boots of Stalking	Movement +10, Cast *Invisibility* Level 10	Feet	All	16-21

Name	Enchantment	Location	Usable By	Where Found
BOOTS OF WITHERING BEAUTY	STR -1, CON -1, CHA +4, Movement +10	Feet	All	6-127
BOOTS OF THE TORTOISE	AC +2, All Saving Throws +2, Movement -20	Feet	All	13-20
DROW BOOTS OF DISPLACEMENT	Movement +5, Cast *Displacement* Level 10	Feet	All	16-87
FARLIAND'S FABULOUS FOOTWEAR	CON +3, CHA -2, Willpower Saving Throws +1, Cast *Heal* Level 20	Feet	All	23-3
LENORE'S SANCTUARY	Protection from Undead +4, Movement +10	Feet	All	8-28
MAGICIAN'S BOOTS	DEX +2, CHA +2, Movement +30	Feet	All	6-36
SNAKESKIN BOOTS	+2 vs. Reptiles, AC +2 vs. Reptiles, Double Damage vs. Reptiles, Protection +6	Feet	All	6-116
VICTORIA'S BOOTS OF BEGUILING GAIT	DEX +2, Reflex Saving Throws +2, Movement +10, Cast *Displacement* Level 10	Feet	All	18-33

Shields
Large Shields

Name	Enchantment	Base AC Bonus	Dex Check Penalty	Spell Failure %	Location	Usable By	Where Found
ANCIENT DWARVEN SHIELD OF PROTECTION +1	AC +1, Saving Throws +1	2	-2	15	Left Hand	Fi, Ba, Ra, Pa, Cl	6-97
FALDIS'S DEFENDER	AC +3, Init +3	2	-2	15	Left Hand	Fi, Ba, Ra, Pa, Cl	8-31
LARGE SHIELD	up to AC +4	2	-2	15	Left Hand	Fi, Ba, Ra, Pa, Cl	Common

Name	Enchantment	Base AC Bonus	Dex Check Penalty	Spell Failure %	Location	Usable By	Where Found
Miners' Ward of Invulnerability	AC +1, Cast *Minor Globe of Invulnerability* Level 15	2	-2	15	Left Hand	Fi, Ba, Ra, Pa, Cl	6-108
Runic Shield	AC +2	2	-2	5	Left Hand	Fi, Ba, Ra, Pa, Cl, So	8-42
Shield of House Stayrm	AC +3, INT +3, WIS +3	2	-2	15	Left Hand	Fi, Ba, Ra, Pa, Cl	15-20
Shield of Purity	AC +3, All Saving Throws +1	2	-2	15	Left Hand	Fi, Ba, Ra, Pa, Cl	16-36, 16-45
Spellfoil	AC +5, All Saving Throws +1, Protection from Undead +4, Cast *Silence* Level 10	2	-2	15	Left Hand	Fi, Ba, Ra, Pa, Cl	19-62
Sylmorrir–Shield of Power	AC +6, DEX +3, CON -2, Fortitude Saving Throws -1, Reflex Saving Throws +2, Cast *Shield of Faith* Level 15	2	-1	10	Left Hand	Fi, Ba, Ra, Pa, Cl	21-37
The Wraithmael Shield	AC +6, CON +3, -WIS 2, Fortitude Saving Throws +3, Willpower Saving Throws +2, Cast *Vampiric Touch* Level 15	3	-2	10	Left Hand	Fi, Ba, Ra, Pa, Cl	19-114

Small Shields

Name	Enchantment	Base AC Bonus	Dex Check Penalty	Spell Failure %	Location	Usable By	Where Found
Lancer's Guard	AC +3, STR +2, CON +2	1	-1	5	Left Hand	Fi, Ba, Ra, Pa, Cl	15-20

Name	Enchantment	Base AC Bonus	Dex Check Penalty	Spell Failure %	Location	Usable By	Where Found
Nightshade	AC +4, CON -2, Reflex Saving Throws +1, Cast *Improved Invisibiliy* Level 10	1	0	0	Left Hand	Fi, Ba, Ra, Pa, Cl	16-55
Ricimer's Barrier	AC +2, +3 to Hit	1	-1	5	Left Hand	Fi, Ba, Ra, Pa, Cl	14-11
Small Shields	up to AC +4	1	-1	5	Left Hand	Fi, Ba, Ra, Pa, Cl	Common
Stalwart Shield	AC +2, Fortitude Saving Throws +3	1	-1	5	Left Hand	Fi, Ba, Ra, Pa, Cl	15-10

Consumables
Arrows

Name	Enchantment	Usable By	Where Found
Arrows of Dire Flatulence	+3 to Hit, Cast *Stinking Cloud* Level 10	Fi, Ba, Ra, Ro, Pa	16-47
Drow Quiver of Arrows	up to +3	Fi, Ba, Ra, Ro, Pa	18-57
Drow Quiver of Assassin's Arrows	+2, Double Damage	Fi, Ba, Ra, Ro, Pa	19-23
Quiver of Arrows	up to +5	Fi, Ba, Ra, Ro, Pa	Common
Quiver of Arrows of Second Death	+5 vs. Undead, Double Damage vs. Undead	Fi, Ba, Ra, Ro, Pa	18-51
Quiver of Arrows of Speed	-1 to Hit, +3 Damage	Ro	8-5

Potions and Salves

Name	Enchantment	Usable By	Where Found
POTION OF BLINK	Cast *Blink* Level 15	All	Common
POTION OF BULL'S STRENGTH	Cast *Strength* Level 20	All	Common
POTION OF CAT'S GRACE	Cast *Cat's Grace* Level 5	All	Common
POTION OF CRITICAL HEALING	Cast *Cure Critical Wounds* Level 20	All	Common
POTION OF CURE BLINDNESS	Cast *Cure Blindness* Level 10	All	Common
POTION OF DARK NAGA POISON	Cast *Poison* Level 10	All	Common
POTION OF DELAY POISON	Cast *Delay Poison* Level 15	All	Common
POTION OF DISPLACEMENT	Cast *Displacement* Level 10	All	Common
POTION OF FREEDOM OF MOVEMENT	Cast *Freedom of Movement* Level 10	All	19-63
POTION OF FULL HEALING	Cast *Heal* Level 20	All	Common
POTION OF GLOBE OF INVULNERABILITY	Cast *Globe of Invulnerability* Level 15	All	Common
POTION OF HASTE	Cast *Haste* Level 10	All	Common
POTION OF HOLD POISON	Cast *Hold Poison* Level 10	All	Common
POTION OF IMPROVED INVISIBILITY	Cast *Improved Invisibility* Level 10	All	19-23
POTION OF INVISIBILITY	Cast *Invisibility* Level 5	All	Common
POTION OF LIGHT HEALING	Cast *Cure Light Wounds* Level 5	All	Common
POTION OF MAGE ARMOR	Cast *Mage Armor* Level 5	All	Common
POTION OF MODERATE HEALING	Cast *Cure Moderate Wounds* Level 10	All	Common
POTION OF NEUTRALIZE POISON	Cast *Neutralize Poison* Level 10	All	Common
POTION OF POISON	Cast *Poison* Level 10	All	Common
POTION OF POWER	Cast *Divine Power* Level 15	All	Throughout Ch. 6
POTION OF PRAYER	Cast *Prayer* Level 10	All	23-10
POTION OF PROTECTION FROM POISON	Cast *Protection from Poison* Level 10	All	Common
POTION OF REMOVE FEAR	Cast *Remove Fear* Level 5	All	Common
POTION OF RESTORATION	Cast *Restoration* Level 15	All	Common
POTION OF SERIOUS HEALING	Cast *Cure Serious Wounds* Level 15	All	Common
POTION OF SHIELD OF FAITH	Cast *Shield of Faith* Level 15	All	Common
POTION OF SLEEP	Cast *Sleep* Level 5	All	Common
POTION OF SLOW	Cast *Slow* Level 10	All	Common
POTION OF SPELL RESISTANCE	Cast *Spell Resistance* Level 10	All	Common
POTION OF TRUE SEEING	Cast *True Seeing* Level 20	All	18-33
SALVE OF CRITICAL HEALING	Cast *Cure Critical Wounds* Level 20	All	Common
SALVE OF SERIOUS HEALING	Cast *Cure Serious Wounds* Level 15	All	Common
SALVE OF FULL HEALING	Cast *Heal* Level 20	All	Common
SALVE OF LIGHT HEALING	Cast *Cure Light Wounds* Level 5	All	Common

274

NAME	ENCHANTMENT	USABLE BY	WHERE FOUND
SALVE OF MODERATE HEALING	Cast *Cure Moderate Wounds* Level 10	All	Common
SALVE OF REMOVE PARALYSIS	Cast *Remove Paralysis* Level 20	All	Common
SALVE OF UNDEAD REPAIR	Cast *Inflict Serious Wounds* Level 10	All	18-51

Miscellaneous
Misc.

NAME	ENCHANTMENT	USABLE BY	WHERE FOUND
AASIRAK'S BRAIN	INT +3, Willpower saving throws +2, Cast *Mass Suggestion* Level 15	All	21-33
BEACON OF GRIGORI	DEX +1, WIS -1, Reflex Saving Throws +1, Willpower Saving Throws -2, Cast *Searing Light* Level 5	All	19-25
DROW LAMP OF DARKNESS	Cast *Darkness* Level 5	All	16-89
ELHRAIN'S LANTHORN	Reflex Saving Throws -3, Willpower Saving Throws +4, Cast *Restoration* Level 10	All	17-44
STONE OF THE FATES	CON +1, All Saving Throws +1, Spell Resistance +1	All	21-41

Books

NAME	ENCHANTMENT	USABLE BY	WHERE FOUND
AASIRAK'S BOOK OF DANCING DEAD	+1 Damage vs. Undead, Protection from Undead +4, Cast *Control Undead* Level 20	So, Cl, Mo	16-74
CLERICS' TOME OF TRUTHS	WIS +1, Spell Resistance +10, Init +1, Cast *Prayer* Level 15	Cl	16-55
DRAUDE'S ILLUSTRATED CODEX MALEFICUS	CON -2, Init +1, Cast *Repulsion* Level 15	All	16-61
DROW SPINNAN TRISAGION	Willpower Saving Throws +3, Init +3, Spell Resistance +14, Cast *Restoration* Level 15	Cl	16-83

NAME	ENCHANTMENT	USABLE BY	WHERE FOUND
RANMAN'S MEDITATIONS	+3 to Hit, Double Damage, Init +3	Mo	15-20
SORCERERS' CYCLOPEDIA ILLUMINATI	INT +1, Spell Resistance +12, Cast *True Seeing* Level 20	So	16-55

Rings

NAME	ENCHANTMENT	LOCATION	USABLE BY	WHERE FOUND
AASIRAK'S EBONY TWIN RING OF POWER	AC +5, STR +5, DEX -5, All Saving Throws -5, Init +5, Movement -40, -250 Weight Limit, Cast *Finger of Death* Level 25	Left Finger	All	18-24
AASIRAK'S IVORY TWIN RING OF POWER	AC -5, STR -5, DEX +5, All Saving Throws +5, Init -5, Movement +40, +249 Weight Limit, Cast *Heal* Level 20	Right Finger	All	17-44
ARKNOR'S VILE VOICE	STR +2, CON +3, Cast *Melf's Acid Arrow* Level 18	Finger	All	11-11
BECKON OF KELEMVOR	+3 Damage vs. Undead, Cast *Cure Serious Wounds* Level 15	Finger	All	11-11
BONE OF MYRKUL	Protection -4, Cast *Resurrection* Level 15	Finger	All	11-11
BREATH OF KOSSUTH	Protection +3, Protection from Fear -5, Cast *Flame Strike* Level 15	Finger	All	11-11
BRIGHT BANE OF MELLIFLEUR	+4 Damage vs. Undead, Cast *Searing Light* Level 10	Finger	All	11-11
CEGILUNE'S PERFUME	CHA -2, Cast *Repulsion* Level 20	Finger	All	11-11
CERULEAN RING	WIS +2	Finger	All	12-1
COMBAT RING	STR +1, CON +1, DEX +1	Finger	All	In Emmeric's equipment at 12th and 15th levels
DEATH'S HEAD RING	CON +2, Cast *Raise Dead* Level 10	Finger	All	23-10

Name	Enchantment	Location	Usable By	Where Found
DYDIMM'S RING OF FALSE HOPE	-2 to Hit, -2 Damage, AC -2, CON -3, INT +2, CHA +4, All Saving Throws -1, Init -2, Spell Resistance -6, Cast *Cure Light Wounds* Level 5	Finger	All	23-9
FEATHER OF SHAR	+5 to Hit vs. Light Sensitive, Cast *Divine Power* Level 15	Finger	All	11-11
FIST OF SAINT CUTHBERT	+7 vs. Undead, Protection from Undead +5, Cast *Searing Light* Level 20	Finger	All	11-11
GARRAS' KEEN SIGHT	+7 to Hit, DEX +3, Cast *Cat's Grace* Level 15	Finger	All	11-11
GEARS OF GRUMBAR	Init -3, Spell Resistance -5, Cast *Destruction* Level 15	Finger	All	11-11
GONG OF TYR	Spell Resistance -4, Cast *Disintigrate* Level 10	Finger	So	11-11
GORGOL'S ASYLUM	Protection from Magic +3, Cast *Globe of Invulnerability* Level 15	Finger	So	11-11
LENS OF OGHMA	+4 to Hit, Cast *True Seeing* Level 15	Finger	So	11-11
MILLA'S BLESSING	AC +2, DEX +1, Protection +4	Finger	All	8-12
MISERY'S EMBRACE	Spell Resistance +16, Draining Touch	Finger	All	11-11
OBERON'S AIRY LASH	Init +2, Spell Resistance -4, Cast *Chain Lightning* Level 15	Finger	So	11-11
OLIDAMMARA'S WHISPER	DEX +2, Cast *Invisibility* Level 10	Finger	Ro	11-11
RING OF AZULAR	INT +1, Reflex Saving Throws -1, Willpower Saving Throws +1, Cast *Disintegrate* Level 20	Finger	All	19-24
RING OF BATTENING	+5 to Hit, Init +4, Spell Resistance -5, Cast *Vampiric Touch* Level 15	Finger	So	11-11
RING OF BLESSING	Cast *Bless* Level 10	Finger	All	18-29
RING OF BRUTE STRENGTH	STR +3, INT -1, WIS -2	Finger	All	6-127
RING OF CALLING	Opens the Seal of Mythanthor	Finger	All	13-3
RING OF CALMING	All Saving Throws +3	Finger	All	6-124
RING OF CHARISMA	CHA +1	Finger	All	6-78
RING OF CLOUDY MIND	-1 to Hit, Willpower Save +3	Finger	All	8-67
RING OF COLD	Protection -2, Cast *Cone of Cold* Level 15	Finger	All	6-34
RING OF CONFUSION	Cast *Confusion* Level 10	Finger	All	19-30

NAME	ENCHANTMENT	LOCATION	USABLE BY	WHERE FOUND
RING OF CONSTITUTION	CON +1	Finger	All	6-59
RING OF CURSING	Cast *Bestow Curse* Level 10	Finger	All	6-85
RING OF DEXTERITY	DEX +1	Finger	All	16-37
RING OF DODGING	AC +2, DEX +1, Reflex Saving Throws +1, Movement +5	Finger	All	23-14
RING OF ELECTRA	Cast *Lightning Bolt* Level 20	Finger	All	16-21
RING OF EQUILIBRIUM	STR -3, DEX +3, Reflex Saving Throws +1, Cast *Cat's Grace* Level 10	Finger	All	16-55
RING OF FREEDOM	Cast *Freedom of Movement* Level 10	Finger	All	16-66
RING OF HARVEST	Cast *Circle of Death* Level 15	Finger	All	18-10
RING OF HEALTH	CON +1, Cast *Cure Serious Wounds* Level 20	Finger	All	18-38
RING OF HOLD PERSON	Cast *Hold Person* Level 15	Finger	All	23-14
RING OF HUSHING	Cast *Silence* Level 10	Finger	All	21-20
RING OF INTELLIGENCE	INT +1	Finger	All	6-98, 6-124
RING OF MOTHERS	Cast *Charm Monster* Level 10	Finger	All	16-56
RING OF NAGA'S KISS	CON +2, Protection +5	Finger	All	7-15
RING OF PRECISION	+1 to Hit, DEX +1	Finger	All	16-89
RING OF PROTECTION +1	AC +1, All Saving Throws +1	Finger	All	5-8, 5-10, 6-85
RING OF PROTECTION +2	AC +2, All Saving Throws +2	Finger	All	Common
RING OF PROTECTION +3	AC +3, All Saving Throws +3	Finger	All	Common
RING OF PROTECTION +4	AC +4, All Saving Throws +4	Finger	All	Common
RING OF PROTECTION +5	AC +5, All Saving Throws +5	Finger	All	Common
RING OF PROTECTION FROM PARALYSIS	Protection from Paralysis +1	Finger	All	6-114
RING OF THE PROTECTED	AC +1, All Saving Throws +3	Finger	All	16-36
RING OF RELINQUISHMENT	+4 to Hit, +4 Damage, AC +4, 80% of spells fail	Finger	So	11-3
RING OF RESTORATION	Cast *Restoration* Level 10	Finger	All	17-59
RING OF SEARING LIGHT	Cast *Searing Light* Level 10	Finger	All	19-107
RING OF SILENCE	Cast *Silence* Level 5	Finger	All	18-46
RING OF SLOWING	Cast *Slow* Level 10	Finger	All	23-14
RING OF SOULS	Cast *Halt Undead* Level 15	Finger	All	17-67
RING OF STAMINA	Fortitude Saving Throws +1	Finger	All	16-9
RING OF STRENGTH	STR +1	Finger	All	6-77

Name	Enchantment	Location	Usable By	Where Found
Ring of Teeth	Cast *Inflict Serious Wounds* Level 10	Finger	All	6-122, 16-6
Ring of Truesight	Cast *True Seeing* Level 20	Finger	All	16-20
Ring of Wisdom	WIS +1	Finger	All	6-77
Serpent's Ring	Damage +3, Spell Resistance -4	Finger	All	8-10
Stillness of Dawn	+7 vs. Dragonkind, Cast *Firestorm* Level 20	Finger	All	11-11
Talona's Lashing Tongue	+5 to Hit vs. Reptiles, Fires Poisonous Missiles	Finger	All	11-11
The Tremble Ring	CON -1, Protection from Fear -2, Cast *Fear* Level 20	Finger	All	11-11
Topaz Band	AC +1	Finger	All	9-38
Torm's Tiny Circlet	CON +1, Init -4, Cast *Dominate Person* Level 15	Finger	All	11-11
Touch of Cyric	Protection from Fear -5, Cast *Finger of Death* Level 15	Finger	So	11-11
Turabin's Cleansing Trinket	Protection from Magic +3, Cast *Dispel Magic* Level 15	Finger	All	11-11
Veil of Vanity	INT -1, WIS -2, CHA +2	Finger	All	7-38
Whip-Ring of Loviatar	DEX +2, Init +2, Cast *Inflict Critical Wounds* Level 15	Finger	All	11-11

Necklaces

Name	Enchantment	Location	Usable By	Where Found
Alaric's Charm	CON -2, INT +2	Neck	All	13-20
Amulet of Constitution	CON +1	Neck	All	5-8
Amulet of Intellect	INT +1	Neck	All	In Kellan's equipment at 9th level
Amulet of Invulnerability	AC +3, Cast *Globe of Invulnerability* Level 10	Neck	All	18-11
Amulet of Perfect Health	CON -4, Cast *Heal* Level 20	Neck	All	18-19
Amulet of Protection +1	Protection +1	Neck	All	Common
Amulet of Protection +2	Protection +2	Neck	All	Common
Amulet of Protection from Paralysis +1	Protection From Paralysis +1	Neck	All	Common

Name	Enchantment	Location	Usable By	Where Found
AMULET OF ROLLING SMOKE	Cast *Cloudkill* Level 15	Neck	All	10-3
AMULET OF STRENGTH	STR +2	Neck	All	6-21
CRIMSON BROOCH	AC +2, Spell Resistance +2	Neck	All	8-56
DRAGONBONE TALISMAN	STR +1, INT +1, Fortitude Saving Throws +3, Spell Resistance +12, Cast *Firestorm* Level 20	Neck	All	23-14
ELENA'S PEWTER LOCKET	INT +1, WIS +1	Neck	All	7-42
EYE OF RANMAN	WIS +2, Movement +10	Neck	Mo	15-4
EYE OF THE WITCH	INT +1, WIS +1, Cast *Divine Power* Level 10	Neck	All	19-24
FRUHVOGEL'S PENDANT	Init +5	Neck	All	9-39
GHOUL STOPPER	Protection from Undead +4	Neck	All	6-81
JEWEL OF SAMMASTER	Cast Breath of an Ancient Dracolich	Neck	All	13-3
KLUUSAR'S BLOODSTONE AMULET	AC +1, STR +2, CON -2, Reflex Saving Throws +1, Willpower Saving Throws +1, Init +1, Spell Resistance +5, Cast *Vampiric Touch* Level 10	Neck	All	8-4
KLUUSAR'S CHAIN OF WARDING	AC +1, Fortitude Saving Throws +1, Spell Resistance +13, Cast *Minor Globe of Invulnerability* Level 10	Neck	All	16-57
LYSTAN'S EXCORIATA	AC -4, CHA +4, Movement -50, Cast *Mass Suggestion* Level 15	Neck	All	19-31
MEDALLION OF DEFENSE	AC +1, All Saving Throws +1	Neck	All	6-119
MEDALLION OF LOLTH	DEX +1, Cast *Control Undead* Level 20	Neck	All	19-63
MORTISSA'S BEADS OF RIGOR	Cast *Hold Undead* Level 15	Neck	All	18-29
NECKLACE OF CONFIDENCE	Willpower Saving Throws +3	Neck	All	16-71
NECKLACE OF MAGIC RESISTANCE	Spell Resistance +5, Cast *Spell Resistance* Level 10	Neck	All	16-89
NECKLACE OF PRAYER BEADS	Cast *Prayer* Level 10	Neck	All	16-49

Name	Enchantment		Usable By	Where Found
Necklace of Protection	AC +3, All Saving Throws +3	Neck	All	6-83
Necklace of Safe Footfalls	AC +2, All Saving Throws +2, Protection from Traprunes	Neck	All	13-19
Necklace of Spiritual Weapon	Cast *Spiritual Weapon* Level 5	Neck	All	19-47
Necklace of the Dead	CON -1, Protection +3	Neck	All	6-96
Onglore's Amulet of War	STR +2, CON +2, Movement +30	Neck	All	6-21
Onyx of the Richest Wort	CON +2, All Saving Throws +2, Spell Resistance +7, Cast *Neutralize Poison* Level 10	Neck	All	9-21
Theodore's Token of Luck	AC +1, All Saving Throws +1, Init +1, Spell Resistance +6, Cast *True Seeing* Level 20	Neck	Ro	8-27
Tyr's Locket of Justice	WIS +2, Cast *Halt Undead* Level 15	Neck	All	7-27

Wands

Name	Enchantment	Usable By	Where Found
Sceptre of Leogans	WIS -2, CHA +3, Fortitude Saving Throws -1, Willpower Saving Throws +1, Cast *Mass Suggestion* Level 15	So	17-83
Terrilan's Crimson Wand	CHA +6, Fortitude Saving Throws -2, Cast *Finger of Death* Level 15	So	16-57
Wand of Chain Lightning	Cast *Chain Lightning* Level 20	So	6-42
Wand of Cloudkill	Cast *Cloudkill* Level 15	So	17-79
Wand of Command	Cast *Command* Level 10	Cl, Pa, Ra	16-93
Wand of Cure Serious Wounds	Cast *Cure Serious Wounds* Level 20	Cl, Pa, Ra	16-84, 17-57
Wand of Electra	Cast *Chain Lightning* Level 20	So	16-52

Name	Enchantment	Usable By	Where Found
WAND OF FIREBALL	Cast *Fireball* Level 10	So	19-55
WAND OF FIRESTORM	Cast *Firestorm* Level 20	Cl, Pa, Ra	19-55
WAND OF FLAME STRIKE	Cast *Flame Strike* Level 15	Cl, Pa, Ra	18-11, 22-10
WAND OF HEAL	Cast *Heal* Level 20	Cl, Pa, Ra	18-4
WAND OF HOLD PERSON	Cast *Hold Person* Level 10	Cl, Pa, Ra	11-2
WAND OF MAGIC MISSILES	Cast *Magic Missile* Level 5	So	9-36, 18-38
WAND OF MAGUS	CON -1, WIS +3, Cast *Searing Light* Level 5	Cl, Pa, Ra	23-10
WAND OF MELF'S ACID ARROW	Cast *Melf's Acid Arrow* Level 15	So	6-46, 19-47
WAND OF RESTORATION	Cast *Restoration* Level 15	Cl, Pa, Ra	6-59
WAND OF RESURRECTION	Cast *Resurrection* Level 20	Cl, Pa, Ra	6-55
WAND OF SLAY LIVING	Cast *Slay Living* Level 10	Cl, Pa, Ra	16-12
WAND OF SLEEP	Cast *Sleep* Level 10	So	16-9
WAND OF STINKING CLOUD	Cast *Stinking Cloud* Level 10	So	16-9
WAND OF UNDEAD CONTROL	Cast *Control Undead* Level 20	So	18-51

Appendix B: Spells

Character
Sorcerers
Cantrips
Daze
Detect Magic
Disrupt Undead
Light
Resistance

Level 1
Burning Hands
Charm Person
Chill Touch

Mage Armor
Magic Missile
Protection from Evil
Protection from Good
   (reverse of *Protection from Evil*)
Shield
Shocking Grasp
Sleep

Level 2
Blindness
Bull's Strength
Cat's Grace
Darkness
Ghoul Touch

Invisibility
Melf's Acid Arrow
See Invisibility
Web

Level 3
Blink
Dispel Magic
Displacement
Fireball
Haste
Hold Person
Hold Undead
Invisibility Sphere
Lightning Bolt
Slow

Stinking Cloud
Vampiric Touch

Level 4
Charm Monster
Confusion
Fear
Fire Shield
Improved Invisibility
Minor Globe of
  Invulnerability

Level 5
Cloudkill
Cone of Cold
Domination
Feeblemind
Hold Monster

Level 6
Chain Lightning
Circle of Death
Disintegrate
Globe of Invulnerability
Mass Suggestion
Repulsion
True Seeing

Level 7
Control Undead
Finger of Death

Level 8
Incendiary Cloud

Clerics
Orisons
Cure Minor Wounds
Detect Magic
Light
Resistance

Level 1
Bless
Cause Fear (reverse of
  Remove Fear)
Command
Cure Light Wounds
Curse (reverse of Bless)
Entangle
Inflict Light Wounds (reverse
  of Cure Light Wounds)

Protection from Evil
Protection from Good
  (reverse of Protection
  from Evil)
Remove Fea
Shield of Faith

Level 2
Aid
Bull's Strength
Cure Moderate Wounds
Darkness
Delay Poison
Find Traps
Hold Person
Inflict Moderate Wounds
Remove Paralysis (reverse
  of Hold Person)
Silence
Spiritual Weapon

Level 3
Bestow Curse Americana
  Remove Curse
Blindness (reverse of Cure
  Blindness)
Cure Serious Wounds
Dispel Magic
Hold Poison
Inflict Serious Wounds
Prayer
Remove Blindness
Remove Curse
Searing Light

Level 4
Cure Critical Wounds
Divine Power
Freedom of Movement
Inflict Critical Wounds
Neutralize Poison
Poison (reverse of
  Neutralize Poison)
Restoration

Level 5
Flame Strike
Magic Resistance
Raise Dead
Slay Living (reverse of
  Raise Dead)
True Seeing

Level 6
Harm (reverse of Heal)
Heal

Level 7
Destruction
Resurrection

Level 8
Firestorm

Paladin
Level 0
Resistance

Level 1
Bless
Cure Light Wounds
Protection from Evil

Level 2
Cure Moderate Wounds
Delay Poison
Remove Paralysis

Level 3
Cure Serious Wounds
Dispel Magic
Prayer
Remove Blindness

Level 4
Free Action
Neutralize Poison

Ranger
Level 1
Cure Light Wounds
Entangle

Level 2
Delay Poison
Sleep

Level 3
Cure Serious Wounds
Hold Poison

Level 4
Free Action
Neutralize Poison

Appendix C: Character Stats

Monsters

NAME	XP	HD	MOVE	AC	# ATT	DAMAGE/ATTACK
ANCIENT ZOMBIE	900	4d12+4	60	11	2	1d8+1/1d8+1
ARCHLICH	18,000	16th Sorcerer	30	29	2	Weapon
ARRACCAT	825	7d10+7	60	18	2	2d4+4/2d6+4
ARRACCAT MOTHER	14,400	20d10+6	60	21	2	4d8+4/4d10+4
BLACK ARRACCAT	8,400	16d10+32	70	24	2	3d10+3/3d12+3
CULT ARCHMAGE	3,600	12th Sorcerer	60	15	2	Weapon
CULT BRIGADIER	18,000	15th Fighter	60	30–32	3	Weapon
CULT MAGE	1,500	8th Sorcerer	60	12–14	1	Weapon
CULT OVERSEER	14,400	16th Sorcerer	60	17–20	2	Weapon
CULT SOLDIER	1,000	7th Fighter	60	19-22	2	Weapon
DARK MAGE	600	2nd Sorcerer	60	11	1	Weapon
DARK NAGA	9,000	13d8+26	80	14	2	2d4+2/1d4+2
DRAGON-KIN	1,800	10d12+7	40	25	2	1d8+8/1d8+8
DRAGON-KIN CAPTAIN	5,850	14d12+9	40	28	2	1d10+10/1d10+10
DWARVEN STATUE	12,000	14d10	40	26	2	2d10+9/2d10+9
ENTHRALLED DROW	1,200	9d12+9	60	27	3	Weapon

Key

Name: Name of the character
Comment: Other important background information (if any)
XP: Experience Points
HD: Hit Dice expressed in the number of sides of a dice
MOVE: Movement ability
AC: Armor Class
 # ATT: Number of attacks per round
DAMAGE/ATTACK: Damage per attack, given a certain weapon, if you can equip the character with a weapon

SPECIAL ATTACKS: Special attack abilities inherent to the character
SPECIAL DEFENSES: Special Defenses inherent to the character
+ NEEDED TO HIT: Hit bonus required for an attack to hit and damage this character
MR: Magic Resistance (if any)
FORT: Fortitude saving throw bonus
REFLEX: Reflex saving throw bonus
WILLP: Willpower saving throw bonus

SPECIAL ATTACKS	SPECIAL DEFENSES	+ NEEDED TO HIT	MR	FORT	REFLEX	WILLP
—	Standard Undead; +2 vs. Turning	0	0	0	-1	3
Fear Aura/ Paralyze	Standard Undead; +8 vs. Turning	1	0	10	15	20
—	Immune to Paralysis and Poison	0	0	4	4	0
Paralyze	Immune to Paralysis, Poison, and Critical Hits	0	12	5	5	0
—	Immune to Paralysis and Poison; +5 vs. Critical Hits	0	10	6	6	2
—	—	0	0	4	4	8
—	—	0	0	9	5	5
—	—	0	0	2	2	6
—	—	0	0	5	5	10
—	—	0	0	5	2	2
—	—	0	0	0	0	3
Spit Poison	Immune to Poison, +2 vs. Charm	0	0	5	7	8
—	—	0	0	5	6	7
—	—	0	0	6	7	8
—	Immune to All Special Attacks and Magic	2	0	4	3	4
—	Standard Undead, +4 vs. Turning	0	17	8	5	7

NAME	XP	HD	MOVE	AC	# ATT	DAMAGE/ATTACK
FRETH DROW ASSASSIN	21,600	17th Rogue	60	26–30	3	Weapon
FRETH DROW COMMANDER	3,600	12th Fighter	60	27	3	Weapon
FRETH DROW HIGH PRIEST	14,400	16th Cleric	60	18–23	3	Weapon
FRETH DROW PRIEST	3,600	12th Cleric	60	14–19	2	Weapon
FRETH DROW WARRIOR	1,100	8th Fighter	60	20–24	2	Weapon
GARGOYLE	1,500	5d10+16	90	16	4	1d4+4/1d4+4/ 1d6+6/1d6+6
GARGOYLE LEADER	2,250	6d10+20	90	16	4	1d6+6/1d6+6/ 1d8+8/1d8+8
GHAST	1,200	5d12	60	16	3	1d4/1d4/1d8
GHOUL	750	3d12	60	14	3	1d3/1d3/1d6
GUARD ARRACCAT	2,200	10d10+10	60	20	2	3d4+3/3d6+3
LICH	12,000	12th Sorcerer	30	23–25	1	Weapon
LIZARDFOLK–ARMED	300	2d8+2	60	15	1	Weapon
LIZARDFOLK–UNARMED	300	2d8+2	60	15	2	1d6+1/1d6+1
LIZARDFOLK FAITH HEALER	1,500	5d8+6	60	17	1	Weapon
LIZARDFOLK GEOMANCER	3,000	7d8+4	60	17	1	Weapon
LIZARDFOLK TASKMASTER	1,200	5d8+8	60	18	1	Weapon
LIZARDFOLK WARRIOR	1,800	6d8+6	60	19	2	1d6+6/1d6+6
MARGOYLE	825	7d10+24	90	19	4	2d4+4/2d4+4/ 2d6+6/2d6+6

SPECIAL ATTACKS	SPECIAL DEFENSES	+ NEEDED TO HIT	MR	FORT	REFLEX	WILLP
—	—	0	21	5	10	5
—	—	0	13	8	4	4
—	—	0	19	10	5	10
—	—	0	15	6	3	6
—	—	0	10	6	2	2
—	—	1	0	8	6	1
—	—	1	0	9	7	2
Paralyze	Standard Undead, +2 vs. Turning	0	0	1	3	6
Paralyze	Standard Undead, +1 vs. Turning	0	0	5	4	3
—	Immune to Paralysis and Poison	0	5	4	4	0
Fear Aura/ Paralyze	Standard Undead, +6 vs. Turning	1	0	5	10	15
—	—	0	0	1	3	0
—	—	0	0	1	3	0
—	—	0	0	5	4	5
—	—	0	5	3	4	5
—	—	0	0	2	4	1
—	—	0	0	5	4	1
—	—	1	0	10	7	2

287

NAME	XP	HD	MOVE	AC	# ATT	DAMAGE/ATTACK
MARGOYLE QUEEN	1,800	10d10+32	90	20	4	2d6+6/2d6+6/ 2d8+8/2d8+8
MASTER SHADOW	1,000	7d12	60	15	2	0/0
MASTER SPECTRE	12,000	14d12	80	17	2	2d6+1/2d6+1
MASTER WIGHT	1,100	8d12	30	17	3	1d4+1/1d4+1/ 1d4+1
MASTER WRAITH	3,000	10d10	60	16	2	2d4+2/2d4+2
MOHRG	3,600	14d12	90	15	3	1d6+5/1d6+5/ 1d6+5
ORC	150	1d8	60	14–16	1	Weapon
ORC CAPTAIN	4,500	7d10+4	60	23	2	Weapon
ORC SHAMAN	600	4d8	60	17	1	Weapon
ORC WARLOCK	2,250	6d6+6	60	19	1	Weapon
ORC WITCH DOCTOR	600	4d6	60	19	1	Weapon
ORMYRR	4,800	10d10+10	60	18	5	1d6+1/1d6+1/ 2d6+2/Weapon/ Weapon
OROG	500	3d10+3	60	20–23	1	Weapon
OROG CHIEFTAN	9,000	10d10+10	60	24–27	1	Weapon
OROG GUARDSMAN	1,200	dd10+5	60	25–27	1	Weapon
OROG HEALER	1,000	d4d10+4	60	20–24	1	Weapon
OROG HUNTER	1,500	5d10+5	60	20–24	1	Weapon
OROG MARAUDER	1,500	7d10+16	60	29	2	Weapon

SPECIAL ATTACKS	SPECIAL DEFENSES	+ NEEDED TO HIT	MR	FORT	REFLEX	WILLP
—	—	2	0	11	8	3
Strength Drain, Non-corporeal	Standard Undead, +4 vs. Turning, Non-corporeal	0	2	4	5	4
Drain 2 Experience Levels, Non-corporeal	Standard Undead, +6 vs. Turning Non-corporeal	1	0	3	6	8
Drain 1 Experience Level	Standard Undead, +5 vs. Turning	0	0	2	4	7
Constitution Drain, Non-corporeal	Standard Undead, +5 vs. Turning, Non-corporeal	1	0	2	5	7
Paralyze	Standard Undead, Can't Be Turned	0	0	4	5	9
—	—	0	0	2	0	-1
—	—	0	0	4	3	3
—	—	0	0	2	1	2
—	—	0	0	1	2	3
—	—	0	0	1	2	3
—	+4 Save vs. Poison	0	0	5	1	4
—	—	0	0	4	1	1
—	—	0	0	8	8	8
—	—	0	0	5	2	1
—	—	0	0	3	4	5
—	—	0	0	5	4	1
—	—	0	0	6	3	3

NAME	XP	HD	MOVE	AC	# ATT	DAMAGE/ATTACK
Orog Marauder Boss	3,000	9d10+18	60	29–31	2	Weapon
Orog Marauder Hoodoo	6,000	12d8+11	60	24	2	Weapon
Revenant	3,000	12d12+3	90	14	3	2d8+8/2d8+8/ 2d8+8
Shadow	750	3d12	60	13	1	0
Shambling Ghast	1,000	7d12	60	18	3	1d4+2/1d4
Skeleton	100	1d12	60	14	1	Weapon
Skeleton Knight	500	2d12	60	22–25	2	Weapon
Skeleton Lord	1,200	6d10	60	25–28	2	Weapon
Soulless Orog	825	7d12+7	60	17	2	1d6+1/1d6+1
Spectre	1,650	9d12	80	15	1	1d8
Wight	413	5d12+15	30	15	2	1d4+1/1d4+1
Wraith	825	7d12	60	15	1	1d4
Zombie	150	3d12+3	60	11	1	1d6+1
Zombie Lord	2,000	9d12+3	80	14	2	2d6+10/2d6+10

SPECIAL ATTACKS	SPECIAL DEFENSES	+ NEEDED TO HIT	MR	FORT	REFLEX	WILLP
—	—	0	0	7	4	4
—	—	0	0	4	4	8
Paralyze	Standard Undead, Can't Be Turned	0	0	10	8	12
Strength Drain Non-corporeal	Standard Undead, +2 vs. Turning, Non-corporeal	1	0	1	3	4
Paralyze +2/1d8+2	Standard Undead, +3 vs. Turning	0	0	1	3	6
—	Standard Undead	0	0	0	1	2
—	Standard Undead, +2 vs. Turning	0	0	1	2	3
—	Standard Undead, +4 vs. Turning	0	0	4	3	4
—	Standard Undead, +3 vs. Turning	0	0	8	0	6
Drain 2 Experience Levels, Non-corporeal	Standard Undead, +4 vs. Turning, Non-corporeal	1	0	2	5	7
Drain Experience Level	Standard Undead, +3 vs. Turning, Non-corporeal	0	0	1	2	5
Constitution Drain, Non-corporeal	Standard Undead, +4 vs. Turning, Non-corporeal	1	0	1	4	6
—	Standard Undead	0	0	0	-1	3
—	Standard Undead, +4 vs. Turning	0	0	2	1	6

NPCs Who Can Join Your Party

NAME	COMMENT	XP	HD	MOVE
ATHAN	Cult's Prisoner in Passage to Castle Cormanthor	120,150	16th Fighter	60
BRONWYN	Sister of the Silver Fire, Elven Ranger	68,900	12th Ranger	60
EADRED	Human Paladin Locked Away in Tomb	29,469	8th Paladin	60
EMMERIC	One of Athan's Band; Captured by Cult	13,004	5th Fighter	60
FAERIL	Half Elf Fighter/Cleric	97,801	5th Fighter/9th Cleric	60
JARIAL	Half Elf Sorcerer	3,300	3rd Sorcerer	60
KELLAN	Sister of the Silver Fire, Human Fighter/Sorcerer	85,800	7th Fighter/ 6th Sorcerer	60
TUDO	Flamboyant Human Rogue	67,801	12th Rogue	60

Good NPCs

NAME	COMMENT	XP	HD	MOVE
ANORRWEYN EVENSONG	Ancient Spectral Priestess	—	—	0
BERIAND	Blind Elven Cleric, Always of Help	—	—	60
CAALENFAIRE	Sedentary Seer	—	—	0

AC	# ATT	DAMAGE/ATTACK	SPECIAL ATTACKS	SPECIAL DEFENSES	+ NEEDED TO HIT	MR	FORT	REFLEX	WILLP
8	4	—	—	—	0	0	9	5	5
11	3	—	—	—	0	0	8	4	4
10	2	—	—	—	0	0	6	2	2
11	1	—	—	—	0	0	5	2	2
10	3	—	—	—	0	0	6	2	6
15	1	—	—	—	0	0	1	1	3
10	3	—	—	—	0	0	5	2	4
11	2	—	—	—	0	0	4	8	4

AC	# ATT	DAMAGE/ATTACK	SPECIAL ATTACKS	SPECIAL DEFENSES	+ NEEDED TO HIT	MR	FORT	REFLEX	WILLP
14	0	—	—	—	0	0	0	0	0
10	0	—	—	—	0	0	10	5	10
10	0	—	—	—	0	0	5	1	7

NAME	COMMENT	XP	HD	MOVE
ELENA	Elven Spectral Cleric	—	—	60
ETHE	Guardian Naga of the Silver Fire	—	—	80
GARRAS	Elven Spectral Archer	—	—	60
GLORAN	Guardian Naga of the Silver Fire	—	—	80
HARLDAIN IRONBAR	Crazy Old Dwarf Lord	—	—	60
MIRODEN SILVERBLAD	Undead Elven Sorcerer/Cleric	—	—	60
NOTTLE	Halfling Trader	—	—	60
ODELINDE	Helpful Guardian Naga	—	—	40
VOLUN	Caalenfaire's Skull Sidekick	—	—	10

Major Named Enemies

NAME	COMMENT	XP	HD	MOVE	AC
BERGOS	Drow Leader	6,000	12th Fighter	60	32
CHIEF PUJIK	Ormyrr Chief	18,000	15d10+10	60	20
DREYDRE	Leader of the Freth Drow	14,400	16d8a	30	16

AC	# ATT	DAMAGE/ATTACK	SPECIAL ATTACKS	SPECIAL DEFENSES	+ NEEDED TO HIT	MR	FORT	REFLEX	WILLP
16	2	—	—	—	0	0	7	3	7
18	1	—	—	—	0	0	7	7	11
22	2	—	—	—	0	0	7	3	3
18	1	—	—	—	0	0	7	7	11
15	2	—	—	—	0	0	7	3	3
20	0	—	—	—	1	5	9	4	9
10	0	—	—	—	0	0	4	9	4
18	1	—	—	—	0	0	7	7	11
10	0	—	—	—	0	0	1	-3	5

# ATT	DAMAGE/ATTACK	SPECIAL ATTACKS	SPECIAL DEFENSES	+ NEEDED TO HIT	MR	FORT	REFLEX	WILLP
3	Weapon 1d8+1/1d8	—	—	0	21	8	4	4
5	6+1/2d8+2/ Weapon/Weapon	—	+4 Save vs. Poison	0	0	6	2	4
3	Weapon	Spells per 16th Level Cleric	—	0	27	10	5	10

NAME	COMMENT	XP	HD	MOVE	AC
FOLUBEN	Drow; Greyanna's Bodyguard	14,400	16th Fighter	30	32
GREYANNA	A Leader of the Freth Drow	33,600	10th Fighter/ 12th Cleric	30	32
GULRITHI	Dark Naga—Captor of Ethe and Gloran, Guardian Nagas	4,500	20d8+40	80	14
KOG	Leader of the Dark Nagas Who Captured Anorrweyn's Shrine	3,000	10d8+20	80	16
KYA MORDRAYN	Supreme Leader of the Cult of the Dragon	65,000	14th Fighter/ 24th Sorcerer	60	29
LIFESPRING GUARDIAN	Giant Guardian Golem	4,500	8d10	20	20
MALGI HI	Evil Human Lizardfolk Master	18,000	8th Rogue/ 10th Sorcerer	60	23
ONGLORE	Dwarf Lord Ghast	1,350	4d12	60	16
PELENDRALAAR	Great Red Wyrm Dracolich	75,000	64d12+255	80	36
PREYBELISH	Dark Naga, Covertor of Necklaces	5,400	9d8+18	80	14

# ATT	DAMAGE/ATTACK	SPECIAL ATTACKS	SPECIAL DEFENSES	+ NEEDED TO HIT	MR	FORT	REFLEX	WILLP
4	Weapon	—	—	0	27	7	3	3
3	Weapon	—	—	0	33	10	7	7
2	2d4+2/1d4+2	Spit Poison	Immune to Poison, +2 vs. Charm	0	0	5	7	8
2	2d4+2/1d4+2	Spit Poison	Immune to Poison +2 vs. Charm	0	0	5	7	8
3	Weapon	—	—	0	20	12	10	14
2	1d10+9/1d10+9	—	Immune to All Special Attacks and Magic	2	0	4	3	4
1	Weapon	—	—	0	15	3	6	7
3	1d4/1d4/1d8	Paralyze	Standard Undead, +2 vs. Turning	0	0	1	3	6
3	5d6+17/5d6+17/ 4d8+8	Detect Invisible, Fear Aura Paralyzing Gaze, Melee Chill Damage Paralysis, Breath Weapon	Standard Undead, plus Cold, Fire, +4 vs. Magic	0	35	32	22	30
2	2d4+2/1d4+2	Spit Poison	Immune to Poison, +2 vs. Charm	0	0	5	7	8

NAME	COMMENT	XP	HD	MOVE	AC
THE DEMON RIVENER	Demon-like Creature of Unknown Origin	12,000	19d12+24	15	25
THYAAST AMMATH	Powerful Sorcerer Spectre	0	20d12	30	31
TUSK-LORD	Ultra-Strong Gargoyle Leader	19,200	14d10	90	22
ZUD	Local Orc Chief	900	4d10	60	21

Major NPCs You Can Fight or Befriend

NAME	COMMENT	XP	HD	MOVE	AC
FLEM	A Chatty Ormyrr	4,800	10d10+10	60	18
GEB	Lost Ormyrr	3,600	7d10+7	60	15

# ATT	DAMAGE/ATTACK	SPECIAL ATTACKS	SPECIAL DEFENSES	+ NEEDED TO HIT	MR	FORT	REFLEX	WILLP
6	1d6+2/1d6+2/ 1d6+2/1d6+2/ 1d6+2/1d6+2	Detect Invisible, Fear Aura, Poison Spit, Paralyze	Immune to Charm, Enfeeblement, Paralysis, Poison Sleep; +2 vs. Acid, +3 vs. Cold, +4 vs. Fire, +1 vs. Magic	3	15	10	12	14
3	Weapon	Fear Aura, Paralyze	Standard Undead, Immune to Cold, Electricity, and Turning	1	0	15	20	25
4	2d4+4/2d4+4/ 2d8+6/2d8+6	Paralyze	—	2	0	8	8	8
1	Weapon	—	—	0	0	1	3	1

# ATT	DAMAGE/ATTACK	SPECIAL ATTACKS	SPECIAL DEFENSES	+ NEEDED TO HIT	MR	FORT	REFLEX	WILLP
5	1d6+1/1d6+1/2d6+2/ Weapon/Weapon	—	+4 Save vs. Poison	0	0	5	1	4
5	1d6+1/1d6+1/2d6+2/ Weapon/Weapon	—	+4 Save vs. Poison	0	0	5	1	4

NAME	COMMENT	XP	HD	MOVE	AC
NATHLILIK	Surviving Kilsek Drow Leader	6,000	10d10+12	30	20
RETHA	Leader of the Ormyrr Sharpstick Clan	4,500	10d10+12	60	19

Multiplayer Only

NAME	COMMENT	XP	HD	MOVE	AC	# ATT
ANCIENT DRACOLICH	As Powerful As It Sounds	100,000	42d12+255	80	41	3
ANCIENT SHADOW	A Bigger, More Difficult Shade	2,700	9d12	60	19	2
BLACK NAGA	The Most Powerful Naga	16,000	23d8+46	80	14	2
LICH PRIEST	Powerful Undead Cleric	46,800	20th Cleric	30	25	3
ORC TRACKER	A Ranger/Cleric Orc	2,000	5d10	60	17	1
SKELETAL ZOMBIE	Unusual Undead; Hard to Turn	600	3d12+3	60	14	1

Standard Undead Immunities:
Charm, Critical Hits, Death, Enfeeblement, Hold, Paralysis, Poison, Sleep

# ATT	DAMAGE/ATTACK	SPECIAL ATTACKS	SPECIAL DEFENSES	+ NEEDED TO HIT	MR	FORT	REFLEX	WILLP
3	Weapon	—	+6 vs. Fire, +2 vs. Magic	0	2	7	3	3
5	1d6+1/1d6+1/2d6+2/Weapon/Weapon	—	+4 save vs. Poison	0	0	5	1	4

DAMAGE/ATTACK	SPECIAL ATTACKS	SPECIAL DEFENSES	+ NEEDED TO HIT	MR	FORT	REFLEX	WILLP
5d7+5/5d7+5/6d8+8	Detect Invisible Aura, Fear Paralyzing Gaze, Melee Chill Damage, Paralysis, Breath Weapon	Standard Undead, plus Cold, Fire, +4 vs Magic	0	30	28	19	26
0/0	Strength Drain, Non-corporeal	Standard Undead, +5 vs. Turning, Non-corporeal	1	0	3	5	6
2d8+2/1d8+1	Spit Poison	Immune to Poison, +2 vs. Charm	0	0	8	10	11
Weapon	Fear Aura/Paralyze	Standard Undead, +8 vs. Turning	1	0	12	6	12
Weapon	—	—	0	0	5	3	5
1d8+1	—	Standard Undead, +5 vs. Turning	0	0	0	0	4

301

Index